TEACHING VISUAL METHODS IN THE SOCIAL SCIENCES

Teaching Visual Methods in the Social Sciences presents a practical and theoretical framework for those wanting to introduce visual methods into their curricula. Drawing on the expertise of contributors from across the social sciences, the book provides a comprehensive introduction to visual methodology, learning and teaching theory, and the ethical considerations involved.

Divided into three parts, the book begins with an overview of how visual methods have been used in academic research, and how this can be applied to teaching and pedagogy. It then goes on to introduce different methods, including photography, film and drawing, describing how they can be used in various locations. Finally, the book pulls everything together, advocating the wider use of teaching visual methods in further and higher education curricula across the social science subjects.

The book features a plethora of examples, as well as practical resources for FE and HE teachers, making it an essential companion for anyone interested in utilising visual methods in their teaching.

Sal Watt is a Senior Lecturer in the Sociology Department at Manchester Metropolitan University. Her expertise is in pedagogical practice and the teaching of research methods. Sal is a Fellow of the HEA and a Chartered Psychologist in learning and teaching.

Caroline Wakefield is an Associate Professor in the Faculty of Science at Liverpool Hope University. Her research and teaching expertise lie in performance enhancement, health and research methods. Caroline is a Fellow of the HEA and is a Chartered Psychologist in learning and teaching.

TEACHING VISUAL METHODS IN THE SOCIAL SCIENCES

Edited by
Sal Watt and
Caroline Wakefield

Routledge
Taylor & Francis Group

LONDON AND NEW YORK

First published 2017
by Routledge
2 Park Square, Milton Park, Abingdon, Oxon OX14 4RN

and by Routledge
711 Third Avenue, New York, NY 10017

Routledge is an imprint of the Taylor & Francis Group, an informa business

British Library Cataloguing-in-Publication Data
A catalogue record for this book is available from the British Library

Library of Congress Cataloging-in-Publication Data
A catalog record for this book has been requested

ISBN: 978-1-138-10134-0 (hbk)
ISBN: 978-1-138-10135-7 (pbk)
ISBN: 978-1-315-65701-1 (ebk)

Typeset in Bembo
by Florence Production Ltd, Stoodleigh, Devon, UK

For Connah and Kaida:
The little people who bring love, joy and laughter

For Phil, Imogen and Oliver:
The ones I laugh with, dream with, live for, love

CONTENTS

FIGURES

TABLES

ABOUT THE EDITORS

Sal Watt is a Senior Lecturer in Sociology within the Faculty of Humanities, Languages and Social Science at Manchester Metropolitan University where she specialises in teaching research methods. Her areas of expertise and research interests include organisational change, health and well-being and research into learning and teaching. In respect of professional commitment to learning and teaching, Sal is a Chartered Psychologist and a Fellow of the HEA. She has a strong profile in pedagogical research that focuses on embedding research methods into curricula design and enhancing student experience.

Caroline Wakefield is an Associate Professor in the Faculty of Science at Liverpool Hope University. Her background and expertise are in the area of performance enhancement using motor imagery and observation. Further research interests centre on body image, research methods, and health psychology. Caroline is a Fellow of the HEA and is a Chartered Psychologist in the respect of learning and teaching. Caroline has a strong interest in developing pedagogies through a variety of approaches, particularly those utilising visual methods as a tool for learning.

CONTRIBUTORS

Lorna J. Bourke is a Principal Lecturer in Psychology at Liverpool Hope University. Her main field of expertise is in the understanding of the cognitive skills that underpin the development of children's writing skills. Lorna has worked in a number of different resource-challenged countries through her involvement with the university's overseas education charity, Global Hope. This has extended her research profile to using interview techniques to examine the psycho-social impact of disablement in those countries as well as visual methods to investigate ideas related to identity and being within the Tibetan diaspora in India.

Simon J. Davies is a Lecturer in Cognitive Psychology and Research Methods at Liverpool Hope University. His background and expertise is in visual cognition. He has worked on several international charitable projects. Most recently this has involved working with artists from the Tibetan diaspora. This work has been developed alongside Liverpool Museums on a project to research and analyse visual representations of identity in a refugee community.

Moira E. Lafferty is one of the Deputy Heads of the Psychology Department at the University of Chester with responsibility for the postgraduate taught courses. Moira has a keen interest in pedagogical practice and has published and presented in the area at national and international events. She has also been in receipt of two HLTSN grants to explore teaching and learning in higher education, specifically focusing on students' perceptions of research and the dissertation process.

Edd Pitt is Programme Director for the PGCHE and Lecturer in Higher Education and Academic Practice at the University of Kent. Edd has worked in academia for 12 years in various teaching and research roles. His principal research field is assessment and feedback with a particular focus upon students' emotional processing during feedback situations. His current research utilises visual methods of drawing and Lego Serious Play to foster deeper participant engagement within the research interview.

Joel Rookwood is a Senior Lecturer in the Faculty of Business, Sport and Enterprise at Southampton Solent University, UK, and a Visiting Fellow in Sport Management at the University of Vic, Spain. He has conducted research and written for various media publications. He has worked in and published widely on sport-for-development, football fandom, violence, peacebuilding, sports mega events, and sport and social identity.

Julie Scott Jones is the Associate Head of the Department of Sociology, and Professor of Sociology at Manchester Metropolitan University. She was the Head of Ethics for the Faculty of Humanities, Languages and Social Science, 2010–15. She recently edited the three-volume *Research Ethics in Context* (2015, Sage) and the three-volume *Research Ethics in Practice* (2015, Sage).

Janet Speake is Associate Dean for Postgraduate Research Students and Principal Lecturer in the Department of Geography and Environmental Science at Liverpool Hope University. Her research interests centre on the contemporary transformations of urban areas, spaces of affectivity, the role of geography and geographers in the creation and production of new GPS-based cartographies and the impacts of satellite navigation technologies on cartographic literacy and spatial awareness.

Julie Taylor is a Principal Lecturer in the Health, Psychology and Social Studies Department at the University of Cumbria. Julie is a Chartered Psychologist who has been working in higher education, research and practice contexts for over 20 years. Julie has particular interests in research methodologies that are sensitive to a range of populations, developing approaches to meaningful service user participation and exploring ways to foster social connection through outdoor activities in nature.

Caroline Wakefield is an Associate Professor in the Faculty of Science at Liverpool Hope University. Her background and expertise are in the area of performance enhancement using motor imagery and observation. Further research interests centre on body image, research methods and health psychology. Caroline is a Fellow of the HEA and is a Chartered Psychologist in the respect of learning and teaching. Caroline has a strong interest in developing pedagogies through a variety of approaches, particularly those utilising visual methods as a tool for learning.

Sal Watt is a Senior Lecturer in Sociology within the Faculty of Humanities, Languages and Social Science at Manchester Metropolitan University where she specialises in teaching research methods. Her areas of expertise and research interests include organisational change, health and well-being and research into learning and teaching. In respect of professional commitment to learning and teaching, Sal is a Chartered Psychologist and a Fellow of the HEA. She has a strong profile in pedagogical research that focuses on embedding research methods into curricula design and enhancing student experience.

PREFACE

In conception, this book came about quite by chance. Over a period of time we had presented work that drew on visual methods at various psychology conferences. In particular, we had started to question why our own training in psychology and sociology had not included the use of visual methods as a valid and useful data collection technique. Indeed neither of us was aware that such methods could be used, let alone had knowledge of it as a genre that was supported by a theoretical framework that was multi-disciplinary and complex in nature. Our venture into visual methods was not planned; it just sort of happened. Caroline as a keen photographer had agreed to take photographs of a friend who had been training in excess of a year for an Ironman Triathlon. The competitor had the parallel semi-objective of compiling documentary evidence of his Ironman challenge; the end result was 252 photographs charting the day-long event. It occurred to us that his record of the achievement could be supplemented still further through a reflective account, and before we knew it, we were designing a visual methods study that our Ironman was keen to participate in. We became aware of other visual methods and studies largely through conference attendance but these studies were few and far between and the methods seemed diverse. It led us to question the degree to which visual methods are taught in higher education and whether that was reflected in the scarcity of conference papers. We learned that while visual methods were embedded in the curricula of some universities, in others they are not, and certainly this had been our experience as both students and academics. The use of visual methods in our own research had been such a positive experience that we wanted to share it with our students and ensure that their research toolbox was wider than the one we had graduated with.

Active in pedagogical research, we set about designing curricula that married our interest in visual methods with our interest in enhancing the student experience. By then, we had both had a long and avid interest in photographs and the messages that they can portray. However, it was our research experience of using photographs (Wakefield and Watt, 2012) that led us to develop curricula and assessment that involved students, using either pre-existing photographs or taking new photographs as part of an assessed group project. These formed the basis of conducting research using visual methods as a pedagogical tool. The student response was both overwhelming and inspiring. It was the resultant pedagogic papers (Watt and Wakefield, 2014; Wakefield and Watt, 2015) and presentations at various conferences that found us being asked on several occasions to write a text on teaching visual methods. We recognise that there are some excellent texts written by world-leading experts in the field (many of which are drawn upon in this book). However, the intended focus of this text is to equip, and we hope motivate or inspire, other teachers to consider visual research methods as a viable and valuable addition to their higher education curriculum. Our experience is based strictly on photographs and therefore, we have brought together contributors who are actively engaged in higher education teaching with varied specialisms within the field of visual methods, to honestly and reflexively share and evaluate their experiences. This book, then, is for like-minded practitioners who are interested in the possibility and potential of teaching visual methods but perhaps for a plethora of reasons are yet to take the first or next step on a visual journey. We hope that this book inspires and challenges practitioners to incorporate visual methods into their practice in creating exciting and vibrant curricula that adds to the student experience and to their portfolio of research skills.

ACKNOWLEDGEMENTS

We would like to thank all the staff at Routledge who have assisted us through the various preparatory stages of this book. In particular, our thanks go to Michael Strang and Libby Volke who were of immense help in the early commissioning and development of this book and Lucy Kennedy, Liz Rankin and Ceri Griffiths for their editorial advice and fielding our many questions as the book progressed.

Sincere thanks go to our respected colleagues who generously gave their time in contributing to this text in producing honest and reflective accounts of their experiences of teaching visual methods. On this note, we would like to thank all of the students whose experiences have been drawn upon and whose work has been explored within this text. We are also grateful to our respective institutions and colleagues for their continued support, namely the Department of Sociology within the Faculty of Humanities, Languages and Social Science at Manchester Metropolitan University and the School of Health Sciences within the Faculty of Science at Liverpool Hope University. In particular we must extend our thanks to our students who were both the participants and the inspiration in our work: Their honesty and generosity provided the foundations for our explorations and curriculum development.

A special thank you goes to our families for their persistent support, belief and patience. Both at our respective homes and The Old Bank Tea Rooms, Helsby, we appreciate the coffee and cake that seemed to magically appear during the writing process, affording us both the space and time to complete the project.

Finally, going forward, we would like to thank all of the teachers and practitioners that have the conviction to go on to use these ideas as they are intended: As a starting point to incorporating visual methods into your curricula and pedagogy. We wish you an enjoyable and fruitful journey.

PART I

Thinking through the use of visual methods in learning and teaching

1

INTRODUCTION

Sal Watt and Caroline Wakefield

The use of visual methods as a research tool is not new, with instances dating back to the mid-nineteenth century. However, its transference into the classroom as a valid research technique is less commonplace in contemporary curricula. Certainly in our own experience of education and training, visual methods were absent. It is fair to say that we have both harboured and shared an interest in visual communication, primarily photography, for many years. Additionally, having gained many years' experience in the delivery of educational programmes, we recognise the different learning styles adopted by learners and recognise that many of our students were visual thinkers. As such, we have always been interested in designing visual curricula (from flow charts to the inclusion of photograph and film extracts) to that end.

In terms of our own journey, the engagement and use of visual methods became of particular research interest to us through the personal photographic documentation of a competitor in an Ironman Triathlon. While the photographs were comprehensive in their (semi)objective account of the day, we were struck by the visual story they told. As such, we wondered what the participant's reflections on these photographs would be, and whether the participant extracted similar meaning from the photographs as we had, given that he had experienced it 'first-hand'. We asked the participant to write a reflection on each one of seven chosen photographs, with particular emphasis on his sense of achievement. We were unsure how the participant would respond and whether he would be able to engage with his feelings on achievement. We anticipated that potentially his accounts might veer towards the descriptive or focus on the procedural aspects of the event. In reality, we were blown away by the depth of his reflections and his engagement with the task, coupled with an unrivalled eloquence of expression about his achievement. We felt compelled to share his story and promote this research method within our then home discipline where this is an often neglected research tool. This first work was published in an Olympic special issue of the Qualitative Methods in Psychology (QMiP) bulletin (Wakefield and Watt, 2012) and from there we disseminated our experience further at the British Psychological Society Sport and Exercise Psychology Conference (Manchester, 2013). In many ways, therefore, our first encounter with visual methods was a happy accident.

Our research experiences then alerted us to the potentially powerful nature of the tool in eliciting participant cathartic reflections. As such, this sparked our enthusiasm to consider how to expose and engage our students with photography as a visual method. It also offered a counterpoint to the traditional research methods that they were currently being taught. Here, the students completed their own visual methods group projects as part of a postgraduate assessment. Students could take (or use existing) photographs to form reflective pieces about various aspects of family, environment or culture within which they live. For example, some students chose to use childhood photographs and others used photographs that represented emotions. The students engaged in reflections on their own photographs, before sharing these with the other group members and noting similarities and differences of opinion in each other's perceptions of the photographs and associated meanings.

We talk more about our pedagogic experience in Chapter 4 but for now it is enough to say that student engagement and commitment to these projects exceeded our expectations and underpins the aim of this text in encouraging the wider teaching of visual methods as an exciting and rewarding means of data collection. That is one that can be utilised in both higher and further education but also importantly, one that engages students with the research process by tapping into the visual practices that students ordinarily engage in via social media.

Alongside innovations in technology, it is evident that visual methods are advancing (Pink, 2012) but dissemination of such techniques through to the classroom and through subsequent application across the social sciences can be less common. Important to our learning and teaching has been first defining the scope of visual methods that we might use as social researchers and which can successfully be transferred through to our pedagogic practice. This is an important point because it is beyond the scope of this book to cover the many visual methods used in research today. Instead we focus simply on two- and three-dimensional methods that we believe can be incorporated into curricula, namely drawing, film, video, photographs and bricolage.

To this end, this book has two overarching aims: (1) to theoretically ground the use of visual methods as a highly innovative and useful means of data collection, (2) to inform pedagogic practice around the use of visual methods in the classroom and in so doing, provide sound guidance and practical advice to practitioners. The focus of this edited text is therefore to promote the use of visual methods more widely in the social sciences but, in particular, to encourage its use in HE programmes, to equip practitioners with the theoretical knowledge and pedagogic confidence to explore its potential through to the classroom and ultimately to enhance student experience of research data collection through its usage.

We recognise that there are some excellent texts on visual methods of data collection across the social sciences (e.g., Reavey, 2011; Spencer, 2011; Pink, 2012; Emmison, Smith and Mayall, 2012; Rose, 2013; Banks and Zeitlyn, 2015). The objective and justification for the text is to bring together the underpinning theoretical framework of visual methods. However, its overarching focus is as a teaching text: one that encourages the teaching of visual methods in the classroom but also sets out to pedagogically equip HE practitioners with the knowledge and confidence to design courses that disseminate visual methods as an appropriate and relevant data collection technique; also, one which gives direction to practitioners to promote students' hands-on practical experience through classes and assessment.

The book comprises three parts. In Part I, which consists of four chapters, we focus on the theoretical and practical application of visual methods, the related ethical issues and how it can be meaningfully embedded into higher education curricula. In Chapter 2 we consider visual research in the social world and contextualise its historical roots. This briefly explores the origins of visual methods, how these developed and evolved into the methods used in social science research today. Further it goes on to outline contemporary theoretical frameworks that we have found highly valuable in our own research and teaching and, which have added a critical dimension to our work. Chapter 3 goes on to explore the ethical considerations of using visual methods and related challenges, critically considering questions of ethical practice. Necessarily it explores the use of visual methods alongside the relevant codes of conduct (for example, the British Sociological Association and British Psychological Society codes of practice) and offers subject-specific guidance for its use in the classroom alongside practical pedagogic advice for practitioners. Chapter 4 focuses on the development of pedagogical application. This chapter turns its gaze to the design of curricula that include visual elements. It focuses first on models of learning and how teaching can be best structured in the enhancement of learning. The focus then moves to how visual methods can be incorporated into the curriculum as a vehicle for learning and teaching but one which also provides a unique opportunity for students to engage in creative and practical assessment. Further, in this chapter we discuss the pedagogical implications of assessing work that goes beyond set parameters and suggest ways in which assessment criteria can mediate this.

Part II is made up of pedagogical case studies where practitioners have incorporated visual methods into their curricula and teaching. Part II is further divided into two discrete sections that in the first instance look at case studies that utilise different visual methods, as distinct from the second part which focuses on different student populations and environments. In Chapter 5, the use of film in the assessment of undergraduate programmes is considered. The chapter explores how clips from feature films can enhance the student understanding of phenomenon, particularly in relation to assessment. Of key focus, this chapter explores the interpretation that students attribute to fictional footage based on the subjective nature of their worldviews, followed by prospective thoughts on how film can promote and enhance the development of empathetic understanding and reflection. Chapter 6 focuses on a drawing-based intervention. It explores the experience of social science students required to draw visual representations of their emotional experiences in relation to feedback and assessment within higher education. This chapter then unpacks how drawing can empower and enable students to critically reflect on their learning experiences and in turn engage in the reflexive process. Chapter 7 focuses on a range of techniques associated with intervention design and evaluation of using creative arts within undergraduate teaching and assessment. The chapter further explores the challenges faced by both the student and the teaching and learning practitioner in the context of engagement, performance and the development of graduate employability skills.

Moving on to focus on different population groups, Chapter 8 discusses visual methodological tools and considers the challenges and possibilities associated with film and photo-ethnography, as legitimate data sources and teaching resources in undergraduate teaching. It explores whether these methods can offer students a degree of insight that may be unavailable via alternative means, pertaining to the underpinning values, socio-political context, opportunities, possibilities and challenges of the projects discussed. Chapter 9 focuses on curriculum design but in particular the related pedagogic, practical and ethical issues of using visual techniques while undertaking field work with students. Specific attention is paid to the positive and rich experiences that students subsequently report when given the opportunity to incorporate visual methods when collecting field data. Finally, Chapter 10 considers the use of visual methods when crossing over cultures. This chapter explores the use of visual methods such as photographs and drawings in respect of working with students in an extended field trip to an Asian country. More specifically it will unpack and discuss the collection of visual data while at the same time addressing considerations around cultural and ethical responsibility.

Part III considers the overarching benefits and challenges of using and teaching visual methods in higher education curricula. Through critical discussion it focuses on the preceding case studies, giving examples of good practice and offering practical advice and potential solutions for common arising issues. Going full circle this final chapter then focuses on the use of visual methods in the social sciences, suggesting ways in which their usage could be embraced more fully. The necessity of the inclusion of a range of visual methods across both undergraduate and postgraduate curricula is highlighted in respect of developing students with balanced and well-rounded research methods training and the necessary skills to utilise visual methods as a meaningful qualitative technique in collecting data. The final chapter contains a range of practitioner resources. These resources are designed to form a basis for reference for practitioners who are considering implementing visual methods into their curricula. Here, templates and idea banks are provided to assist with this journey, and can be adapted according to individual preference and need.

References

Banks, M. and Zeitlyn, D. (2015). *Visual methods in social research*. London: Sage.

Emmison, M., Smith, P. and Mayall, M. (2012). *Researching the visual* (2nd edn). London: Sage.

Pink, S. (2012). *Advances in visual methodologies*. London: Sage.

Reavey, P. (2011). Back to experience: psychology and the visual. In P. Reavey (ed.), *Visual methods in psychology: using and interpreting images in qualitative research* (pp. 1–13). New York, NY: Routledge.

Rose, G. (2013). *Visual methodologies*. London: Sage.

Spencer, S. (2011). *Visual research methods in the social sciences: awakening visions*. London: Routledge.

Wakefield, C. and Watt, S. (2012). 'There will always be a part of you that wants to return': a reflective photo elicitation of an Ironman triathlon. *Qualitative Methods in Psychology, Special Issue: Focus on Sport and Performance, 2*(14), 40–52.

2

LOOKING BACK

The use of visual methods in the social sciences

Sal Watt and Caroline Wakefield

Background

Engaging our students in subject matter can sometimes be challenging, particularly so when it comes to teaching research methods. This could be for a variety of reasons including: Students would perhaps prefer not to engage in the respective philosophical approaches that underpin research methods; lack of understanding regarding the relevance of research methods to students' chosen disciplines; or simply the practicalities of actually conducting research. Whatever the resistance, when designing curricula this presents us with thought-provoking but also creative opportunities to engage students in research methods learning that importantly speaks to students at a level they understand and can experience alongside their everyday life and practices. Different learning styles and the range of these across and among the student body add to the challenge with some students preferring the rigidity or certainty of scientific or experimental methods of gathering and analysing data, while others prefer the more fluid nature of qualitative methods. In our own experience as students (in different subject areas), curriculum experience of qualitative methods equated to a brief introduction to observation and interviews. However, as teachers we wanted our own students to have a much wider experience of qualitative methods, and so a number of years ago we started to design curricula that extended qualitative provision at our home institution to include project work based on visual methods of data collection.

Through our own research experience, we found ourselves falling into the use of visual methods quite by chance. As it turned out, a fortuitous research opportunity subsequently went on to inform our pedagogy and enhanced the desire to engage students in a data collection method that spoke to them alongside their everyday practice of taking photographs. As regular consumers of social media and related technological applications such as 'Instagram' and 'Snapchat' our students are socially competent photographers, and the practice of taking and sharing photographs is an everyday norm. It therefore made perfect sense to us to align our teaching with this cultural shift by extending our qualitative provision to include the visual method of photography as a medium highly familiar and engaging to our students. While photography or the use of photographs has been the visual method of data collection that we favour, there are, of course, a number of visual methods or techniques that can be utilised, some of which are outlined within this text. However, it is important that primarily we talk about what we know; therefore, this exploration of the area of visual methods is predicated largely on our own research experience and classroom practice. Therefore, the following overview will first look at the origins of demographic map-making followed by the introduction of photographic evidence as research data. In addition to early origins of visual methods of data collection, this chapter will then move on to chart the usage of photography in social science research and address some of the related considerations and challenges regarding its usage.

Overview

Mapping out social issues

In origin, visual methods and the type of emergent data gathered is discipline specific but generally across the social sciences we would look to anthropology as the forerunners who harnessed the utility of photography (Knowles and Sweetman, 2004; Harper, 2012; Banks and Zeitlyn, 2015). Arguably, some of the ethnographies subsequently introduced in this chapter typically identify seminal points in time when the development and potential of photography to capture real world data was utilised. Typically, early ethnographic studies focused on indigenous tribes often in far-flung climes; however, early social data, which was both ethnographic and visual, can also be found much closer to home in the form of demographic maps that visually depicted data on social issues of the day. For example, John Snow is considered one of the founders of epidemiology whose initial research interest focused on respiration and theories of miasma. In 1849 (Snow, 1855), following an outbreak of cholera, *On the Mode of Communication of Cholera* was originally published, which suggested cholera was a water-borne disease. In 1854 when a further outbreak of cholera took hold in Snow's home locality of Soho, 550 people died across a 2-week period. Snow systematically identified and mapped the location of each of these deaths within the Soho area (see Figure 2.1). One exception was a death that fell beyond the locality and this death was that of a former wealthy resident of Soho who, on moving out of the area, insisted on consuming the preferred water of the old neighbourhood. In constructing a map of the deaths in the area, this one isolated case proved to be the key in Snow affirming cholera as a water-borne disease. In insisting on the water from the public water supply in Soho, the death of the wealthy former resident established the link between the cases and the root cause of the spread of cholera as emanating from a contaminated public water pump in Broad Street. Once the handle of the water pump was disabled, the number of reported cases of cholera went into immediate decline. Snow's theory

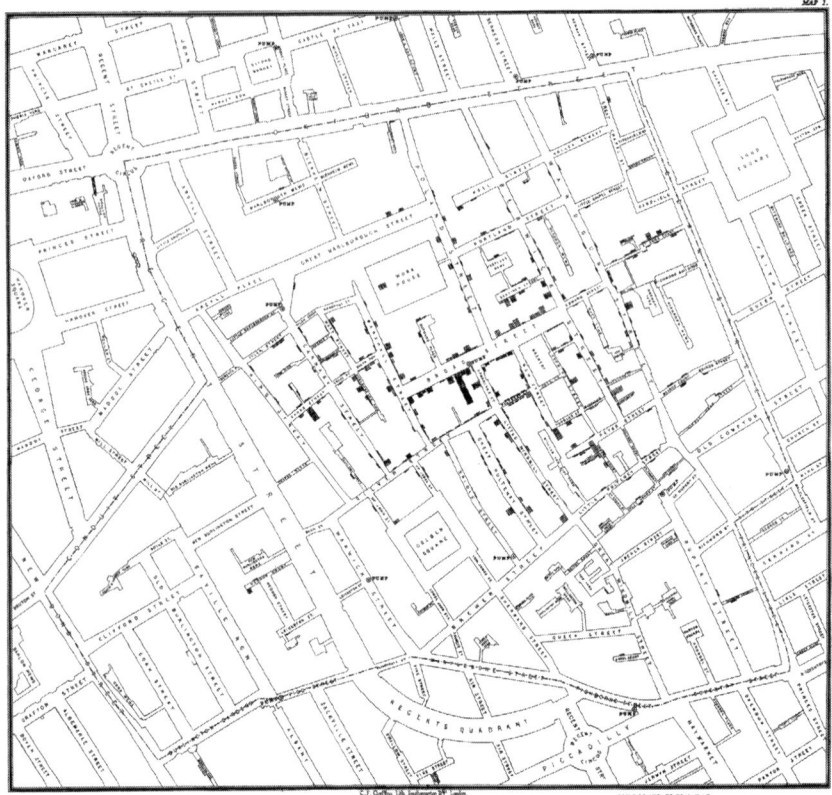

FIGURE 2.1 Original map made by John Snow in 1854. Cholera cases are highlighted in black.

Source: John Snow – Published by C.F. Chiffins, Lith, Southampton Buildings, London, England, 1854 in Snow, John. *On the Mode of Communication of Cholera*, 2nd edn, John Churchill, New Burlington Street, London, England, 1855. (This image was originally from storybench.) http://storybench.org/a-dummys-guide-to-mapping-daesh

of cholera as a water-borne disease was finally supported and later, so too was his theory of germs being responsible for the spread of disease more generally.

Snow's idea of visually mapping data is not an isolated example of a visual method of data collection around this time. Closer to the social sciences is the work of Charles Booth (1889) who initially investigated the class structure and therein poverty in the East End of London. Based on a quantitative and ethnographic approach, streets and residents therein were assigned a class status that indicated a level of affluence or poverty. A colour-coded system was applied that drew on a range of colours from yellow through to black, each of which denoted and classified the perceived social demographic of the respective streets. For example, a street or area identified as yellow indicated upper-middle and upper-class wealthy residents, a red street denoted middle-class residents considered 'well to do', through to streets classified in black in which residents were deemed as the lowest class with the potential to

FIGURE 2.2 Cropped section of Charles Booth's map of Whitechapel 1889. Darker shades indicate lower class areas.

Source. https://booth.lse.ac.uk/map/IS/-01499/51.5221/100/0

be vicious and semi-criminal. These colour-coded maps (see Figure 2.2) provided a visual representation of data that revealed the shocking depths of poverty and deprivation experienced in parts of the East End of London and went on to subsequently inform policy decision making around social intervention.

Booth's work continued across many more volumes (1891–1903), classifying and producing social demographic maps for other parts of London (for more on the work of Charles Booth, see Fried and Ellman, 1969; O'Day and Englander, 1993). Both case studies detailed here are invaluable in illustrating the use of visual maps as a data collection technique, but Booth's work, in particular, illustrates that in the social sciences there is a history of demographically collating data, the legacy of which is still in common use today. They also serve in demonstrating that visual methods can take many forms; forms that we might not necessarily or immediately identify as a visual method of data collection.

Visual representation: Photographic frames

Creative analytic practice

Earlier we mentioned that our own student training was limited and confined to simple observations or interviews. Our PhD training extended beyond this but it was the British Psychological Society's Inaugural Qualitative Methods in Psychology (QMiP) Conference in 2008 that opened up a world of other qualitative possibilities. In particular, the power of the visual was illustrated through a performative paper presented by Mary Gergen in 2008 (see Gergen, 2012 and Gergen in Willig and Stainton-Rogers, 2008 for wider information on feminist perspectives on qualitative methods and performance). Performative psychology was new to us but it fuelled our interest in different ways of expressing or disseminating data, ultimately leading us to creative analytic practice (CAP). CAP is an approach that seeks to reflect data within personal, social, political and cultural contexts. In doing so it pulls on various means of expression, and can take the form of poetry, drama, auto-ethnography, fiction stories, satire and visual representations such as photographs, films and videos (Willig and Stainton-Rogers, 2008) to name but a few. A developing interest in visual representation and in particular photographs, the process of photo-elicitation and photo-voice went on to influence our own research and subsequent pedagogic practice (Wakefield and Watt, 2012; Watt and Wakefield, 2014; Wakefield and Watt, 2015). This chapter will return to the process of photo-elicitation and photo-voice but first it is helpful to locate and chart the use of photographs in research and their influence in social science research.

Anthropological lens

The invention of photography can be traced back to the early experimentation of light and exposure by Thomas Wedgewood through to the work of Niepce (1826/7) and the daguerreotype process developed by Niepce's associate, Louis Daguerre in 1839 (Knowles and Sweetman, 2004; Harper, 2012). Commercialised photography subsequently became established and it is to the discipline of anthropology and its ethnographic approach that we first turn our gaze, as the discipline that harnessed its usefulness as a data collation tool. Observation as the key method of ethnography has already been illustrated through the work of social scientist Charles Booth. Sketching out a visual map of an environment for example is commonplace within field notes. However, the potential to supplement field note narrative with photographs provided an exciting dimension to research, which brought words, and worlds, to life. These early photographs supplemented the anthropological accounts of distant lands and the lifestyles of indigenous people (Harper, 2012) and photographs as documentary evidence of a one-dimensional narrative became normative practice. In contemporary society where information and knowledge can be sourced almost instantaneously through the internet, it is perhaps hard for us to imagine the impact of photographs as documentary evidence on a nineteenth- and twentieth-century audience. This was the first opportunity people had to view photographs of indigenous tribes and, while they served in widening understanding of cultural difference, it can be argued that they stimulated euro-centric interest and curiosity in what was perceived as alien or exotic culture. This perception is something we will return to later in the chapter but suffice at this point is to say that early anthropological ethnographic studies help us in understanding how photography began to inform social research and visual methods as a means of data collection.

Notable examples of ethnographic work in the twentieth century that employed photography as a data collection technique can be seen through the work of Bronislaw Malinowski (1922) and Margaret Mead (1928, 1942), who both drew on photographic documentary evidence when investigating the cultural and sexual practices of indigenous people in, for example, the Trobiand Islands. Still in print today, Malinowski's (1922) seminal text *Argonauts of the Western Pacific: An Account of Native Enterprise and Adventure in the Archipelagoes of Melanesian*, remains relevant today and is credited for contributing to theory on exchange and reciprocity. Considered as founding 'participant observation' as the key method in ethnographic work it is not surprising that Malinowski's work is supplemented by photographic evidence that allows the reader to become a remote observer of his experience of island life. Mead and Bateson (1942) similarly undertook work in the Pacific region studying the cultural and sexual habits of the people of Samoa and later, through Mead's work with Gregory Bateson, on Balinese culture more generally (for details of Mead and Bateson's work see Harper, 2012, pp. 10–17). These classic studies supplemented ethnographic field notes with photographic images opening up the viewfinder to other ways of being. For example, Mead's work on the pre-marital sexual habits and practices of Samoan women contributed widely to debates ongoing in the West, and in particular in the United States at that time, in relation to the sexual revolution of the 1960s and 1970s.

It is important, however, to see these early anthropological accounts in context. While these accounts were of general interest and shed new light and understanding of different cultures and cultural contexts they remained discipline specific. Relatedly Emmison, Smith and Mayall (2012), drawing on the words of Ball and Smith (2007), make the point that the use of photography has been more easily justified in anthropology than in sociology. The use of photographs as artefacts that provide evidence of cultural difference on topics or tribes perceived as 'exotic' is very different to sociological usage where the focus is often on normative society and/or societal issues or concerns. Therefore, a distinct disciplinary difference existed in the use of photographic evidence between sociology and anthropology, which revolved primarily around intent. The focus of photographs in anthropological accounts is typically one of trustworthiness whereby photographs provide evidence to substantiate or verify cultural context and locate the physicality of the ethnographer and anthropology itself. Conversely, sociological photographic evidence was, and still is, used more widely to support the need for reform or the repair of broken and problematic elements of society (Becker 2004; Knowles and Sweetman, 2004). Necessarily these two distinct usages have affected the popularity of using visual methods as a means of data collection.

This is not to say that sociology has not played its part in using visual methods, simply that its usage has been more conservative and subjected to scrutiny that is more critical. While Charles Booth in 1889 gathered data to construct demographic maps of London, during the same decade Riis and Hine in the United States similarly identified slum conditions in New York through photographic images (Knowles and Sweetman, 2004). Emmison, Smith and Mayall (2012) make the point that the use of photographs in American sociology became more commonplace at the turn of the century with the publication of 31 articles containing 244 photographic illustrations in the *American Journal of Sociology* between 1896 and 1916. However, as Stasz (1979) points out, on closer analysis, the publishing of the articles that drew on photographic illustrations was sporadic across this 20-year period. In 1905, an editorial shift began, that asserted a more scientific focus and which saw the eventual cessation of photographic material in papers from 1916 onwards (see Stasz 1979; Emmison, Smith and Mayall, 2012 for a more in depth account). This editorial decision intended to reposition sociology as being scientific similarly mirrors the positioning of psychology as a science. However, in sociology, it had the dramatic effect of largely quashing visual methods for over four decades. It was not until the 1970s that visual sociology began to re-emerge through the work of Howard Becker and Erving Goffman. Interestingly and somewhat ironically, Becker's article, 'Photography and sociology' (1974) was published in an anthropological journal. That said, in this article Becker (1974, p. 11) is highly critical of documentary photographers whose work relies on images to make a point, which he argued rendered them theoretically naive and under developed or, as Becker put it, 'intellectually and analytically thin'.

From the 1970s onwards, photographs as documentary evidence soon became established as a social research technique more widely across the social sciences. However, popularity over time has both wavered and varied with a number of different approaches emerging in respect of how photography can best be utilised. Becker (2002, 2004) makes the point that when we look at photographs we should first take a cursory look at the focus of the photograph followed by a closer inspection that importantly focuses on and studies its detail. This ensures that the content and understanding of the photograph is fully engaged with, thus exploring its full potential. As Becker (2002) points out, it is not sufficient to look at a photograph in isolation, we must also locate it within society and its societal and cultural context. It is perhaps hardly surprising in a fast-paced society where we are deluged with visual stimuli that too often we take a cursory look at images only to see what we expect to see, accepting photographic evidence as a given, without studying the minutiae of its detail, its context or its intended motivation. These are just a few considerations that hold the potential for misinterpretation of visual imagery and which contemporarily we see everyday examples of in the media and, perhaps closer to home, through the sometimes negative use of photographs on social media. The chances are most of us have had a direct negative experience of being, for example, tagged in an undesirable photograph, most probably our students have. Looking beyond social and/or personal experience, the potential to skew research data brings with it many considerations that need to be addressed and identified as possible issues to our students. Therefore, we need now to turn our gaze to the different ways in which visual data collection or representation is approached and the many associated issues and considerations.

Different ways of seeing

At the start of this chapter we suggested that visual data can come in different forms and we drew on the early construction of maps as a means of identifying, for example, outbreaks of cholera and social deprivation respectively. In the social sciences, such demographic maps continue to identify, for example, areas of deprivation or crime and so on, but contemporary methods draw on sophisticated and evolving technology such as Global Positioning Systems (GPS) in helping to monitor and track data in furthering the construction of social life. As the chapters in this text go on to illustrate, methods of visual data collection are many and varied, as too are the underpinning approaches. However, in our own research and teaching we have found the approach framework identified by Emmison, Smith and Mayall (2012) particularly helpful and one that students can negotiate when planning their own research. Emmison, Smith and Mayall (2012) make clear distinctions between:

- the use of researcher-produced visual materials;
- participant-centred approaches to the use of visual materials;
- the analysis of existing visual materials;
- the use of materials generated by video technology.

The examples drawn upon in this chapter so far squarely fall into the first category of '*researcher-produced visual materials*' both in the demographic maps referred to, the early use of photography in anthropology and, later, other social science disciplines such as sociology. As we have seen, this approach can be criticised around its scientific rigour and the potential to fall foul of accusations of documentary journalism. However, that said, when it comes to learning and teaching, this is a gentle way to introduce students to visual methods. Of course, alongside this is the need to adopt a reflective and reflexive approach that considers issues of, for example, subjective framing of a visual image. This is a point we will explore more later in this chapter and in subsequent chapters more generally.

Conversely a '*participant-centred approach*' puts participants at the heart of the research inquiry, whether that be in negotiating what visual imagery is possible, the framing of a photograph or its interpretation. There are numerous possibilities in this respect but essentially it is a collaborative process between the researcher and the participant that can facilitate processes such as 'photo-voice' (see Wang and Burris, 1997) or 'photo-elicitation' (see Harper, 2002). For example in our own research of an Ironman Triathlon event, the participant taking part in the event was collaboratively consulted regarding the intention to take photographs of him throughout the event and that later he would be asked to reflect on a small sample of the photographs through the process of 'photo-elicitation'. Such collaborative participation holds the potential to benefit the participant, for example, it can be meaningful, cathartic or empowering for the participant. Garrod (2007) suggests it provides useful opportunity for experiential reflection of the photograph's focus and importantly, the decision-making process of how and, to whom, it is disseminated. With this approach the participant's voice becomes central to the research and often it gives voice and access to topics and cultures that would otherwise be more difficult to access or study; as Behar would say of qualitative research more generally, 'the voices that often go unheard' (2003, p. 16). An example of this can be seen through the work of Anna Graham (in Graham and Kilpatrick, 2010) who ethnographically investigated social deprivation in an inner-city suburb. In her research, children were issued with disposable cameras and asked to take pictures of their life. This later allowed Graham to talk to each of the children about their home and what was important to them (Graham and Kilpatrick, cited in Scott Jones and Watt, 2010). The opportunity for the child to tell the story of their home and the personal objects through the photographs they took provided insight into their home life; detail that ordinarily would not be easily accessed or heard.

The third approach identified by Emmison, Smith and Mayall (2012) is '*the analysis of existing visual materials*'. Never before has so much visual imagery been available for us to examine and interpret. The traditional approach of looking to the arts or theology as a way of understanding our world has been superseded by technological development. The introduction of the camera, the later development of film and television through to the internet and the power of social media culminate in a proliferation of visual data, all of which inform and construct our social view of the world and its cultures. In short, it is a secondary-data approach that is popular in media and communication studies through to cultural and social geography, sociology and psychology alike (see Pink, 2012, 2015; Rose, 2013) which incorporates Emmison, Smith and Mayall's final approach, that of '*the use of materials generated by video technology*'. We have yet to venture into this final approach of data collection in our own research or teaching but again the possibilities with hand-held devices of this approach speaking to our students is multiple and Moira Lafferty's chapter later in this book illustrates the good use that can be made of film in the classroom.

From theory to application: Issues and consideration

In framing our own research and later when teaching visual methods we heavily relied upon the framework put forward by Gillian Rose (2012), that when working with a visual methodology we first need to think about the production of a visual image, the actual image itself and its audience. In deconstructing the process that underpins a visual methodology it helps us to critically reflect on the constituent parts of the process. As suggested at the beginning of this chapter, the taking of visual imagery has become an automatic and everyday process facilitated by the 'very' smartphones that we carry around with us. However, the problem in snapping away with our smartphone cameras is that often the minutiae, or possibly even the mundanity, of life are missed as we career to the next image. This holds the potential for us to become less critical or less observant of the images we take or who they are intended for. Rose's (2012) framework details the three sites of production, image and audience, each of which help focus and ensure we tread a critical path, a path that is crucial when teaching visual methods to our students. Beyond these sites fall what Rose calls 'modalities', each of which can be applied to the respective three sites. These modalities are: Technological, compositional and social. It is the interaction between the respective sites and modalities that facilitates a critical approach.

For example if we take '*site of production*', then a visual image can be taken by various means, composed under different conditions or parameters, and for various audiences. When teaching we find it useful to apply Rose's (2012) framework through personal and social application that students can identify with. For example, if someone uploads an unflattering photograph of us onto social media, or one that we were unaware had been taken, then it raises personal and social issues that students can identify with and map onto Rose's (2012) framework. The scenario exemplified raises questions such as: How has the image been produced? Has it been air-brushed or photo-shopped? How was it composed? What was the compositions purpose? What was the intention behind the focus? What was the social motivation for its production? Who was the intended audience? And why? In demonstrating the potential for interaction between the respective sites and modalities, Rose produced an excellent illustration that encapsulates the sites and the modalities (see 2012, p. 21). Beyond using this in our own research, we have adapted Rose's (2012) illustration for teaching purposes as below (see Figure 2.3).

In terms of the '*image*' itself, equally there are many considerations to take into account. Too often when teaching qualitative interviews, students have reported back that participant interviewees 'didn't give me what I wanted', which begs the question why would you think they knew what you wanted? Why should or would they? In the same vein, teaching visual methods to students can be equally challenging because they can either take the 'what should I photograph?' approach or conversely fall into the trap of only photographing the images that best suit their own purpose – often a subjective purpose. Therefore, in much the same way as an interviewee not 'giving what was wanted' we also need to critically challenge what images are taken and why. What is the purpose or motivation of the chosen setting? Is it typical or representative? In a culture of 'selfies' which has a tendency to privilege perfection, it is really important that we challenge the focus of our intention in order that photographic evidence does not become a product of self-fulfilling prophecy that suits our own ends or more generally fulfils societal or cultural stereotypes. When working with students this can be both thought-provoking and

SITE / MODALITY	Production	Image	Audience
Technological	How was the image made? e.g. camera/mobile phone camera?	Were there any effects applied to the image? e.g. air brushed or photo-shopped?	How was it transmitted or disseminated? e.g. social media?
Compositional	Intended genre? e.g. moody → black and white?	Why was the image composed? e.g. special event, graduation?	What was the image's context? Overt or covert?
Social	Who was the image intended for? Why?	What was the apparent visual meaning? e.g. celebratory event?	Who and how was it interpreted?

FIGURE 2.3 Sites and modalities: Adapted from Gillian Rose's model (2012).

problematic; drawing on Rose's (2012) framework necessarily evokes a reflective and reflexive approach that gives thought and voice to how images are determined and used.

We do, of course, also need to think about who takes a photograph and what his or her underpinning motivation may be. If we reflect back to anthropological work then early photographic evidence affirms the difference between western societal and cultural norms, and those found in far-away destinations or cultures. While our horizons were widened about previously unknown cultures and/or tribes, one only has to look at the photographs to recognise a potential hierarchical power relation at work. Becker's (2002) criticism of the journalistic-like qualities of documentary photographers serves as a warning that photographic evidence must be critically scrutinised not just in terms of its visual quality but the motivation that lies beneath the focus of the topic. This can be particularly demanding but also a rewarding activity to engage students in, for example, one that works beyond methodological consideration but through to application of their personal photographic practices in terms of their motivation, the frequency of the images they take and importantly the dissemination of their images.

The visual focus of this chapter has highlighted early demographic map-making and photography, but of course, as later chapters illustrate, other sites of visual production also include film, drawing and drama. What should underpin all these creative sites of production is the practice of reflection and reflexivity. Whatever the form of visual image making, there is the ongoing need to critique our own motivational practice, something that is not simply a visual or qualitative practice but something that should apply to all research whether that be qualitative, quantitative or mixed method. We do not design or undertake any form of research that is not a product of our own social reality and the way that social reality is constructed (Berger and Luckman, 1975, 1991; Gergen, 2001; Burr, 2003; Gergen, 2015). Therefore, we need to think about our own reality, the ways in which it has been influenced, by whom and the impact that has on our research or photographic practices. From research design through to dissemination, the need for reflective and then reflexive practice must underpin the data we collect, the findings we interpret and the pathways we choose for dissemination. This is crucial when it comes to visual images because, as seen too often in the media, the scope for misrepresentation can have negative and deleterious consequences. This is complex and deep 'stuff' to deal with especially for our students and Rose's (2012) framework helps enormously in compartmentalising the many aspects that need to be considered.

Audience effects

This brings us to Rose's (2012) final site, the '*audience*'. Whatever the creative form, whether it be a piece of writing, a painting, a drama, a drawing or a photograph, once it is disseminated out into the ether by whatever means, it takes on a life of its own. The very nature of social construction means any intended meaning by the producer is superseded by the social construction of reality the interpreter brings to it. The hierarchical power relation that we speculated about earlier in this chapter with regard to early anthropological photographs is our interpretation of a hierarchical power relation at work. Conversely, another interpretation might be one of tribal homage being, ceremoniously bequeathed on a revered anthropological visitor. As beauty is in the eye of the beholder, so too is the interpretation of any visual stimulus. How something is known and subsequently disseminated to an audience revolves around the subjective self and the social reality it has known and experienced. Issues of subjectivity regarding the production and use of visual imagery result in perennial problems which can stifle the creative process. Indeed with regard to the site of production and technological modality, Becker (2004) comments that subjective concerns around framing, focus and exposure of photographs hold back the potential use of visual imagery. Highlighting those journal papers that do emerge with visual images, Becker (2004) notes that authors have a tendency to overly angst about issues such as social reality and subjectivity. Certainly, in our own work and that of our students we have noticed this tendency to overthink related issues of subjectivity or subjective focus. Arguably, this prevails across qualitative research generally as we nonsensically seem to strive to align qualitative or visual methods alongside a scientific model which, when all said and done, is not a good fit for qualitative research by its very nature. However, Rose's (2012) framework of the *sites of production, image* and *audience* together with the interacting modalities does provide solid and practical opportunity to critically challenge and question the purpose, use and dissemination of visual images.

From process to practice

However, to be aware, reflective and reflexive of our ethical practice is crucial to all research but perhaps especially so when it comes to visual methods. Whatever discipline we research and teach in, we will be bound by an ethical code of practice that is discipline specific. The scope of ethical bodies and codes of conduct across the social sciences is beyond the capacity of this chapter. However, in our own disciplines of sociology and psychology we are bound by the British Sociological Association and the British Psychological Society codes of practice, both of which determine that we must be mindful of individuals' private space and non-infringement of personal right to privacy. In our respective disciplines, visual imagery and photographs in particular can only be taken in public spaces where people might expect to be photographed and in these instances, for example, individuals must not be captured in the foreground of a photograph. The exception to this general code of practice is, of course, where fully informed consent has been obtained. It is unlikely that codes of conduct will vary to any great degree across social science disciplines because all will be intent on protecting individuals and their basic human rights but practitioners must always consult their disciplinary ruling body before conducting research or before teaching visual methods. However, it must be noted that here we are talking about general guidelines; it should not be assumed that 'one size fits all'. Julie Scott Jones unpacks ethics in far more detail in the following chapter but until then, when thinking about ethics, we need to revert to issues of subjectivity and social construction. While we have guidelines that inform our ethical standpoint, these do so in alignment with our own social environment and habitat. Such familiarity subsequently informs our own ethical standpoint, however, we also need to think about ethical implications regarding the unfamiliar. What might be acceptable in a UK environment may not be acceptable, and should not be assumed so, in environments that lie beyond the UK. As later chapters will discuss, conducting field research and in particular student field research in countries beyond our shores, brings new ethical dimensions for consideration and adherence.

Conclusion: Our higher education experience of teaching visual methods

At the start of this chapter, we outlined that we began using visual methods after we were inspired by an approach known as CAP which seeks to explore data through political, social, personal and cultural contexts (Willig and Stainton-Rogers, 2008). We were attracted to this approach because it acknowledged the complexity of lived social lives and experiences but it offered a means of expression that was diverse and creative (Richardson, 2000; Schwandt, 2001; Parry and Johnson,

2007). The creative mode of CAP that seduced us was that of photography and in particular the process of photo-elicitation alongside. Over a cup of coffee, we discussed the journey a friend was about to embark upon; an Ironman Triathlon. We knew he was keen to have a record of his Ironman challenge and Caroline had agreed to photograph the all-day event. It occurred to us that this bank of photographs could be a collaborative venture whereby the Ironman could have a reflective record of his day and we could gain insight as to why someone would test their body and endurance to the nth degree; what did it feel like to physically, emotionally and psychologically complete such a challenge? We resolved to ask the Ironman whether he would be interested in engaging in a collaborative piece of research that set about throwing light on some of our questions. Following the event there were 252 photographs, which was clearly unworkable, so we settled on just seven photographs that could be said to encapsulate 'achievement' in some form. We asked our Ironman to reflect on his thoughts and feelings in this respect with regard to each of the seven photographs and he did so most eloquently (see Wakefield and Watt, 2012).

Working with our participant, the generosity with which he shared with us his thoughts and feelings on his sense of achievement was such a rewarding experience. It made us question our own training and want more for our own students; we wanted their research and qualitative toolkit to be more useful and relevant in contemporary society. Over subsequent years we went on to develop curricula that drew upon Emmison, Smith and Mayall's (2012) typology by providing opportunity for students to, either 'use researcher-produced visual materials' or draw on 'existing visual material'; thus engaging our students in photo-elicitation. Photo-elicitation is a process by which participants scrutinise and reflect on a photograph or photographs and then describe what thoughts and feelings the photograph evokes (Collier and Collier, 1999). This could be a subjective interpretation of an unfamiliar scene or activity or it could evoke memories and associated thoughts and feelings of the familiar (Sands, 2002), as was the case with our Ironman triathlete and the participants of Anna Graham's study mentioned earlier. Progressing the process one step further, Harper (2002) makes the point that neural processing of visual information occurs in evolutionary older parts of the brain and as such this evokes 'deeper elements of the human consciousness'; more so than aural processing. Collier and Collier (1999, p. 10) point out that 'photographs are precise records of material reality' and although they go on to say that 'most photographs are a minute time-sample – a hundredth-of-a-second slice of reality', (p. 13) they can nevertheless evoke powerful memories, thoughts and feelings that might otherwise not be expressed.

In Chapter 4 we go on to talk in more detail about the curricula we developed with our students, but for now it is enough to say our experience has been a positive one. Our students have fed back positively about the method of using photographs to elicit reflections and the creativity that the method has allowed them to explore. Knowles and Sweetman (2004) note that there has been an expansion of teaching visual representations in recent years and while some higher education institutions have visual methods embedded in curricula, others simply do not. This could be because of concerns around a lack of academic expertise to teach visual methods, issues of subjectivity, ethical concerns or other related disciplinary constraints. Without doubt, the use of visual methods varies across the social sciences, as does the extent to which visual methods are taught or embedded in the curriculum. The objective of this chapter was to briefly provide an introduction to practitioners who may be unfamiliar with how visual methods have been utilised in the social sciences, to outline how we came to draw on visual methods in our own research and how it inspired us to want to share the creativity of using visual methods with our students. The challenge we throw open to readers of this chapter and those that follow is to consider how you could design curricula that incorporate the option for your students to gain the fulfilling and creative experience of using visual methods.

Suggested reading

Banks, M. and Zeitlyn, D. (2015). *Visual methods in social research*. London: Sage.

Burr, V. (2003). *Social constructionism*. London: Routledge.

Berger, P.L. and Luckman, T. (1991). *The social construction of reality: a treatise in the sociology of knowledge*. London: Penguin Social Sciences.

Harper, D. (2012). *Visual sociology*. London: Routledge.

Knowles, C. and Sweetman, P. (2004). *Picturing the social landscape: visual methods and the sociological imagination*. London: Routledge.

Rose, G. (2012). *Visual methodologies*. London: Sage.

References

Ball, M. and Smith, G. (2007). Technologies of realism? Ethnographic uses of photography and film. In P. Atkinson, A. Coffey, S. Delamont, J. Lofland and L. Lofland (eds), *Handbook of Ethnography* (pp. 301–19). London: Sage.

Banks, M. and Zeitlyn, D. (2015). *Visual methods in social research*. London: Sage.

Becker, H.S. (1974). Photography and sociology. *Studies in the Anthropology of Visual Communication*, *1*, 3–26.

Becker, H.S. (2002). Visual evidence: a seventh man, the specified generalization, and the work of the reader. *Visual Studies*, *17*(1), 3–11.

Becker, H.S. (2004). Afterword: photography as evidence, photographs as exposition. In C. Knowles and P. Sweetman (eds), *Picturing the social landscape: visual methods and the sociological imagination* (pp. 193–7). London: Routledge.

Behar, R. (2003). Ethnography and the book that was lost. *Ethnography*, *4*, 15–39.

Berger, P.L. and Luckmann, T. (1975). *The social construction of reality*. London: Penguin Books.

Berger, P.L. and Luckmann, T. (1991). *The social construction of reality: a treatise in the sociology of knowledge*. London: Penguin Social Sciences.

Booth, C. (1889). *Life and labour of the people* (1st edn), Vol. I.

Burr, V. (2003). *Social constructionism*. London: Routledge.

Collier, J. and Collier, M. (1999). *Visual anthropology: photography as a research method*. Albuquerque, NM: University of New Mexico Press.

Emmison, M., Smith, P. and Mayall, M. (2012). *Researching the visual* (2nd edn), London: Sage.

Fried, A. and Ellman, R. (eds) (1969). *Charles Booth's London*. London: Hutchinson.

Garrod, B. (2007). A snapshot into the past: the utility of volunteer-employed photography in planning and managing heritage tourism. *Journal of Heritage Tourism*, 2(1), 14–35.

Gergen, K.J. (2001). *Social construction in context*. London: Sage.

Gergen, M. (2008). Qualitative methods in feminist psychology. In C. Willig and W. Stainton-Rogers (eds), *The SAGE handbook of qualitative research in psychology* (pp. 280–95). London: Sage.

Gergen, M. (2012). *Feminist reconstructions in psychology: narrative, gender and performance*. London: Sage.

Gergen, K.J. (2015). *An invitation to social construction*. London: Sage.

Graham, A. and Kilpatrick, R. (2010). Understanding children's educational experiences through image-based research. In J. Scott Jones and S. Watt (eds), *Ethnography in social science practice* (pp. 89–106). London: Routledge.

Harper, D. (2002). Talking about pictures: a case of photo elicitation. *Visual Studies*, 17, 13–26.

Harper, D. (2012). *Visual sociology*. London: Routledge.

Knowles, C. and Sweetman, P. (2004). *Picturing the social landscape: visual methods and the sociological imagination*. London: Routledge.

Malinowski, B. (1922). *Argonauts of the Western Pacific: an account of native enterprise and adventure in the Archipelagoes of Melanesian*. London: Routledge and Kegan Paul.

Mead, M. (1928). Coming of *age in Samoa: a psychological study of primitive youth for western civilisation*. New York: William Morrow.

Mead, M. and Bateson, G. (1942). *Balinese character: a photographic analysis*. New York: New York Academy of Sciences.

O'Day, R. and Englander, D. (1993). *Mr Charles Booth's inquiry: life and labour of the people in London reconsidered*. London: Hambledon Press.

Parry, D.C. and Johnson, C.W. (2007). Contextualising leisure research to encompass complexity in lived leisure experience: The need for Creative Analytic Practice. *Leisure Studies*, 29, 119–30.

Pink, S. (2012). *Advances in visual methodologies*. London: Sage.

Pink, S. (2015). *Digital ethnography: principles and practice*. London: Sage.

Richardson, L. (2000). Writing: a method of inquiry. In N.K. Denzin and Y.S. Lincoln (eds), *Handbook of qualitative research* (2nd edn, pp. 923–48). London: Sage Publications.

Rose, G. (2012). *Visual methodologies*. London: Sage.

Sands, R.R. (2002). *Sport ethnography* Champaign, IL: Human Kinetics.

Schwandt, T. (2001). *Dictionary of qualitative inquiry* (2nd edn), Thousand Oaks, CA: Sage.

Scott Jones, J. and Watt, S. (2010). *Ethnography in social science practice*. London: Routledge.

Snow, J. (1855). *On the mode of communication of cholera*. London: John Churchill.

Stasz, C. (1979). The early history of visual sociology. In J. Wagner (ed.), *Images of information: still photography in the social sciences* (pp. 119–36). Beverley Hills, CA: Sage.

Wakefield, C. and Watt, S. (2012). 'There will always be a part of you that wants to return': A reflective photo elicitation of an Ironman triathlon. *Qualitative Methods in Psychology, Special Issue: Focus on Sport and Performance*, 2(14), 40–52.

Wakefield, C. and Watt, S. (2015). A double take: the practical and ethical dilemmas of teaching the visual method of photo elicitation. *Psychology Teaching Review*, 20(2), 143–55.

Wang, C.C. and Burris, M.A. (1997). Photovoice: concept, methodology, and use for participatory needs assessment. *Health Education and Behaviour*, 24, 369–87.

Watt, S. and Wakefield, C. (2014). Picture it!: The use of visual methods in psychology teaching. *Psychology Teaching Review*, 20(1), 28–35.

Willig, C. and Stainton-Rogers, W. (2008). *The SAGE handbook of qualitative research in psychology*. London: Sage.

3

RESEARCH ETHICS AND VISUAL METHODS

Julie Scott Jones

What are ethics?

This chapter will explore what we mean by 'research ethics' and why a consideration of ethics within our research is crucial to contemporary research practice. It will provide an overview of the key ethics concepts and explore some of the central debates in relation to ethics within the social sciences. As pedagogic practitioners teaching contemporary research practice, visual methods of data collection bring a set of unique ethical issues that must be considered in our own work and relayed as good practice to our students. Research ethics are a key element, some would argue *the* core element, of research involving human participants. All academic disciplines that engage in research that involves human participants incorporate ethics into their research training and practice. Increasingly, there is a greater appreciation of shared concepts and practices across academic disciplines; psychologists and sociologists can learn from medical researchers and *vice versa*. The origins of contemporary ethical principles lie in wider ethical debates within philosophy, theology, religion and law. Ethics is a broad category of concepts, principles, and practices; it will become clear that what is and is not ethical is highly contested. It is important to appreciate that 'being ethical' is not an instrumental process and this chapter is not a 'how to' guide; rather ethical practice is highly dependent on the researcher and the research context.

A brief history of ethics

It is important to appreciate the historical context from which contemporary ethical concepts emerge; today's ethical regulations developed in response to specific cases of unethical practices. Additionally an examination of some of the more infamous cases affords us an opportunity to reflect on key concepts and to develop ways to ensure good ethical conduct. The foundational ethical concept can be found in medicine; 'first do no harm', which is the first commitment of the Hippocratic Oath. The minimisation of harm is key to all research practice that we can deem 'ethical'. It is within the field of medicine in the nineteenth century that the first debates regarding what is (and is not) 'ethical' began. Relatedly there was a parallel debate concerning who should regulate this 'ethical practice'. The consensus was that medical researchers, invariably doctors, were inherently 'moral' and scientifically neutral, without bias; thus, they did not need any fixed regulation (Brazier, 2008). Consequently, 'ethical' practice was whatever the medical researchers deemed 'appropriate' within their context. This model can be termed paternalistic and 'expert-centric'; or to put it more colloquially 'Doctor knows best' (Layman, 2009). When social science research emerged in the late-nineteenth century a similar model of the objective, value-neutral, researcher was adopted which had an implicit presumption that there was no need to clearly articulate 'ethics' or 'ethical practice'. This 'researcher knows best' model survived until the latter half of the twentieth century when disquiet at a number of notorious cases of unethical practice in medical and social science research prompted change.

In 1947, the so-called Doctors' Trial in Nuremberg was the first to shine the spotlight on the problem with the 'researcher knows best' approach. This was a trial of Nazi doctors and other medical staff who conducted horrific experiments on concentration camp inmates during the Second World War. It is interesting to note that these Nazi doctors worked within a professional context in Germany, which had tougher ethical guidelines than any other western nation at that time; demonstrating that the existence of guidelines does not mean that people will act ethically. Indeed, it also demonstrates that what is 'ethical' is shaped by specific socio-cultural contexts (Layman, 2009). To illustrate, the Nazi doctors experimented upon concentration camps' inmates because they believed them, based on racialised discourses, to be 'lesser' humans than themselves and therefore lacking in human rights. The use of participants deemed racially inferior is also a feature of the Tuskegee Syphilis Experiment, which ran 1932–72 in the United States. This was a study funded by the US government to examine the long-term consequences of syphilis. Researchers based in Alabama recruited 399 poor, African-American men who had syphilis. In the United States in the 1930s, particularly in the southern states, African Americans were seen as racially inferior to Whites. In return for their participation, the volunteers received free health care and believed themselves to be furthering medical science's search for a cure for syphilis; the original study was to be short term and focused on observing how the disease spread and affected the body. However, the study was expanded and became a 'to-the-death' project; the men were wilfully deceived as to the purpose of the study. The researchers did not intend to treat the men (they were given placebos) but rather chart the disease's impact on their bodies. A public outcry finally ended the study, by which time over a third of the men had died. If we review the past 150 years of experimentation involving human subjects, we see the recurring use of individuals deemed marginal or 'lesser' within a society, including the mentally ill, physically disabled, homeless, prisoners, and so forth; often the most vulnerable of society are the most open to exploitation by researchers (Brazier, 2008).

One outcome of the Doctors' Trial was the *Nuremberg Code*, which represents the very first attempt to produce a universally agreed list of ethical guidelines for researchers. The defining principles of the *Nuremberg Code* are 'informed consent' and 'avoidance of harm'. However, the *Nuremberg Code* did not seriously alter the approach taken by researchers; it was not legally enforced and researchers were left to 'be moral' and 'ethical'. To illustrate, the *Nuremberg Code* did not stop the Tuskegee experiment from continuing for a further 25 years. In addition, it remained commonplace for doctors in the United States and many other western nations to include patients in medical trials without their consent (Brazier, 2008).

FIND OUT MORE

There are many online resources on the Doctors' Trial and the Tuskegee Syphilis Experiment. Go online and examine these cases in more detail; can you identify the following:

the rationale used by the researchers for their experiments; the unethical practices; public reaction to the cases; what ethical regulations emerged in response to them?

So far, this section has discussed cases within medical research but social science researchers have also participated in unethical practice. Until the 1970s, deception was common within psychology experiments (Herrera, 1997), for example, the Milgram Experiment (1963). In field research within sociology, deception was also commonplace, for example, in the work of Humphreys (1970). Deception is often justified within social science research not just because of a 'researcher knows best' attitude but due to a specific view of data collection that believes people will only behave 'naturally' when they do not know they are being studied or know the true purpose of why they are being studied. This position is problematic because how can we ever truly know if people are acting 'naturally', irrespective of setting (Herrera, 1997)? In the Milgram Experiment (1963), volunteers consented to participate in a 'learning experiment'; they had to administer electric shocks to a 'learner' when the latter failed to answer questions correctly. The volunteers were cajoled to continue to administer the shocks by one of the researchers present even when the 'learner' screamed in pain. Milgram was seeking to explore how ordinary people commit often-atrocious acts when ordered to by authority figures; ironically, he was seeking to account for the behaviour of guards in Nazi concentration camps. However, he deliberately deceived his volunteers as the electric shocks were fake and the 'learner' was pretending to be in pain (Nicholson, 2011). Zimbardo (1973) also wanted to explore the interaction between authority and obedience. In 1973, he set up the Stanford Prison Experiment on campus at Stanford University; a mock prison was constructed and students were either allocated to the role of 'guard' or 'prisoner'. Zimbardo assumed the role of prison governor and the students played out the roles they were given. The experiment was suspended after only a few days due to growing violence among the 'guards' towards the 'prisoners' and increasing emotional distress among the 'prisoners'. The Stanford Prison Experiment, like the Milgram Experiment, is unethical because it caused harm to its participants; neither researcher did little to minimise this harm (Tolich, 2014). Laud Humphreys was a sociologist who wanted to tackle prevailing homophobic attitudes to homosexuality in his 1970 study of illicit sex between men in public toilets (so called 'tea-room trade'). He went undercover and observed men in this setting, taking on a participatory role (as the 'watch-queen'). Humphreys tracked the men's home addresses via their car license plates and conducted 'interviews' with them under the guise of a 'health survey'. Many of his participants were married men and this study occurred at a time when homosexuality was still illegal in the United States. Not only did Humphreys deceive his participants but he also risked harming them in terms of reputational and legal harm (Babbie, 2004). Humphreys, himself gay, justified his approach as vital in demystifying homosexual encounters between men (not all of them gay) and thus challenging homophobia (Babbie, 2004). One interesting thing about these three cases is that each researcher made claims to 'the greater good' (in terms of furthering our understanding) through unethical practice; in a sense a wrong to right a wrong.

EXPLORE IN MORE DETAIL

It can be useful to review some of the infamous cases of poor ethical practice in order to gain a greater understanding of the key concepts. Find out more on the following case studies:

Milgram Experiment (1963)
Stanford Prison Experiment (1973)
Humphrey's 'Tearoom Trade' (1970)

- Can you identify the central elements that make these studies 'unethical'?
- Can you suggest how you might make these studies 'ethical' by today's standards?

The late-1960s onwards saw the emergence of a greater concern with ethics, prompted by the civil rights movements of the era that challenged the representation and treatment of specific communities, challenging long-standing conceptions of power and authority, including 'scientific' authority. New methodological approaches emerged within these movements, including Feminism, and these challenged the paternalistic, 'researcher knows best' model and placed ethics at the heart of research practice. These new methodologies, alongside reaction to a range of cases of unethical practice, including the Tuskegee Syphilis Study, led to more complex and widespread ethical regulations, the most widely accepted being the *Helsinki Protocol* (2013), which operates as a universal ethics code for the medical and social sciences. Today all universities, public organisations, research agencies and professions have ethical codes, most of which derive from the *Helsinki Protocol*. However, it is important to remember that such codes are not usually legally enforceable or binding but instead carry a moral and reputational force.

FIND OUT MORE

Go online and explore some of the ethics guidelines that are available. Start with your own university and subject area (most academic disciplines have a professional organisation, for example, the British Psychological Society). You might then explore more international guidelines, such as the *Helsinki Protocol*.

- What ethical concepts are common to all these guidelines? Are there any that are subject specific?

Teaching research methods itself can often be challenging around student engagement but when we add ethics into the mix, ethical consideration can be perceived by students as a 'tick box' exercise; a process to be complied with but not necessarily engaged with fully at a deeper level. Pedagogically it can be problematic trying to convey the importance of ethics to students as something to be embodied rather than as a process to be tolerated. Ethical consideration of visual methods in itself is challenging because technologically our students are contemporarily so used to taking and sharing photographs via social media; often 'tagging' people with little thought to individual privacy or consent. Nevertheless, as researchers and practitioners, our responsibility is to disseminate key ethical concepts through our teaching. Additionally, the technological familiarity our students have in using images presents us with a unique opportunity for students to consider ethical practice alongside their own social experiences of visual dissemination. For example, many of us have been tagged in a photograph on social media and have not appreciated the image the 'tagger' has chosen. Teaching the key ethical concepts through social experience can provide us with thought-provoking opportunities for our students that bring the following concepts to life.

Key ethical concepts

Informed consent

What is informed consent?

The central ethical concept, to which all other concepts relate, is that of 'informed consent'. Consent simply means 'agreement'; the agreement of an individual to participate in research. However, 'agreement' alone is not sufficient for us to be ethical; participants must first be fully aware ('informed') about the planned research. The onus is on researchers to ensure that their participants are fully 'informed' prior to consenting to participate; failure to do this makes the work 'unethical' and may put participants at risk. If we consider the Milgram and the Tuskegee Syphilis Experiments, researchers gained consent from participants. However, in both cases participants did not know what they were agreeing to, nor were they informed of potential for harm. Researchers must consider two questions when considering 'informed consent'; first, can the research participants understand the concept? Second, can they give their consent freely? This is particularly important when undertaking visual research because not only do we have to think about the informed consent of those participants who have knowingly agreed to take part in a visual research study but also those who have the potential to unknowingly become part of a visual research project. For example, if a student project focuses on family photographs, then informed consent from all family members in the photographs, must be obtained. A further consideration around consent when taking photographs in public places concerns people who are located in the background, and this will be discussed later in the chapter.

Do research participants understand consent?

There are two types of participants who may not necessarily understand the concept of consent; the first are those who have a lack of cognitive development (owing to age or disability), making them unable to understand the concept of 'consent' or the full nature of the research. The obvious members of this group are children (particularly under the age of 11) and adults with learning difficulties and cognitive impairment. Researchers usually seek consent from parents, teachers and caregivers when working with such participants; although increasingly researchers think that it is important that children and adults with learning difficulties be part of the consent process, alongside their primary caregivers. Crucially in relation to visual methods, it is a legal requirement under child protection legislation, that researchers obtain consent from parents and/or appropriate gatekeepers to film/take photographs of children. Further, wherever possible, beyond primary caregivers, assent from a child should also be obtained. It is one thing for a primary caregiver to give consent, but this does not account for whether the child wishes to be part of the study. Consideration should also be given to the child's wishes.

The second category of participants who may not understand consent are those adults who we may deem 'vulnerable' due to their life circumstances and thus may not be sufficiently capable at a specific time to fully give 'consent', for example, substance misusers, the homeless or the bereaved. Researchers must consider their participants and assess whether they are able to give 'informed consent' at the time of asking; appropriate specialists, like doctors, teachers or social workers, may provide advice. Often researchers must use 'gatekeepers' to assist them in gaining consent when dealing with 'vulnerable' participants. However, again any possibility of visual data must be appropriate and handled sensitively.

Is consent given without coercion?

Researchers must ensure that participants give their consent freely, without coercion. Coercive consent is when participants feel real or perceived pressured to agree to take part in research, even when they do not want to. Coercive consent can appear benign, for example, asking your mother to be a participant or offering your friend a free meal for completing your questionnaire. Can they truly say no to you? It can also be more malign, for example, withholding treatment to patients who refuse to participate in medical research. It is important that researchers consider to what extent participants are giving their consent freely, particularly student researchers who may more commonly call on family and friends to participate. This does not mean that you cannot use such participants but it is important that you make it very clear that their participation is optional. With student visual projects as exemplified earlier, student focus might be on family photographs therefore it is really important that family members are not coerced into participating in projects if they do not wish to participate.

How to ensure consent is 'informed'?

In order to ensure that consent is 'informed' researchers should provide prospective participants with information about the research, ideally as much as possible. This may be in the form of briefings, an information sheet, online materials and so forth; indeed this process may involve a combination of methods and can be quite lengthy. Information can be shared with participants face to face or via various online media; the process should be dialogic, in other words, participants should be able to ask questions and seek clarifications. The process should not be a one-way (nor one-off) exchange of information from the researcher to the researched. Indeed with visual research it should be a collaborative process in respect of both the focus of the visual material and its subsequent usage.

The key is to provide as much information as possible and to be as honest as you can with your prospective participants. For example, individuals may still consent to participate in a study where they may feel mild pain or discomfort; the crucial thing is that they knew they would experience this pain. Information sheets should be written in clear, non-technical, non-academic language. It is easy for researchers (and students) to forget that most people do not speak or understand technical, subject-specific jargon.

It is important that you 'future-proof' your research, so that data collected in the present do no future harm to participants. This is particularly pertinent when considering visual data collected from young people or 'vulnerable' adults. For example, a piece of research where teenagers have been filmed expressing extreme political views and participating in anti-social behaviour may continue to be

INFORMED CONSENT

Here are some of the key questions that participants need to ask before participation; they should be answered on an information sheet:

- Why do you want me as a participant?
- What is the research about?
- What is the point of the research?
- What will I have to do?
- How long will it take?
- What sorts of data/information will you be collecting about me/from me?
- How will you keep my information safe?
- What will you do with the information that you collect from me?
- Will others see my information?
- How can I contact you after the research?
- Can I see the completed research?
- Do I have the right to withdraw from the research at any time?
- What if I change my mind about taking part?
- What if I am not comfortable with some of the questions/photos/activities asked of me?

This list is not exhaustive; can you think of other questions?

viewed online when those teenagers are adults who may have abandoned such views and are trying to pursue careers. In this situation, their 'younger' selves are harming the research participants, now adults. Therefore, it is crucial in research featuring visual methods that researchers make three things very clear (i) how the research (and its data) will be disseminated, (ii) the potential longevity of the visual data and (iii) the possible long-term consequences for participants of this visual data. In these cases, the researcher must consider whether the young person's adult self would consent to participate.

Is consent needed in public spaces?

It is commonly accepted that researchers need not necessarily seek consent when conducting observations in public spaces, such as railway stations, shopping centres, or cafes. However, due to increasing legislation regarding surveillance, privacy and child protection, it is important that researchers seek consent prior to filming or photographing people in public spaces. Even if you intend to remove identities via pixilation, it is crucial that you seek consent from whoever manages a specific public space, otherwise you may face removal from that space or even prosecution, particularly if the space features children. Researchers do not have the same rights as photo-journalists in public spaces.

How do you prove you have consent?

Increasingly researchers must provide an audit trail to demonstrate that they have consent. Typically, participants sign a consent form prior to the start of the research. Consent forms can be distributed by hand or online. Consent forms can be quite detailed and should include all the key things to which the participant consents. There should be a space for signatures and the date on which consent was given. If you require your participant to consent to filming/photography then this should be a specific item on the form. You may want to give participants options, for example:

- 'I give consent to my photo being taken as long as it is pixelated.'
- 'I give consent to my photo being taken as long as it is pixelated and only published in a journal article.'
- 'I give consent to my photo being taken as long as it is pixelated and I agree to the researcher using it in a variety of outputs.'

Again, it is important that consent forms are written in clear, non-technical or academic language; key terms such as 'pixelated' should be explained. In relation to data captured on film it is important that all individuals featured have given consent; you might find that some people in a film or photograph wish to be pixelated, while others do not. It can be frustrating for visual researchers to have to delete or pixelate images of specific individuals. Such editing may reduce the impact or significance of the data. However, to not do this would be unethical and a violation of the research participant's rights. If researchers build a dialogic relationship with participants then trust develops which can lead to participants being more comfortable with their images being used within research. Consent is not a one-off event that happens before research starts, researchers must appreciate that as research evolves its focus may change; participants may not have consented to 'new' elements of the research and thus consent should be sought once more.

TIME TO HAVE A TRY

Imagine you wish to research teenagers' use of social media, specifically in relation to friendship networks. The research will involve the collection of interview data and visual data from mobile phones and social networking sites.

- How would you provide information to your prospective participants? What would your information include? What would your consent form look like?

Right to withdraw

The right to withdraw is a concept intrinsically linked to informed consent. If one consents to participate, one also has the right to change one's mind and withdraw from the research. Without the right to withdraw, the research becomes coercive and consent meaningless. When seeking informed consent researchers must ensure that it is clearly stated that participants have the right to withdraw from the research at any time during the research process. Researchers should make it clear that the right to withdraw is not conditional, that is, participants need not provide a reason for their withdrawal nor should researchers insist on one. Once a participant withdraws from research then all their data must be destroyed and cannot be used by the researcher or stored. Good ethical practice in relation to visual data means that the 'right to withdraw' should be available post-research too, specifically in relation to where and when such data are published. This is crucial given the ready availability of digital visual data when posted online.

Avoidance of harm

Types of harm

The very first ethical principles were concerned with the avoidance of harm. The development of subsequent ethical regulations were an attempt to avoid the very real harm done to research participants in the nineteenth and twentieth centuries in the name of medical and social science. Harm was traditionally interpreted as physical harm, but in contemporary research ethics, it is broader:

- **physical harm**: Physical harm to the participant, such as injury, illness, death;
- **emotional harm:** Emotional harm to the participant, such as stress, distress, depression, worry;
- **reputational harm:** The participant's reputation is harmed, for example, their professional standing as a doctor or lawyer;
- **social harm:** The participant's social status is harmed, for example, their status within a specific community;
- **legal harm:** The participant is identified as participating in illegal activities and potentially criminalised.

Researchers must carefully consider all these types of harm within the design and planning of their research and ensure that steps are taken to minimise harm. When seeking consent from participants, researchers should be explicit about potential harm within the research. Increasingly, researchers explore the issue of harm through formal risk assessments, which are a usual requirement of any form of research involving human participants. It is unrealistic to expect researchers to avoid all harm, especially during the research process when situations can change quickly; nevertheless, researchers must be reflective and consider potential harm throughout the process. Again it is important to consider future harm to participants; for example, photos showing illegal behaviour may cause reputational or social harm to participants in the future.

Minimisation of harm

Most research design has specific protocols in place to minimise harm to participants beyond mere reassurances on consent forms. The risk of physical harm is greatest in disciplines which conduct actual physical testing on human subjects, for example, taking blood/tissue samples, body scanning, mental testing and so forth. The physical testing of human subjects particularly where it involves the collection of bodily tissues or fluids is increasingly governed by legislation that dictates specific harm-avoidance protocols. As these usually occur in clinical settings, they are also governed by long-established risk protocols. Physical-harm risks to participants in non-clinical settings, that is, field settings are less easy to control or minimise and researchers may not foresee potential harm. There is also the ethical grey area of participants revealing that they physically self-harm either through alcohol/drug misuse, risky physical behaviours (such as unprotected sex), or forms of deliberate self-harm such as cutting, starving and so forth. Are researchers ethically bound to intervene in such cases and offer support? Alternatively, is that beyond the scope of their role? There are no clear answers and researchers themselves must reflect on what is appropriate.

Emotional harm is also less easy to foresee but researchers examining so-called sensitive topics, for example, bereavement, domestic violence, body image and so forth, should ensure that counselling sessions are available should the participant become distressed. Additionally, good ethical practice would be to offer debriefing sessions at the end of the research to allow potential emotional harm issues to be identified. Reputational and social harm again may be harder for researchers to predict and may only emerge as research ends and is published; the use of anonymity can help alleviate such forms of harm. Legal harm is a grey ethical area in that researchers often witness their participants doing (or indeed talking about) illegal activities and choose not to report them to the relevant authorities. Their rationale is that they have a duty to protect their participants with whom they have built trust and rapport. However, this is a highly contentious approach, which places the researcher in legal harm, and more importantly, perhaps, gives great power to the researcher to decide what is right and wrong. Would for example the commitment to protecting participants from legal harm be acceptable if participants were directly harming others?

Harm and the researcher

Much of this chapter has so far focused on protecting participants, but a consideration of harm should also include protecting researchers. The history of research in medicine and the social sciences features a great deal of harm to researchers.

In the nineteenth century, auto-experiments were commonplace in medicine; researchers used themselves as guinea pigs to test drugs and treatments, often with deadly results. In the twentieth century, social scientists conducting participant observations put themselves at considerable risk of harm; Patrick (1973) was beaten up while studying gangs in Glasgow; Pearson (2009) witnessed illegal activity during his research on football hooligans; and Humphrey's (Babbie, 2004) research involved him in illegal activity and brought him some reputational harm. Increasingly, risk assessment and consideration of harm focuses as much on researchers as participants. Partly this is due to an increasingly risk-averse culture within universities and other research-intensive organisations and partly due to the increasingly litigious contemporary culture.

STUDENT RESEARCHERS AND SAFETY

What sorts of safety protocols and guidance do you think students could build into their research designs to minimise them experiencing the following types of harm:

- physical
- emotional
- legal?

Confidentiality and anonymity

Confidentiality and anonymity are often used synonymously; they are related but different concepts and it is important that they be treated as such. Confidentiality refers to the keeping of the participant's personal information confidential, that is not published or posted publicly. Relatedly it means that the researcher must store the participant's personal information securely and place access restrictions upon it. Participants may itemise what they wish to keep confidential through discussions of consent. Confidentiality may be important in order to protect participants from forms of harm, for example, photographs of illegal activity that may incur prosecution. Researchers using visual data may face the problem of participants insisting on certain images being kept confidential and thus hampering the overall narrative of the research.

Anonymity involves the removal of all elements within a piece of research from which participants could be identified. The most common example of this is the use of pseudonyms (false names) instead of the real names of participants, locations and so forth. Anonymisation can be challenging when the researcher needs to communicate specific contexts for the research in order to provide meaning, yet cannot directly identify specific locations or people. Visual data in particular pose a problem in relation to anonymisation because it can render such data meaningless if images are removed or distorted. Again, the researcher must develop a dialogic relationship with participants in order to explore the extent to which they are comfortable with the use of specific images. The advent of digital media makes anonymisation relatively straightforward; images can be pixelated, voices can be distorted and specific individuals can be deleted from group images. It is important when dealing with images featuring more than one participant that the researcher ensures that all of those featured have given their consent. Even if participants consent to the use of their data, researchers should consider the future impact of visual data, in particular, on participants, given the longevity and accessibility of online media.

Privacy

Participants have a right to privacy; indeed increasingly, there are national privacy laws that enshrine this right in many western nations. Researchers must respect the privacy of participants in several respects. First, research is an intrinsically invasive process and researchers by nature are prone to nosiness; it is important that researchers itemise through the consent process what areas of a participant's life will be examined and which are off limits. Second, researchers must ensure privacy through confidentiality and/or anonymity considerations. Last, researchers must respect established boundaries and avoid coercing participants into consenting to expansion of the research into areas beyond the original remit. This gives us food for thought in respect of taking photographs or film/video footage. As social researchers we are bound by the ethical code of practice of our various disciplines and common across these are guidelines around the taking of images in public spaces. For example in the British Psychological Society's code of practice, it is determined that images can be taken in public spaces where individuals might expect to be photographed; therefore, care and conservative thought needs to be applied when assessing what defines a public space to avoid infringement of people's privacy.

Sensitivity

The last key ethical issue to consider is sensitivity; often sensitivity is taken to refer to being sensitive when researching so-called sensitive topics, for example, sexuality, rape and domestic violence. It is important to note that all topics can be sensitive for specific individuals. In a broader sense, sensitivity refers to the need to be sensitive towards participants when collecting data, for example, asking questions in a non-offensive or threatening manner. However sensitivity is more than that and involves a great deal of reflection on the part of the researcher who should consider if the topic under study may be 'sensitive' for the participant, either in a way that could generate harm, particularly emotional harm, or in a manner that could cause offence. For example, some cultural groups are not comfortable with the taking of photographs. The capturing of visual data can be invasive even in seemingly non-problematic settings and even when consent has been given. For example, filming everyday family life may disrupt established patterns. Researchers must reflect on their behaviour and demeanour within the research setting.

THINKING THROUGH ETHICS ACTIVITY

Consider the following two research scenarios.

1 Police station study
You have been granted full access to a local police station in order to research the everyday workings of the Police. You shadow officers as they do their work and you are allowed to take photographs.

- What ethical issues would you have to consider?
- How would you resolve these ethical issues?

Two months into your research, you witness (and film) an officer being violent towards a member of the public suspected of committing a crime.

- What should you do?
- What do you do?

2 Teenagers and underage drinking
You have been granted full access to a local youth club in order to research teenagers and their consumption of alcohol while underage. You hang out with the teenagers and staff in the club. The teenagers include you in their social media communications and freely exchange text messages and photographs with you.

- What ethical issues would you have to consider?
- How would you resolve these ethical issues?

After 3 weeks, you begin to notice some of the teenagers are exchanging sexually explicit text messages and posting explicit images of some club members.

- What should you do?
- What do you do?

Statutory frameworks

It was noted earlier that all universities, research-intensive organisations and professional bodies have their own ethical codes and regulations. These are usually based upon transnational codes like the *Helsinki Protocol*. Nevertheless, such codes are not legally binding or enforceable, although individuals may incur organisational punishments, for example, students may be failed on a research module if they behave unethically. The past 20 years has seen an increase in ethical regulation within organisations that conduct research on human participants; researchers are required to submit ethical approval forms, risk assessments, insurance assessments and so forth. However, this shift has been driven by external legislation rather than an imperative to be more ethical. Researchers must now consider a range of statutory frameworks within which they must work:

- **Data protection laws**: Such laws seek to ensure that people's data are collected with consent; stored securely; kept confidentially; and that researchers ensure that in all stages of the research cycle data are safeguarded. It is important to note that data protection laws typically view data very broadly, for example, a child's drawing could be deemed data. Researchers must outline to participants exactly how their data will be looked after and used.
- **Privacy laws**: Such laws work to establish boundaries between public and private spaces and to protect the privacy of individuals. It can be difficult to establish what sort of space is 'private' and what is not, particularly in relation to spaces that appear 'public'. Crucially researchers should be aware of the need to avoid violating people's privacy; this is, particularly pertinent for visual researchers as the capturing of people's images can be readily done but can be highly invasive.
- **Child and 'vulnerable' adult protection**: Such laws operate to protect children and 'vulnerable' adults from abuse, ensuring their rights, and establishing mechanisms by which to safeguard them. An obvious example of this is in the need for criminal records searches for those who work with such groups. The filming of children, in particular, is increasingly governed by rules and researchers must ensure that they abide by them.

DATA PROTECTION DILEMMAS

Consider the following scenarios, which ones are 'illegal' or 'unethical' and how might you ensure compliance with the Data Protection Act?

1 You store your data on an open access PC on campus.
2 You film people in a shopping mall.
3 You are socialising with your participants and take a group selfie.
4 You show your best friend a joke on the social media feed from one of your participants.
5 You take photographs of people relaxing in a local park.
6 You make photocopies of some pictures drawn by young adults.
7 You email yourself photographs taken during field research.
8 You tweet a research update that mentions your field setting.

Ethical problematics

This chapter has focused on the core ethical concepts that researchers must reflect upon in research design and management. However, there are a group of related topics, which do not necessarily feature in formal ethics paperwork or indeed in many ethical regulations. Nevertheless, these 'ethical problematics' are important and most researchers reflect upon them in their everyday practice.

Power/authority

Since the 1960s, researchers have increasingly been concerned with examining the dimensions of power within their research. The research relationship is one of power imbalances, with the researcher being the authority figure, with power, and the participants, potentially being powerless. If we consider the 'researcher knows best' attitude of early social scientists, we can perhaps understand why contemporary researchers concern themselves with ways to equalise the power imbalance of the research relationship. Obviously, consent, sensitivity and respect for privacy assist this process, as does the creation of proper dialogue within the research process. In addition, many researchers allow participants a decision-making role within the research, particularly in relation to outputs, for example, allowing participants to choose which images are to be included.

Representation/voice

Another emerging problematic from the 1960s reaction to the 'researcher knows best' attitude is a concern with representation; in other words, how we choose to represent our participants matters. To illustrate, does our use of certain photographs merely support prevailing stereotypes or does it offer a challenge to these stereotypes? This was a primary concern of early feminist researchers who critiqued prevailing academic representations of women that merely reinforced wider social attitudes to gender. Linked to this is the idea of allowing participants 'voice' within the research; this can involve extensive use of their actual words or through allowing them to select their own images. Incorporating participants' voices into visual research is crucial given the interpretative nature of visual data; a photograph of an inner-city wasteland may communicate to a wider 'audience' a sense of poverty, despair or crime, whereas local children may identify it as a positive space, a space for play. Without the voices of participants, such images merely serve to reinforce prevailing stereotypes.

Overt/covert and public/private

All researchers assume a specific position within their research; they either collect data in an open (overt) way, where participants fully understand that they are participating within a piece of research, or they collect data covertly, without informing participants. The latter position is clearly unethical as informed consent cannot be given. However, it is not necessarily as clear-cut as it may first appear. Some spaces are so public that covert research cannot be deemed unethical, such as a railway station, but some public spaces (for example a church) may be a private space for some people. Field research specifically poses dilemmas for the researcher particularly as relationships with participants grow; what if private conversations or observations generate interesting data but consent was not sought? The very nature of social life is that people shift between private and public worlds. This is why it is important for researchers to be reflective and maintain a good dialogue with their participants. The development of social media and the internet has reignited this debate due to the blurring of public and private space. People may view others' conversations on social media or in chatrooms as public because these are public or semi-public spaces, which are easy to join. Some researchers do not think that consent is needed in these research contexts and may choose a 'lurking' stance. However, we should be mindful that the increase of social media has led to people, particularly the young, having a skewed view of privacy leading them to broadcast material that for previous generations would have been deemed very private. Therefore, researchers may find themselves having to impose their own boundaries to prevent future harm for participants. The anonymity of the internet has allowed marginalised groups to find 'safe' gathering spaces and therefore researchers need to consider whether covert stances are unethical violations of such spaces.

Ethics are situational

It will have become apparent that ethics is not an instrumental process that ends with a committee approving an ethics form; if we or our students approach ethics like this then we are not being ethical and as practitioners we are not only neglecting our responsibility to our students' training but also our own research and code of ethical practice. Ethics rather is a process of reflection and dialogue that does not even necessarily end with our work being published or our students being taught; it relies on us as practitioners to lead by example. Contextual matters determine how we behave as researchers, and the ethical choices we make are situational and often pragmatic. Nevertheless, our key value at all times should be that as researchers we ensure that our participants are safeguarded and protected and as practitioners the research toolkit of our students is founded on ethically sound practices; if we cannot guarantee that then we and they should not embark on research in the first place.

Suggested reading

Bulmer, M. (1980). Comment on 'the ethics of covert methods'. *The British Journal of Sociology*, *31*(1), 59–65.

Calvey, D. (2008). The art and politics of covert research: doing 'situated ethics' in the field. *Sociology*, *42*(5), 905–18.

Carrabine, E. (2012). Just images: aesthetics, ethics and visual criminology. *The British Journal of Criminology*, *52*(3), 463–89.

Clark, A., Prosser, J. and Wiles, R. (2010). Ethical issues in image-based research. *Arts & Health: An International Journal for Research, Policy and Practice*, *2*(1), 81–93.

Enyon, R., Fry, J. and Schroeder, R. (2008). The ethics of internet research. In N.G. Fielding, R.M. Lee and G. Blank (eds), *The SAGE handbook of online research methods* (pp. 23–41). London: Sage.

Homan, R. (1992). The ethics of open methods. *The British Journal of Sociology*, *43*(3), 321–32.

Pauwels, L. (2008). Taking and using: ethical issues of photographs for research purposes. *Visual Communication Quarterly*, *15*(4), 243–57.

Wiles, R., Coffey, A., Robinson, J. and Heath, S. (2012). Anonymisation and visual images: issues of respect, 'voice' and protection. *International Journal of Social Research Methodology*, *15*(1), 41–53.

References

Babbie, E. (2004). Laud Humphreys and research ethics. *International Journal of Sociology and Social Policy*, *24*(3–5), 12–19.

Brazier, M. (2008). Exploitation and enrichment: the paradox of medical experimentation. *Journal of Medical Ethics*, *34*, 180–3.

Herrera, C.D. (1997). A historical interpretation of deceptive experiments in American psychology. *History of the Human Sciences*, *10*(1), 23–36.

Humphreys, L. (1970). *Tearoom trade: impersonal sex in public places*. New York: Aldine.

Layman, E.J. (2009). Human experimentation: historical perspective of breaches of ethics in US health care. *The Health Care Manager*, *28*(4), 354–74.

Milgram, S. (1963). Behavioral study of obedience. *Journal of Abnormal and Social Psychology*, *67*(4), 371–8.

Nicholson, I. (2011). 'Torture at Yale': Experimental subjects, laboratory torment and the 'rehabilitation' of Milgram's 'Obedience to Authority'. *Theory & Psychology*, *21*(6), 737–61.

Patrick, J. (1973). *A Glasgow gang observed*, London: Eyre Methuen.

Pearson, G. (2009). The researcher as hooligan: where 'participant' observation means breaking the law. *International Journal of Social Research Methodology*, *12*(3), 243–55.

Tolich, M. (2014). What can Milgram and Zimbardo teach ethics committees and qualitative researchers about minimizing harm? *Research Ethics*, *10*(2), 86–96.

Zimbardo, P.G. (1973). On the ethics of intervention in human psychological research: with special reference to the Stanford Prison Experiment. *Cognition*, *2*(2), 243–56.

4

VISUAL METHODS

Developing pedagogical application

Caroline Wakefield and Sal Watt

Visual methods are an ever-growing and important part of many academic research projects. Research using such methods has been conducted in sociology (Shrum, Duque and Brown, 2005; Hurdley, 2007), anthropology (Collier and Collier, 1986), psychology (Frith, Riley, Archer and Gleeson, 2005), sport science (Wakefield and Watt, 2012) and geography (Oldrup and Carstensen, 2012) and is embedded into the associated curricula with varying degrees of success in different subject groups.

As time progresses, it has become imperative for graduates to demonstrate the ability to transfer knowledge and skills that will subsequently allow them to operate effectively in a work environment. Alongside an increasing focus on employability, there has been a 'new emphasis on generic learning outcomes' (Boud, Cohen and Sampson, 1999, p. 415) whereby the skill base developed as a result of studying a particular subject is often of equal importance to a student's career prospects as the subject content itself. Both field- and class-based activities can assist in the teaching of subject material and enhance students' own research skills, with increasing degree of competence (Willison and O'Regan, 2007). The learning and practice of visual methods provides a strong opportunity to develop two of the key crucial qualities among modern graduates, that is, responsivity and a flexible transferable skill set (Harvey 2000). Indeed, Grady (2004, p. 18) promotes the usefulness of 'visual evidence' when communicating ideas. However, the teaching of visual methods often remains an emergent part of social science curricula, particularly at undergraduate level. This chapter explores the use of visual methods in learning and teaching. This is achieved first by examining appropriate learning and teaching models and providing examples of how such methods can be incorporated into the curriculum. The chapter then considers how the most rewarding and fruitful environment can be created, along with points for consideration when implementing visual methods.

Learning and teaching

Traditional approaches

Much of the research methods material taught in social science curricula is delivered in a traditional manner, that is, through creating a balance between the delivery of quantitative and qualitative methods. This is often achieved with differing degrees of success both dependent on the subject in question and the department (and associated staffing) within which it is housed. Indeed it appears that many departments are driven by a style that is predominantly positivistic in approach.

While research methods are undergoing significant change across numerous academic departments (Scarles, 2010), a dominance of quantitative methods remains apparent and many of the research skills and techniques taught conform to a traditional positivist discourse. This is further emphasised via the specific approaches typically taken to the teaching of research methods and training, and the material published by the major journals themselves (Bhati, Hoyt and Huffman, 2013). However, engagement with a wider range of research methods can enable and promote a deeper understanding in undergraduate study while at the same time equipping students with a wider toolkit that they can utilise when entering the workplace (Walkington *et al.*, 2011).

Guba and Lincoln (1994) remind us that the terms qualitative and quantitative describe methods that are not exclusive to any particular approach to inquiry. However, when choosing an appropriate method, it is crucial to develop an understanding of the philosophy of science and the key underpinning principles first: An area that is also often under-represented in HE curricula. That is, usually preceding the teaching of quantitative methods is a brief introduction to positivism as the underpinning philosophy of science and research, often with scant regard for the underpinning philosophy of qualitative approaches, that is, interpretivism. Developing this understanding of the distinction between these philosophies and their usage across social science disciplines is crucially important preparation for teaching qualitative methods and important in ensuring students are fully informed both in philosophical origins and subsequent research techniques (Morrow, 2007). However the reality is that often the underpinning philosophies of research approaches remain an alien concept to students. With a brief introduction to research as being scientific in approach, this leaves no counterpoint to offer students regarding a qualitative approach, thus limiting both their knowledge and understanding. Therefore we argue that this spectrum of understanding spanning both qualitative and qualitative philosophies must be developed and achieved as a precursor to the examination of the specific methods themselves. To this end, Poulin (2007) recommends that we should teach 'to convey, not convert' adding that 'to draw students into the kind of curiosity that is consistent with a qualitative stance, I suggested that interpretive research is one but not the only viable approach to inquiry' (p. 455).

Indeed, many techniques can be used to introduce qualitative and interpretive processes. For example Poulin (2007) describes how she asked her students to introduce themselves within the class, prior to giving an introduction of her own. On reflection the students expressed a degree of discomfort at the task and an uncertainty about what was expected. However this was then used as a discussion point which allowed the students to consider and explore their previously held assumptions about who they were and who they were expected to be in various different situations. This emphasises the necessity of interconnected learning and provides an example of how students can struggle to grasp information or tasks that exist in a vacuum without the associated contextual information. This is particularly relevant to the study of visual methods which, owing to the lack of grounding in qualitative methods that is often encountered among students, can appear abstract and difficult to comprehend.

In undergraduate provision the idea is to introduce concepts, develop skill sets and challenge existing approaches. It is worth noting that, to this end, even traditional qualitative techniques (questionnaires, interviews etc.) may present barriers to meaningful engagement. However, in many disciplines, visual methods are marginal, with reluctance among staff to adopt such methods. Such reluctance or lack of confidence in adopting visual methods could even be a product of the personal learning journey of the staff themselves and their own education or training. This should be avoided and as educators we can only enable the most effective and convincing critique among students by striving to provide a comprehensible grounding in several different research methods, including visual methods. Staff training, education and prior experience should be overcome to enable the students to experience visual methods as an exciting way of generating knowledge. Providing this range of opportunity will ultimately enable the students to create a fit between research purpose and design, rather than being confined to methods linked to their own enjoyment, satisfaction and/or competence.

Learning models

A great deal of research has been conducted on the efficacy of different pedagogies, with particular attention paid to how to maximise student learning. Bruner (1960) explored the concept of spiral learning. Spiral learning and scaffolded structures are used to underpin the formal development of knowledge and understanding of research (Tweed and Boast, 2011; Walkington *et al.*, 2011) (see Figure 4.1). This is achieved, not through repetition, but through continually revisiting topics and building on the previous encounter (Harden and Stamper, 1999) at a higher level of difficulty and in greater depth.

Bruner believes that when students discover knowledge independently, it increases the responsibility to learn on their own and their subsequent motivation to learn more. A further model of learning focuses on what is termed 'constructive alignment'.

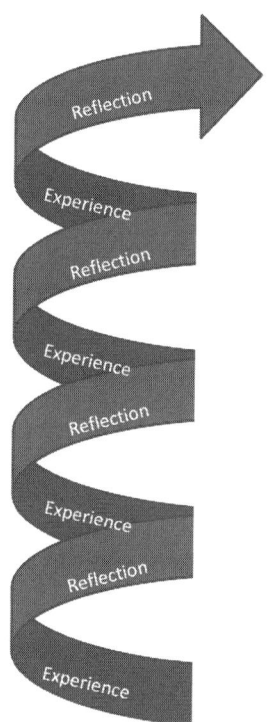

FIGURE 4.1 Spiral learning.

Constructive alignment is 'a principle used for devising teaching and learning activities, and assessment tasks, that directly address the learning outcomes intended in a way not typically achieved in traditional lectures, tutorial classes and examinations' (Biggs and Tang, 2011, p. 7). Here, meaning is not transmitted to the student but rather the student creates it within a supportive and appropriate environment fostered by the tutor (Vitiello, 2009). Such an approach cultivates Marton and Saljo's (1976) deep approach to learning; one which enables students to understand the personal significance of the learning, adopt meaning and construct knowledge based on this meaning. This is in direct contrast to a surface approach to learning, whereby students are able to remember information on cue but do not engage with the material as part of a wider learning journey. Indeed, Biggs (1999) points out that 'good teaching is getting most students to use the higher cognitive level processes that the more academic students use spontaneously' (p. 58).

In modern fast-paced higher education environments, broad, skill-based learning outcomes are a priority, and as such the environment should be created that naturally leads the students to these learning outcomes (see Figure 4.2). It is then the role of the teacher to elaborate on the learning outcomes to make them specific for the assignments within the module and task briefs. This is useful both in terms of

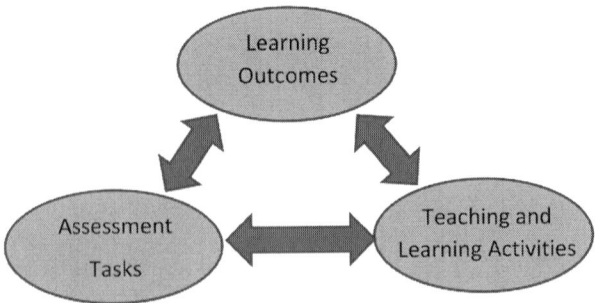

FIGURE 4.2 Biggs (1999) constructive alignment between learning outcomes, teaching and learning activities and assessment tasks.

developing the requisite skills for the student beyond graduation and also in the design and marking of assessments. Indeed, both formative and summative assessments need to be clearly aligned with the learning outcomes (Biggs and Tang, 2011) to create the optimal learning environment. Earl (2003) points out that

> Learning is not a linear process. Assessment doesn't come at the end. Teaching is not the filling in the sandwich between curriculum and assessment. Taken together, curriculum, teaching, learning, and assessment interact in an iterative and sometimes cyclical process. They feed into one another and sometimes dart back and forth in seemingly unpredictable patterns. This does not mean that they are independent of or disconnected from one another. On the contrary, the interconnections are the key.
>
> (p. 83)

Through this approach, students develop the ability to work holistically and conceptually rather than with isolated knowledge (Ramsden, 2003). Visual methods provide an excellent example of promoting this inter-reliability between teaching, learning and assessment, and enhancement of the student experience. In fact, active methods such as problem-based learning require students who typically adopt a surface approach to learning to question, generate solutions and begin to use the high-level process that is required for a deep approach to learning (Biggs, 1999). This reinforces the concept of researchers as 'active agents' (Spry, 2001) as students themselves act as both the researchers and the researched in curriculum-based work, effectively experiencing the research environment from multiple perspectives. Visual methods can also be beneficial in supporting learners whose preferences lie along the learning-style spectrum. That is, the method will have particular appeal to visual learners who may find this method to be more accessible than some of the other research methods taught within the curriculum.

How visual methods can be incorporated into the curriculum: The example of photographs

Despite a present and growing interest in visual methods within social science research, consideration must be given to how this can be translated into meaningful classroom activities. After having typically been taught a number of qualitative approaches and techniques, students would benefit greatly from the incorporation of visual methods into the curriculum. Indeed, 'experiences and meanings become tangible through visual representation and may be understood in ways that other conventional forms of communication may not necessarily allow' (Liebenberg, 2009, p. 445).

The photograph itself

Photographs used in photo elicitation can be pre-existing or taken primarily for the use of the research. In either of these two scenarios, when viewing and subsequently analysing an image, a good starting point is the SHOWeD acronym (Wang, 1999). Here, each letter signifies an important consideration when analysing an image (see Figure 4.3).

Later, Smith, Bratini and Appio (2012) suggested that the previously undesignated E should stand for Exploration in the here and now. Of course, in addition to what is shown in the photograph, there are many more key considerations and reflection should be conducted on the decision making of the photographer regarding what to include within the frame (and therefore what to omit) (Garrod, 2007). Indeed, Pink (2003) highlights that 'a researcher should attend not only to the internal "meanings" of an image, but also to how the image was produced and how it is made meaningful by its viewers' (p. 186).

In the case of pre-existing photographs, these can act as 'restatements of reality' (Collier, 1957, p. 859) and memory prompts in interview settings, retrieving something that has otherwise disappeared (Harper, 2002) and offering a greater opportunity for reflection. Here, in the experience of Hurdley (2007, p. 366), 'as the photographs became productions in their own right, they invited speculative editing'.

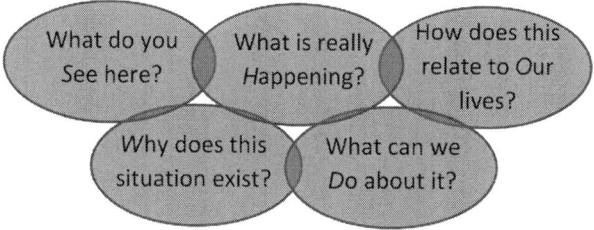

FIGURE 4.3 Considerations when analysing images (based on Wang, 1999).

Interview data

Auto photography (or photo-voice; Wang and Burris, 1997) is becoming increasingly popular (Phoenix, 2010) as it involves the participant having control over what images they chose to document. After deciding upon or taking the image, this can then be used in subsequent interview or reflection tasks. This is particularly useful because while the photograph itself can act as data, it is often the rich description, that is the respondent reflexivity, which accompanies the photograph that provides the greatest insight. Here, the visuals 'become more than merely prompts or "safety nets", but offer gateways for merging reflexive subjectivities' (Scarles, 2010, p. 912). Pink (2007) explains that visual methods cannot be used independently of other methods because of the associated cultural ties and thus it is important to incorporate a reflective component to assessments of this type to fully ensure that the benefit is being maximised.

Although the photographs can be extremely powerful in eliciting experiences in interview settings (Radley and Taylor, 2003) they also have the added benefit of slowing down the pace of the interview while the participant fully considers the image (Liebenberg, 2009). Furthermore visual auto-enthnography can develop understanding by 'transcending the limitations of verbal discourse and opening spaces for creativity and appreciation' (Scarles, 2010, p. 906). This ensures that it is a positive influence within the classroom environment and allows a natural and easy incorporation of visual methods without it becoming overly onerous for the tutor.

Our case study

In our own experience, the exploration of teaching visual methods began several years ago, using photo elicitation as a research tool and as such we will use one of these examples as a case study here. In 2012, we completed a research project using visual methods, specifically on a photo-voice project that we conducted with an Ironman Triathlete (Wakefield and Watt, 2012).

Photo-voice aims to 'to enable people (1) to record and reflect their personal and community strengths and concerns, (2) to promote critical dialogue and knowledge about personal and community issues through group discussion of photographs, and (3) to reach policy makers' (Wang, 1999, p. 185). During this particular research project, we provided the participant with a researcher-selected seven of the 252 photographs taken of his completion of the Ironman Triathlon and asked him to reflect on the photographs around the theme of achievement. Three examples of these photographs appear in this section. Five main premises emerged from these reflections: Life-Changing event, personal challenge, sense of achievement, change in well-being and sense of loss.

This research paper was then used as the basis of activities for a postgraduate visual methods teaching session (for extended discussion, please see Watt and Wakefield, 2014). After being given the background to visual methods and

FIGURE 4.4 Examples of the Ironman photographs.

exploring its roots, students were introduced to the photographs and reflections from the Ironman participant, thus providing an example of how photographs can elicit participant reflections.

At this point, we had the opportunity to raise with the students potential issues and pose important questions, such as those suggested by Rookwood and Palmer (2009, p. 205):

> Does the photograph add value in some way? If so, how? What are the lenses that frame and describe the images? How much contextual information may be required to understand the photograph? Does it protect the identities and well-being of the participants?

These are all key considerations when undergoing, and indeed teaching, a project of this nature and students can have a two-way dialogue with the tutors, as researchers, making them more likely to engage with the method in a meaningful and critical way. Once we were satisfied that such considerations could form an integral part of our students' research methods training, we decided to devise an assignment that was compatible with and built on the contemporary cultural practice of taking and sharing photographs.

FIGURE 4.5 Achievement.

Therefore, we developed an assessment that drew on photo elicitation as the specific method whereby our students worked in small groups of two or three members. The students collaboratively negotiated topic areas with each other which were then agreed with us as appropriate. The students were tasked with completing a visual methods project for which they were required to either take original, or source pre-existing, photographs. The students first wrote a personal reflective account based on each of their own photographs before collaboratively sharing them with their group members who similarly wrote a reflective account of what thoughts and emotions the photographs elicited. In short then, all photographs were shared and reflected upon by each group member and then the group of students got together to share and discuss their reflective comments with each other. Throughout the process students were supported and their learning scaffolded by us. A strict ethical code regarding confidentiality and mutual respect was enforced, which complied with our professional code of practice determined by the British Psychological Society (BPS). We wanted to give the students involved as much freedom as we could regarding the topic area because we wanted the work to be participatory but also to allow them to be collaboratively included in the topic choice within the assessment task, thus making them more likely to be motivated and interested and their work to be all the more creative as a result (Rust, 2002). Assessment of this work consisted of three elements that met the learning outcomes and took a three part form:

1   a group photo board (A3; displaying the group photographs to prompt informal discussion);

2   a group presentation platforming and exploring the group photographs and associated reflections;

3   an individual written report that critically evaluated their experience of using photo elicitation for this project and reflected on their experience of using the method generally; furthermore, a reflexive narrative was also included in the report, charting the working process of the group and their experiences of collaboratively using photo elicitation.

Our students were extremely successful in their assessments, and engaged on a level that we had not predicted. Many students chose topics that were highly emotion laden, including existing photographs of relatives who had since passed away and in one case exploration of life-changing injuries sustained as a result of a car accident. We were staggered by the engagement and emotional charge of the presentations and how well the students had adapted to using the method. Indeed, Scarles (2010, p. 906) points out that 'new and alternative methods are required that engage with research participants in ways that move beyond the realms of representation to access the haptic, non-representational spaces of encounter and experience', and certainly this was our experience of this group of postgraduate students.

Fanning (2011) also used photo elicitation in an assignment. In Fanning's study student feedback indicated that there was an overall sense that this assignment format was a welcome break from the traditional essay. Analysis of student responses to completing the assessment indicated that a number of recurring themes emerged, including learning as a journey, increased focus on effective group work, importance of planning, a sense of accomplishment and increased effort. When asking our own students to reflect, they too contemplated their sense of accomplishment alongside their perceived level of success (or otherwise) with the method. However, despite the level of support and scaffolding available, some students felt that the concept was too creative and would have preferred more clearly defined boundaries, while others reflected on the frustrating, yet valuable, processes involved when acting as both a participant and a researcher.

Our students also expressed similar feedback to those in the Fanning (2011) study through their reflective reports, exploring the potential that they believed the method allowed. However, they raised some concerns regarding the emotive content of both the photographs and the presentation, where students had spoken freely about highly emotive and personal issues. While the work and its strong emotional content ignited a connection between the group members and ourselves as tutors, we felt that we had almost 'gone too far' in allowing the students as much freedom as we had regarding their chosen topic area. As such, we angst over the question of responsibility and duty of care in respect of taking closer control over the topic areas when working with future cohorts. Therefore, the following year we enforced the brief of 'place and space' when working with the next cohort of students. That is, the students retained freedom to choose their own topics, but within this more specific and closely monitored brief.

The resultant student work (detailed in Wakefield and Watt, 2014) was much safer in terms of emotional content, focusing on photographs of technology and inanimate objects, with basic, descriptive accompanying reflections. In short, the assessment brief did not seem to allow the students the creative space to fully engage with the task to the same degree as the first group of students had. The student reflections on the method, however, showed greater comfort at the task set and an appreciation of the potential benefits of using visual methods. Therefore, we offer a 'cautionary tale' when designing assessment. In our experience, a balance must be gained between safety, commitment, engagement and creativity, and therefore assessments of this kind should be reviewed and revised on a regular basis.

Assessment design

When introducing visual methods into curricula, a key consideration must be how this work should be assessed. Owing to the great deal of emphasis placed on assessment by students, how such assessments are designed, implemented and marked is worthy of deliberation. Indeed, Brown (2004) explains that we need to consider not just what we are assessing but how we are assessing it.

Overarching module aims are prominent in the development of both learning outcomes and subsequent module content. This stepped process is essential when marking student work as it is by these learning outcomes that student work must be appraised. That is, if student work is deemed to have met the learning outcomes, then it warrants a pass mark. This makes the development of learning outcomes that are closely linked to the module aims imperative, particularly for projects involving visual methods, owing to the creative element which may not be easy to assess compared to more positivist 'right/wrong' answers. Biggs (1999) points out that in a system where the objectives (or outcomes) are rooted in the assessment task, then a situation develops whereby when students focus on the assessment, they are necessarily learning in line with the objectives. This is beneficial as 'from our students' point of view, the assessment always defines the actual curriculum' (Ramsden, 1992, p. 187). In this case, therefore, any developments (subtle or otherwise) in content and assessment need to promote student engagement with the module aims and ensure the overarching module objectives are not compromised. In our own experience of teaching visual methods, this deep and inseparable connection between the assessment task and learning outcomes was paramount and provided the students with structure and context regarding the work to be completed.

Earl (2003, p. 25) explores the concept of assessment *as* learning, explaining that

> Students, as active, engaged, and critical assessors, can make sense of information, relate it to prior knowledge, and master the skills involved. This is the regulatory process in metacognition. It occurs when students personally monitor what they are learning and use the feedback from this monitoring to make adjustments, adaptations, and even major changes in what they understand. Assessment as learning is the ultimate goal.

Garde-Hansen and Calvert (2007) explored a project where students were encouraged to be research-active and found that 'these students were so assessment-driven they sought a paint-by-numbers approach to gaining knowledge' (p. 112). Furthermore, students engage with and 'largely study what is assessed, or more accurately, what they perceive the assessment system to require' (Gibbs, 2006a, p. 15). Assessment, therefore, must have meaning for students (Biggs, 1999) and thus it is important that the assessment undertaken bears a strong relationship to the students' ability to undertake the associated research methods. For example, in the case of visual methods, an examination would not be an effective or meaningful mode of assessment.

As difficulties in research are not widely acknowledged, discussed or published, a culture is created among students who are fearful of acknowledging weakness in their own practice among a 'façade of infallible research practice' (Ryan-Flood and Gill, 2010). This, along with the creative elements of this approach can sometimes unnerve or 'throw' students who are traditional in their approach to their studies and assessments. This was certainly the case in our experience, whereby some of the students clearly identified with a more traditional approach and the creativity of our chosen visual method did appear to inhibit some of our students. Therefore, based on our own work, the thinking behind assessment design and clear explicit assessment briefs and guidelines must be made available and disseminated effectively to the students.

If assessment is conducted effectively, it should link to the module outcomes and serve in equipping students for future study or employment. When students move forward to do their own research or work in associated professions, they must use the most appropriate method for the research question and the participants. However, in order to do that, they must have a wide range of methods to choose from. As such, a diversity of methods across the spectrum, including visual methods, should be delivered to students. Students then can become 'informed consumers' (Poulin, 2007, p. 437). The assessment design employed should account for this and equip students to employ the best-suited method to the participants and the scenario. To reiterate the points made earlier in the chapter, sound design of the teaching and assessment of visual methods will allow the students to develop their knowledge in this area, but also enable a clear understanding of the application of visual methods in the wider sense of the word, enhancing their employability and future career prospects.

Assessment marking and assessment of work beyond traditional parameters

One key consideration when incorporating visual methods into the curriculum and assessment pattern is how this work will be linked directly and coherently to marking criteria and learning outcomes. Such criteria are often used to assess work which falls within traditional parameters and often feedback is (and should be) given in direct relation to these criteria. Brown (2004, p. 84) explains that 'assessment criteria must be designed to ensure that all students have an equal chance of achieving high grades'.

In recent years there has been a call to make the process more equitable (Williams, 2005). However, in order for the process to be sound, both staff and students need to be absolutely clear on what it is that is being assessed. In methods such as this, whereby there is a research process followed by a written report or presentation, 'criteria need to take account of any distinctions between the final product and the process involved in its production' (Hanson, 2013, p. 1). Indeed when performance is assessed, this is 'frequently multidimensional' (Yorke, 2003, p. 484). In our experience, when teaching and assessing visual projects, the perceived vagueness of the assessment criteria and absence of a 'right' answer can unnerve some students. However, despite the attention to detail given during the production of comprehensive marking schemes, students often appear to be unaware of, or disengaged with, the criteria. As such, Brown (2004) points out that it is often helpful to involve students in the process of developing and negotiating criteria so that everyone knows what is expected. Furthermore the marking criteria can be embedded within the delivery of one or more of the teaching sessions, in addition to the assessment. This will also have the added benefit of creating an obligatory awareness of the criteria, making engagement unavoidable.

Within the bounds of institutional factors, student receptiveness of tasks and associated assessments can be related to positioning within the course. Visual assessments often rely on the sharing of interview data plus the visual tools themselves (photographs, drawings, film). As such, assessments should be conducted when there is a level of familiarity among the group to allow them to maximise both the process and the final piece of work. However, it is possible that the students will perform better in tasks such as this and Gibbs (2006b, p. 33) suggests that 'social pressures to deliver . . . through making the products of learning public (in posters, or through peer assessment) may induce more care and pride in work than "secretly" submitted assignments to the teacher'.

Criteria should then be devised that provide sufficient guidance to achieve, but without constraining the students and thus negating the key benefits of the work. Any alterations made to the task brief need to be well thought through because, as in our experience (Wakefield and Watt, 2014), if not, the concern around enabling the students to have freedom may lead to a task brief that is too prescriptive and stifles creativity.

Another point worthy of note is the potential challenges involved in second-marking or moderation processes. Visual methods teaching often produces work that is highly creative, but which is subjective in nature and contains highly emotionally charged content. In our experience, marking such work can make it difficult to separate objective criteria and academic content (reading, depth of reflection etc.) from the more subjective (emotional content of the stories). This can lead to difficulties in second-marking processes as tutors may respond differently to the work presented. Through our own experience, we realised that these issues can be overcome with further consideration of the formation of clear and transparent marking criteria and a thorough second-marking protocol. Please refer to Part III of the book for samples of the criteria that we employed.

Creating the necessary environment

In order for visual methods to be fully and meaningfully incorporated within the student experience and learning, several considerations need to be made with regard to the environment. Poulin (2007, p. 433) points out that 'consideration of relevant contextual factors promotes successful teaching and learning'. In this case, these include understanding of reflexivity, delivery mode, level of introduction and departmental considerations.

Reflexivity

In promoting reflexivity within the student body and the assignments, it was first crucial to ensure that a distinction was made between reflection and reflexivity. That is, while reflection is a process of retrospective consideration involving experiences, memories and emotions, reflexivity,

> is first about reflection but then relies on us being introspective, that is, looking inward and taking responsibility for our own thoughts, feelings and action, and asking ourselves probing questions about our own motivation and involvement.
>
> (Scott Jones and Watt, 2010, p. 188)

One of the key elements of visual research is the ability and the willingness to engage in good and meaningful reflexivity. Training is required to gain a competence in this skill and this is commonplace in social science curricula. This is important as 'reflexivity is a key concern in most recent literature on visual research, indispensable to any contemporary research project and often cited as the virtue that distinguished between good and bad research' (Pink, 2003, p. 87). Therefore, through the project described as a case study above, we were asking the students to *reflect* on their photographs, but to be *reflexive* regarding their practice. This responsibility also extended to ourselves as tutors as we needed to consistently engage in reflexivity regarding our practice and the teaching and assessment of the students in this context.

In our experience, students have a tendency to overlook their dual role as both the researcher and the participant. That is, while acting as the researcher, their role in the production and presentation of images needs to be addressed. This can be achieved through effective reflexivity, which can be integrated to 'reveal the very processes by which the positionality of researcher and informant were constituted and through which knowledge was produced during the fieldwork' (Pink, 2003, p. 189). Through visual methods projects, students can develop skills in image creation and critique, and develop their reflexive skills by engaging in such processes both on an individual level and as part of a group. This adds to a heightened awareness that different people may view and interpret images differently. Indeed, 'we need to link our statements about what we study with statements about ourselves, for in reality neither stands alone' (Krieger, 1996, pp. 191–2).

Reflexivity played a hugely important part in our journey, with assignments and teaching changing depending on our previous experiences. As discussed earlier in the chapter, in our use of visual methods, students were given a range of examples and free reign to explore their agreed topic of choice (after ethical and tutor approval). However, upon reflection the next cohorts were restricted to that of 'place and space' (see Wakefield and Watt, 2014 for an in-depth discussion). While changes can, and should be, implemented within and between academic years, this must be juxtaposed with the students not feeling like they are experimental in any way. For them, preoccupation with their own qualifications is prevalent over a concern with the potential benefits for future cohorts.

Therefore, while promoting reflexivity among students as a crucial element of using visual methods, tutors must also assume this undertaking. We have found that there is often a tendency to avoid this in case there is criticism of individual staff approaches. However, it is only by experimenting and being willing to engage in open and honest reflection that curricula will change and adapt to continually ensure that students are equipped for future employment. Grady (2004) cautions that teaching in this way is a continual and life-long learning journey. Indeed, we would view the accounts of anyone who got it perfectly right the first time with a healthy suspicion. Furthermore, Grady (2004) also cautions that tutors should be prepared to undertake visual methods teaching as a life-long learning journey, and one which involves careful planning and practice.

Delivery mode

Throughout the higher education sector, didactic lectures remain a popular mode of delivery. However, when teaching visual methods, where the key skills are self-directed learning, group work, self-awareness and reflective practice, this may not be the most appropriate method. Furthermore, 'it is important to remember that what the student does is actually more important in determining what is learned than what the teacher does' (Shuell, 1986, cited in Biggs, 1996, p. 349). In our experience it seemed inappropriate to use a didactic lecture when we were asking the students to be so creative. In short, we did not want to stifle the creativity and discussion that was resultant from our session. Therefore, we briefly outlined the background, explored some of our own research that incorporated visual methods (while warning of the challenges that we had faced), and allowed the students to discuss their ideas and project outlines in small groups. Then, as with the work of Flick (2002), the participants essentially took the role of the teacher, as experts of their own stories and projects.

Through these sessions, we tried to engage the students themselves with the photographs that we had used in our research, to form their own viewpoints before our reflections were revealed. Furthermore, when completing the assessments, the students were required to complete a photo board alongside their work, displaying only their photographs. This was designed to provide the other students with the opportunity to interpret the photographs themselves and led to a realisation that meaning from the photographs was derived from imposition of their own worldviews and prior experiences and thus would inevitably be different from person to person. This was particularly critical as there is a difference between involvement and engagement (Harper and Quaye, 2009). Furthermore, Owen and Riley (2012, p. 63) point out that

> embedding activities allows us to identify any gaps between what we thought we've taught the students and what they've taken from our teaching; and gives students ownership over their learning as they become coparticipants in the creation of meaning and learning. Practical activities therefore offer a crucial space for students to put theory into practice and to start developing key embodied and relational understandings of conducting visual research.

Thus, engaging students with the process as early as possible allows them to become familiar with the methodology and philosophy of the method, as they are engaged in a way that promotes this familiarity. This then becomes a good starting point for their own projects and associated assessments.

Level of introduction

The level at which methods are introduced is of critical importance. Owing to their backgrounds, it may be that some undergraduates do not have the capability to think in a way that is reflective or creative enough for such work. Aside from the mature students, typical undergraduate students may not have enough life experience to draw upon to fully explore the arising issues. In our experience, which was one of postgraduate study, there were several highly emotionally charged pieces of work that developed into deep (and sometimes dark) reflections. However, we (Watt and Wakefield, 2014) concluded that at postgraduate level, students should have the opportunity to experience all forms of research methods and that denying them the opportunity may in itself be unethical. Nevertheless, if visual methods are not introduced early on enough in a student's academic journey, then students cannot gradually develop these skills in the same way that they do with quantitative methods. Indeed Ponterotto and Grieger (2007) warn that 'one can become so confused by the myriad qualitative traditions and methods that it may be tempting to retreat to the comfort of familiarity of the post-positivist paradigm and quantitative methods' (p. 411). The concern at this point is that students are so ingrained and familiar at using hypothesis-testing models of research methods that they may not be comfortable in extending those boundaries. This raises questions rather than providing answers, but one suggestion could be that students are exposed to a graduated progression across the different levels. That is, through introducing visual methods that are prescribed and more simplistic at undergraduate level with a greater focus on description rather than reflective and reflexive use, which would then pave the way in giving opportunity for more freedom for exploration and increased reflexivity and academic challenge as they move towards postgraduate study.

Departmental considerations

One of the main departmental considerations is receptiveness of other members of the host department. All members of staff, regardless of whether they are directly involved in the process should be able to demonstrate justification of the academic rigour of visual methods. It is through this support that a consistent message is given to the students and that they will be able to see the value of the methods and trust in their rigour and equitability. In our experience, students are wary of curriculum changes and new content, particularly if this is perceived as being experimental, as they harbour concerns regarding their own work, and transferability into the world of employment. Therefore, introduction of new and less traditional methods may 'throw' students who know how to get a good mark in traditional assignments. This pressure makes them less likely to flow creatively and inhibits the process, while they are searching for prescribed and standardised instructions regarding the assignments. As mentioned above, this can be pacified by the cre-ation and use of open, transparent and structured marking criteria. This will give the students confidence that they are working towards set and well-thought-out, approved criteria that will undergo the same academic quality testing (e.g., through second marking and external examiners) as traditional assessments. When implementing visual methods into the curriculum ourselves, there was little reluctance but also an apparent lack of active support. However, as the students engaged and became enthused by the projects, we noticed a change in the practice of other people. For example, staff within the department began to discuss the incorporation of visual methods with us and it became evident that aspects of visual methods were subsequently being utilised in the practice of others.

Conclusion

Visual methods, in our experience, have been under represented in both undergraduate and postgraduate curricula in the social sciences. Through our own research we have found that the use of visual methods can be a great source of engagement for the students and provide meaningful data and a strong connection between the tutor and the students. However, we would warn against including such methods for their own sake. While this can be an extremely worthwhile, challenging and enjoyable part of the curriculum, it is crucial to ensure that the pedagogical benefits are justified and that assessments and marking criteria are well thought through. The incorporation of visual methods with the sole aim of appearing innovative and creative will simply dilute the benefits of powerful and meaningful visual methods research. Therefore, we urge you to experiment, be bold and creative and provide the students with sufficient grounding in visual methods research to ensure that they are equipped to use the methods if their research question allows.

Suggested reading

Biggs, J. and Tang, C. (2011). *Teaching for quality learning at university: what the student does.* Maidenhead: McGraw-Hill Education.

Rose, G. (2013). *Visual methodologies.* London: Sage.

Scott Jones, J. and Watt, S. (2010). *Ethnography in social science practice.* London: Routledge.

Wakefield, C. and Watt, S. (2012). 'There will always be a part of you that wants to return': a reflective photo elicitation of an Ironman triathlon. *Qualitative Methods in Psychology, Special Issue: Focus on Sport and Performance, 2*(14), 40–52.

Wakefield, C. and Watt, S. (2014). A double take: the practical and ethical dilemmas of teaching the visual method of photo elicitation. *Psychology Teaching Review, 20*(2), 145–57.

Watt, S. and Wakefield, C. (2014). Picture it! the use of visual methods in psychology teaching. *Psychology Teaching Review, 20*(1), 68–77.

Yorke, M. (2003). Formative assessment in higher education: moves towards theory and the enhancement of pedagogic practice. *Higher Education, 43*(4), 477–501.

References

Bhati, K.S., Hoyt, W.T. and Huffman, K.L. (2013). Integration or assimilation? Locating qualitative research in psychology. *Qualitative Research in Psychology, 11*, 98–114.

Biggs, J. (1999). What the student does: teaching for enhanced learning. *Higher Education Research and Development, 18*(1), 57–75.

Biggs, J. and Tang, C. (2011). *Teaching for quality learning at university: what the student does.* Maidenhead: McGraw-Hill Education.

Boud, D., Cohen, R. and Sampson, J. (1999). Peer learning and assessment. *Assessment and Evaluation in Higher Education, 24*(4), 413–26.

Brown, S. (2004). Assessment for learning. *Learning and Teaching in Higher Education, 1*, 81–89.

Bruner, J (1960). *The process of education,* Cambridge, MA.: Harvard University Press.

Collier, J. (1957). Photography in anthropology: a report on two experiments. *American Anthropologist, 59*(5), 843–59.

Collier, J. and Collier, M. (1986). *Visual anthropology: photography as a research method.* Albuquerque: University of New Mexico Press.

Earl, L.M. (2003). *Assessment as learning: using classroom assessment to maximize student learning.* London: Sage.

Fanning, S. (2011). Visual methodologies: photo-elicitation in the university classroom. Paper presented at the 10th European Conference on Research Methodology for Business and Management Studies, Normandy Business School, Caen, France.

Flick, U. (2002). *An introduction to qualitative research.* Thousand Oaks, CA: Sage.

Frith, H., Riley, S., Archer, L. and Gleeson, K. (2005). Imag(in)ing visul methodologies. *Qualitative Research in Psychology, 2*(3), 187–98.

Garde-Hansen, J. and Calvert, B. (2007). Developing a research culture in the undergraduate curriculum. *Active Learning in Higher Education, 8*(2), 105–16.

Garrod, B. (2007). A snapshot into the past: the utility of volunteer-employed photography in planning and managing heritage tourism. *Journal of Heritage Tourism, 2*(1), 14–35.

Gibbs, G. (2006a). Why assessment is changing. In C. Bryan and K. Clegg (eds), *Innovative Assessment in Higher Education* (pp. 11–22). Routledge: London.

Gibbs, G. (2006b). How assessment frames student learning. In C. Bryan and K. Clegg (eds), *Innovative assessment in higher education* (pp. 23–36). Routledge: London.

Grady, J. (2004). Working with visual evidence: an invitation and some practical advice. In C. Knowles and J. Sweetman (eds), *Picturing the social landscape: Visual methods and the sociological imagination* (pp. 18–32). London: Routledge.

Guba, E.G. and Lincoln, Y.S. (1994). Competing paradigms in qualitative research. In N.K. Denzin and Y.S. Lincoln (eds), *Handbook of qualitative research* (pp. 105–17). Thousand Oaks, CA: Sage Publications.

Hanson, S. (2013). Assessing and evaluating creativity for undergraduates in media studies and art and design. *Higher Education Academy*. www.heacademy.ac.uk/blogs.

Harden, R.M. and Stamper, N. (1999). What is a spiral curriculum? *Medical Teacher, 21*(2), 141–3.

Harper, D. (2002). Talking about pictures: a case of photo elicitation. *Visual Studies, 17,* 13–26.

Harper, S.R. and Quaye, S.J. (2009). *Student engagement in higher education: theoretical perspectives and practical approaches for diverse populations.* Routledge: London

Harvey, L. (2000). New realities: the relationship between higher education and employment. *Tertiary Education and Management, 6*(1), 3–17.

Hurdley, R. (2007). Focal points: framing material culture and visual data. *Sociology, 7,* 355–74.

Krieger, S. (1996). Beyond subjectivity. In A. Lareau and J. Schultz (eds), *Journeys through ethnography: realistic accounts of fieldwork* (pp. 179–94). Colorado: Westview Press.

Liebenberg, L. (2009). The visual image as discussion point: increasing validity in boundary crossing research. *Qualitative Research, 9*(4), 441–67.

Marton, F. and Saljo, R. (1976). On qualitative differences in learning – 1: outcome and process. *British Journal of Educational Psychology, 46,* 4–11.

Morrow, S.L. (2007). Qualitative research in counselling psychology: conceptual foundations. *The Counselling Psychologist, 35*(2), 209–35.

Oldrup, H.H. and Carstensen, T.A. (2012). Producing geographical knowledge through visual methods. *Geografiska Annaler: Series B, Human Geography, 94*(3), 223–37.

Owen, C. and Riley, S. (2012). Teaching visual methods using performative storytelling, reflective practice and learning through doing. *Psychology Learning and Teaching, 11*(1), 60–65.

Phoenix, C. (2010). Seeing the world of physical culture: the potential of visual methods for qualitative research in sport and exercise. *Qualitative Research in Sport and Exercise, 2*(2), 93–108.

Pink, S. (2003). *Visual research, encyclopaedia of social science research methods.* London: Sage Publications.

Pink, S. (2007). *Doing visual ethnography.* London: Sage Publications.

Ponterotto, J.G. and Grieger, I. (2007). Effectively communicating qualitative research. *The Counseling Psychologist, 35,* 404–30.

Poulin, K.L. (2007). Teaching qualitative research: lessons from practice. *The Counselling Psychologist, 35,* 431–58.

Radley, A. and Taylor, D. (2003). Remembering one's stay in hospital: a study in photography, recovery and forgetting. *Health: An Interdisciplinary Journal for the Social Study of Health, Illness and Medicine, 7*(2), 129–59.

Ramsden, P. (1992). *Learning to teach in higher education.* Routledge: London.

Ramsden, P. (2003). *Learning to teach in higher education.* Routledge: London.

Rookwood, J. and Palmer, C. (2009). A photo-ethnography: a picture-story-board of experiences at an NGO football project in Liberia. *Journal of Qualitative Research in Sports Studies, 3*(1), 161–210.

Rust, C. (2002). The impact of assessment on student learning. *Active Learning in Higher Education, 3,* 145–58.

Ryan-Flood, R. and Gill, R. (2010). *Secrecy and silence in the research process: Feminist reflections*. London: Routledge.

Scarles, C. (2010). Where words fail, visuals ignite: opportunities for visual autoethnography in tourism research. *Annals of Tourism Research, 37*, 905–26.

Scott Jones, J. and Watt, S. (2010). *Ethnography in social science practice*. London: Routledge.

Shrum, W., Duque, R. and Brown, T. (2005). Digital video as research practice: methodology for the millennium. *Journal of Research Practice, 1*(1), M4.

Shuell, T.J. (1986). Cognitive conceptions of learning. *Review of Educational Research, 56*, 411–36.

Smith, L., Bratini, L. and Appio, L.M. (2012). 'Everybody's teaching and everybody's learning': Photovoice and youth counselling. *Journal of Counselling and Development, 90*(1), 3–12.

Spry, T (2001). Performing autoethnography: an embodied methodological praxis. *Qualitative Inquiry, 7*, 706–32.

Tweed, F. and Boast, R. (2011). Reviewing the 'research placement' as a means of enhancing student learning and stimulating research activity. *Journal of Geography in Higher Education, 35*(4), 599–615.

Vitiello, L. (2009). Redesigning a 'quantitative research methods for finance' module. *Investigations in University Teaching and Learning, 5*(2), 128–32.

Wakefield, C. and Watt, S. (2012). 'There will always be a part of you that wants to return': A reflective photo elicitation of an Ironman triathlon. *Qualitative Methods in Psychology, Special Issue: Focus on Sport and Performance, 2*(14), 40–52.

Wakefield, C. and Watt, S. (2014). A double take: the practical and ethical dilemmas of teaching the visual method of photo elicitation. *Psychology Teaching Review, 20*(2), 145–57.

Walkington, H., Griffin, A.L., Keys-Mathews, L., Metoyer, S.K., Miller, W.E., Baker, R. and France, D. (2011). Embedding research-based learning early in the undergraduate geography curriculum. *Journal of Geography in Higher Education, 35*(3), 315–30.

Wang, C.C. (1999). Photovoice: a participatory action research strategy applied to women's health. *Journal of Women's Health, 8*, 185–92.

Wang, C. and Burris, M. (1997). Photovoice: concept, methodology, and use for participatory needs assessment. *Health Education and Behaviour, 24*(3), 369–87.

Watt, S. and Wakefield, C. (2014). Picture it! The use of visual methods in psychology teaching. *Psychology Teaching Review, 20*(1), 68–77.

Williams, K. (2005). Lecturer and first year student (mis)understandings of assessment task verbs: 'mind the gap'. *Teaching in Higher Education, 10*(2), 157–73.

Willison, J. and O'Regan, K. (2007). Commonly known, commonly not known, totally unknown: a framework for students becoming researchers. *Higher Education Research and Development, 26*(4), 393–409.

Yorke, M. (2003). Formative assessment in higher education: moves towards theory and the enhancement of pedagogic practice. *Higher Education, 43*(4), 477–501.

PART II
Teaching visual methods

Case studies

Different visual methods

5

FILM

Using secondary data as a mechanism to support student learning

Moira E. Lafferty

Introduction

This chapter introduces readers to the concept of using feature films as a method for seminar tasks and formative and summative assessment within social science teaching. Drawing on personal experiences, reflection and student feedback examples are given in this chapter as to how feature films have been used in a final-year undergraduate sport psychology module. I begin by charting my own journey discussing how I came to use feature films in assessment. I identify the key literature which provided the evidence base for the task development and review the benefits and caveats to such an approach. Finally, along with a flow chart to help guide those who may wish to use the technique I comment on some future uses of the approach within assessment.

Background to using films in teaching: A personal journey

In many social science disciplines, when lecturing, we often draw upon real-world events as exemplars to explain key theories and theoretical positions. We often teach on modules or courses that have an 'applied' or 'practical' focus but due to the topic nature we are unable to actually provide a real-world experience, as practical or field work are often impossible. In my own field I frequently teach on modules in sport psychology that explore critical factors relating to applied practice and the work of the sport psychologist as a practitioner. The nature and content of such modules suggests there is an element of application of psychological training and working with clients; however, rarely does this happen. In fact reflecting on the module feedback of such modules one of the recurrent themes has been it would be beneficial to actually apply or *do* some real psychological training. Unfortunately, when teaching applied sport psychology and other such areas it is often difficult, due to numerous professional, practical and ethical reasons, to expose students to real-world applied experiences. This is in comparison to other subjects where laboratory and fieldwork is engaged with early on and can facilitate understanding and contextualise theoretical principles. For me, as a sport psychologist and for other colleagues within the social sciences, it is often harder to create the theory in action and/or real-world experience for students. How we can do this has been an intriguing question for me since first being introduced to the concept of ethnodrama (Gilbourne, Triggs and Merkin, 2006) at a conference workshop.

Through watching the performance and discussions with Dave Gilbourne I began to review how I brought my subject 'to life' for my students and reflected on my tendency to use scenarios from text books, students' self-disclosure and my own personal practitioner experiences (described in a manner which protects the privacy and confidentiality of the client) to illustrate key points. It struck me that while all of these methods provide vignettes and narratives of real-world events and can enhance understanding; it could be argued that they fall short of creating for the student the actual physical, social and emotional climate as observed at the critical moment, unlike my experiences of the ethnodrama. This may be because they provide a 'unidimensional' source of information (Higgins and Dermer, 2001) through the medium of the spoken or written word and are therefore reliant on students' auditory and/or comprehension skills. Students miss out on observing body language, facial expressions, participant interactions and the influence of the social environment. This lack of 'visual stimuli' leaves them dependent on their own experiences to construct and create the whole picture with limited scaffolding. This reflection led me to begin to review how other fields akin to my own engage students and use differing media to enhance, encourage and develop the learning experience.

Reviewing pedagogical practice through journal articles and the internet searches on teaching sites such as CROW – Course Resources on the Web (http://jfmueller. faculty.noctrl.edu/crow/) – led to a recurring theme: The use and integration of popular culture, or in real terms, the use of films in the learning environment, a concept in medical teaching known as 'cinemeducation' (Blumer, 2010). First introduced by Alexander, Hall and Pettice (1994), the term cinemeducation described a method of using movie clips and/or whole movies to educate learners about the differing psychological aspects of health care. Enthused by this, I became conscious of the fact that to move away from 'traditional' lecturing approaches there was a need to be cognate of the pedagogical evidence base both to reassure traditionalist colleagues and to be able to contextualise the approach for the students. I thus began to explore the available literature.

Using films in learning and teaching: A review of the literature

From an initial review of the literature, examples of using film in teaching and learning began to emerge from diverse fields including counselling psychology (Higgins and Dermer, 2001), psychiatry (Akram, O'Brien, O'Neill and Latham, 2009), psychotherapy (Edwards, 2010), cognitive psychology (Conner, 1996) and hypothesis testing (Gardner and Davidson, 2010). It became apparent that films were being used in numerous ways to enhance the learning experience and increase students' active participation, with positive responses (Berk, 2009).

Paddock, Terranova and Giles (2001) described how films were used to teach personality theories to undergraduate psychology students. Over the course of two classes, students watched movie clips depicting different aspects of behaviour and personalities. They then participated in group discussions and individual work analysing the film scene and characters portrayed. Results of a short post-activity questionnaire indicated that students found the movie clips interesting and believed them to illustrate the theoretical concepts and increase their understanding of the theory. Paddock *et al.* (2001) argued that this teaching method provided a theoretically rich and intellectually challenging approach, and the use of movies had benefits compared to films obtained through naturalistic observation, although no reasons were offered for this conclusion.

Examples also began to emerge of consistent film use during teaching. Ventura and Onsman (2009) discussed how movie clips were used throughout a lecture series with pharmacology undergraduate students to introduce concepts or drug treatment. Clips were embedded in the PowerPoint lecture slides and lasted on average between 1 and 3 minutes. Student course evaluation indicated that students found the clips interesting, enjoyable and an appropriate form of learning influencing concentration, motivation and attendance.

Edwards (2010) offered a different approach to using film when she described how it could be used to teach non-clinical students about countertransference in psychotherapy. During a seminar, scenes from the film *Morvern Caller* were shown and used as a means to enhance students' understanding and as a catalyst for discussion. Edwards suggested that using film in this way offered students some 'proto-experience of the individual work in the consulting room' (p. 97).

These examples all identified ways in which film could be used and integrated, through a tutor-led approach, as part of a lecture or seminar. Datta (2009) suggested an alternative method of using film where, as well as being part of the actual lecture, it also formed part of the post-lecture work for medical students enrolled on an undergraduate psychiatry module. Each week had a specific theme which was exemplified in the designated film and watched by all students. As well as completing assigned reading, students were also expected to watch at least one further movie from a prescribed list. They then participated in a seminar or lecture which focused on critically reviewing the issues depicted in the films, applying empirical evidence to explain or suggest treatments.

Throughout the initial literature search several papers came to light that reviewed using film as a form of assessment. Blumer (2010) discussed how postgraduate students enrolled on a marriage and family therapy course completed a film review as part of their assessment. While Conner (1996) described how students in an introductory cognitive psychology module had to identify a topic of interest, read a journal article, select and view a feature film, present and then complete an individual report. A format replicated by Akram *et al.* (2009) with medical students studying psychiatry.

Examples also emerged of how films were being used in tandem with other pedagogical techniques to enhance student performance. Hemenover, Castor and Mizumoto (1999) discussed how film viewing and analysis were combined with progressive writing instructions in an assignment for undergraduate students on an introductory psychology course. Student feedback from end-of-module evaluations indicated that students enjoyed the assessment and perceived the progressive writing technique to be beneficial to their development. It therefore became clear that feature films could be used in a variety of ways in both teaching and learning. However, critically from a pedagogical stance, there was a need to review and explore what possible benefits there could be to adopting feature film use.

The benefits of using films in teaching and learning

As illustrated above, numerous authors have suggested that there are benefits to using film as a pedagogical tool. Anderson (1992) reported that students felt more comfortable talking in class using film as a medium for discussion of theoretical topics, and Conner (1996) suggested that students viewed film tasks as fun and that it allowed them to bridge the 'real-world' theory chasm. Scherer and Baker (1999) proposed that this may be because films provide the visual medium to engage students and encourage retention of information. While Ventura and Onsman (2009) argued that the integration of films can provide cognitive reinforcement of theoretical knowledge, and a change in the learning modus operandi can increase motivation and, subsequently, concentration and learning. In turn, this could lead students to an 'Aha' moment where they suddenly understand, grasp or make sense of a concept or idea (Wrobbel, 2003). Akram *et al.* (2009) further supported the use of movies and films, describing them as a 'directly positive tool for educating and generating lively debate' (p. 267).

As well as these generic benefits a number of papers highlighted positive aspects that would be relevant, useful and transferable to applied sport psychology teaching. In a review of film use in marriage counsellor education, Higgins and Dermer (2001) stated that film analysis provided a safe distance from the action and allowed under-represented populations to be observed. These authors also suggested that film use can help explain and explore difficult-to-teach concepts, provides the option of multiple viewings and is an entertaining medium, which people engage with cognitively, emotionally and behaviourally. Research by both Armstrong and Berg (2005) and Blumer (2010) reiterated these positive ideas and highlighted several pedagogical benefits. For example, they believe that integrating film clips can allow complex information to be presented in a simple and engaging manner. They also suggested that film viewing and analysis used in tandem with group activities can provide a social and fun experience for students.

While many articles highlighted the positive aspects of film integration there are obvious caveats to its use and those who oppose the approach. Bhugra (2003) argued that film can both stigmatise and distort the truth, while Akram *et al.* (2009) cautioned practitioners to be mindful of artistic licence, given that feature films are by their very nature stories and not facts. Casper, *et al.* (2003) cautioned those using film to be aware of potentially offending content and the emotional impact that films can have on their audience. They also suggested that the introduction of film into teaching will involve an 'up front' workload in terms of reviewing appropriate films, deciding upon key scenes and developing critical questions if the intention is to run a guided discussion. All of these points are reiterated by Dave and Tandon (2011), though they also suggested that in real terms the time factor is no longer than preparing any new material.

Perhaps the most vehemently opposed to the use of films is Greenberg (2009) who likened the use of film within teaching to 'Tinseltown' teaching. In a damning review of film use in psychiatry, he argued that students learn nothing from movies and can acquire a false understanding of disease complexity and treatment options. He argued that 'the practice of celluloid psycho-pharmacology, if found at all, imparts a morass of misinformation' (p. 243). In actual fact the majority of arguments presented by Greenberg have been highlighted as caveats to film use by a number of authors who, when stressing the benefits, also presented a list of the possible pitfalls (Armstrong and Berg, 2005; Blumer, 2010; Dave and Tandon, 2011). For example Datta (2009) stated that 'films do not pretend to present an accurate portrayal' (p. 265) but argued that this is not really a problem if both students and tutors are aware of this. Jayawickreme and Forgeard (2011) suggested that using non-empirical sources (i.e., in this case feature films) can serve as a catalyst for further empirical exploration and thus deepen knowledge and understanding by analysing the misconceptions portrayed. While Ventura and Onsman (2009) suggested that integrating film clips into lectures retained interest, engagement and motivated students while also breaking up the lecture up into manageable chunks. Therefore, although there are obviously concerns with using film, there also seem to be numerous potential benefits.

Example 1: Using films in seminars a sport psychology example

Rationale, background and purpose

Enthused by the possibilities and mindful of the caveats of using film I began to explore how we could integrate films into one of our Level 6 (third-year undergraduate) modules to provide a practical and enriching experience for the students. A secondary review of the literature drew me back to the work of Anderson (1992) who described how she used films as a catalyst for group discussion in a law and psychology class. Prior to watching the film, students were required to prepare for two types of discussion. One centred around the application of course knowledge while the second was designed to elicit a more critical approach through analysis of the issues portrayed and stance taken. Anderson conducted this task towards the end of the course to ensure that all material relevant to the film had been covered and argued that the discussion acted as a form of revision for the final examination and allowed students a break from the usual assigned readings.

At this time I was leading a Level 6 applied sport psychology module that was arranged around four discrete topic areas which were taught in blocks with the final week of each block devoted to a summary and review of the information and areas covered. This summary lecture presented an ideal opportunity to explore the efficacy of using films in sport psychology in gaining information as to whether students enjoyed and engaged with the activity and, importantly, whether both students and course tutors perceived there to be any identified benefits.

Instigating and running the seminar

Two weeks prior to the final session of the leadership and cohesion topic, students were informed that the summary session would not be based around a vignette, narrative or research paper, but instead film clips would be used as a catalyst to explore and discuss key concepts. Students were told that they had to choose an area covered in the topic, register the area with the module leader and find a 3-minute film clip which showed, identified or explored their chosen issue. During the summary seminar they would each present their clip, briefly highlight the key concepts and research and state how a sport psychologist could use the clip. Mindful of the fact that novel approaches, which differ from the established norm, can evoke increased anxiety (Norton, 2007) students were given a worksheet that provided scaffolding for the exercise and allowed them to frame their discussion points (Table 5.1).

TABLE 5.1 Presentation outline overview and guiding questions

Structure of the presentation	Key question to frame content
Brief overview of chosen clip	Describe what is going on; contextualise in respect of the story
Theoretical position	Be specific; remember to check through topic notes
Research evidence	Which recently published research could you use to explain what you are seeing or may link to the theme shown in the clip?
Application	How as a sport psychologist might you use this clip?

Prior to the seminar the order of presentations was posted on the module virtual learning space. This was based around the students' chosen topic areas (cohesion, leadership, coaches and coaching) to ensure that the session had some structure in terms of material presentation and review with respect to the taught block. During the seminar students introduced their clip, played the clip for the group and then described what they perceived to be the key theoretical issues linking to relevant research. We encouraged the group to challenge the views presented and to suggest alternative interpretations during the open floor discussion towards the end of the seminar. During the final 15 minutes the module tutors summarised each of the core themes within the film clips chosen and linked these to the core topic areas covered in the module to both contextualise the session and reinforce learning.

Reflections on using films in a sport psychology seminar

At the end of the seminar session, we asked students to complete a short feedback form about the exercise, which resulted in numerous positive comments. In line with the research reviewed previously, our students supported the use of film commenting that it *'helps see how theory can be related to real life'*, *'gives you a practical way of thinking about theory rather than being told . . .'*, and *'. . . you begin to see the theory through the film and understand its position within the applied context . . .'*. As well as commenting on what they had learned, the group also made some perceptive comments about student contributions: *'. . . those who do not find the clips/do the work should not have the benefit of taking part'*; about the notion of group work: *'. . . work in pairs to share knowledge and understanding and feedback to the class . . .'*; and, interestingly, about the actual assessment itself: *'can this become summative assessment as we did a lot of work for it?'*.

Reviewing the informal feedback it became obvious that the seminar task had engaged the students, focused their attention and created the theory-practice link, thereby meeting my original goal for the task. However, as we discussed the exercise and task as a teaching team we began to wonder whether we could make more of this exercise. The benefits of this approach for formative assessment were obvious but, responding to student feedback, could it be used as a form of summative assessment?

Example 2: Summative assessment through the medium of feature films

Rationale

Returning to the literature I once again reviewed the work of those authors who reported using film for assessment purposes. Conner (1996) described an assessment strategy for an undergraduate cognitive psychology course where students worked in pairs reviewing a journal article and then selected a film which identified and linked to the critical points in the article. Students then wrote an individual report and presented as a pair their findings to the group. This mixed-method assessment of group and individual work presented a promising approach for our assessment. Combining a group oral presentation with an individual written report would allow us to redress one of the key concerns that many students have when faced with group summative assessment, namely, the equity of marks awarded and parity of actual members' work and contribution (Sharp, 2006).

Blumer (2010) discussed and reflected upon a course where postgraduate students self-selected into groups, reviewed a film from a set list and produced a written review. After the report had been graded it was worked on further by the student group to prepare it for submission to a professional publication. For the initial graded assessment, Blumer reported that the students found the activity enhanced their learning and ability to analyse core concepts, and was enjoyable. With respect to developing our own assessment this paper raised some interesting questions: Do we select a list of films or should we give students the freedom to select their own? Do we select the groups or let the students formulate their own? Reflecting on the feedback from the original task, several students stated that they 'enjoyed finding the clip' and perhaps inadvertently this created a subliminal learning opportunity in its own right. With respect to group formation we decided in the first instance to assign group membership as students taking the module were from both combined and single honours courses. We were also conscious of the fact that unless students are adequately supported when working in groups there can be problems such as group divisions, disagreements, social loafing and the perception of unfairness, in that, potentially weaker students could gain higher marks based purely on group membership and vice versa, with stronger students perceiving that their mark was reduced (Davies, 2009). To promote group cohesion, division of work and allow a transparent process where the individual group members could comment individually on the group's performance we decided to use Altman's 'Rubric for Assessing Group Members – Ability to Participate Effectively as Part of a Team' (http://williamaltman.info/Courses/Scoring%20Guides/GroupProcess Questionnaire.pdf).

I was also guided by the work of Higgins and Dermer (2001). They presented examples that included using film as an exam replacement or supplement, and of direct relevance to our situation, examples of using film for summative written assessment. Interestingly, these authors described how after the individual papers were submitted, class and group-based discussion took place. This allowed students to share their interpretations and learn from each other. Keen to provide a stimulating environment and allow students to actively participate while observing the group presentations, we developed a crib sheet so that students could provide feedback on each other's presentations and reflect on alternative explanations (Table 5.2).

The feature film summative assessment task

Guided by the literature and based on our previous exercise we formulated a summative assessment comprising two components, a group presentation and individual written report constituting 50 per cent of the module mark. For the presentation students were informed that they must work in their group and identify a short clip (3 minutes) from a feature film which depicted one of the key areas covered in the first three topics of the module. The clip could be sourced from YouTube, a DVD or from the internet. They then had to produce a 10-minute

TABLE 5.2 Example of the crib sheet

Group	Film	Key factors identification (what you found interesting)	Alternative explanations/ interpretation
Presentation feedback			

PowerPoint presentation highlighting the psychological theory which could be used to explain what was happening in the film and how the applied sport psychologist might work with the athlete, team or individuals (e.g., coaches, parents and friends). An example of presentation content is shown in Figure 5.1. For the individual written report (Part B) students had to discuss how sports psychology research can be used to explain the actions and reactions of the individuals in their scenario.

Conscious of the need to support the students through this novel assessment and aware that new or innovative methods can sometimes be viewed with a certain amount of trepidation and fear (Cartney, 2010), several key stages were built into the assessment process. Once the groups had been organised they had 3 weeks to choose and register their movie clip. This ensured that no two groups could use the same clip and presented me with an access point early in the process to work with each group. This meant that I could check that they fully understood the task brief and had analysed the clip correctly (for examples of movies chosen and areas see Table 5.3).

During the weeks leading up to the presentation, student groups could book tutorials with any member of the module teaching team. Support information was made available through the university intranet module learning space, including an online example of a film clip and PowerPoint presentation. At the end of each lecture 5 minutes were devoted to answering any assessment-related questions, including the structure of the presentation. The week before the presentations students were reminded to submit their group process rubric sheets in the folder

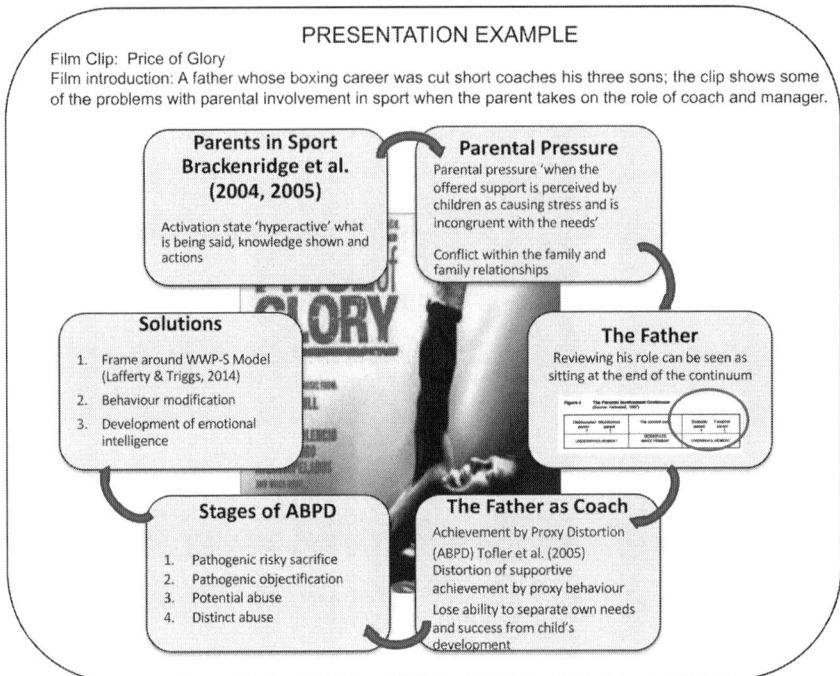

FIGURE 5.1 Example of presentation.

TABLE 5.3 Topic areas and chosen films

Area	Examples of films used
Coaches and coaching	Longest Yard, Coach Carter
Leadership	Miracle, Facing the Giants
Cohesion	Varsity Blues, Remember the Titans, Coach Carter

outside of the module tutor's room. Presentations took place mid-way through the winter term and were formally assessed by three members of staff, with students using the pre-designed crib sheet (Table 5.2). The individual written report was submitted 1 week later.

Reflections on the summative assessment task

It would be easy to say that the students enjoyed the task, the mean module mark increased and there seemed to be engagement with the process, all of which could support the assumption that the integration of feature films into the assessment process was a success. In essence, this is all true: I believe the journey from initially searching for ways of bringing sport psychology alive through film to developing a summative assessment task has been logical, systematic and informed by a wealth of research and positively appraised through student feedback. In end-of-year evaluations students commented favourably on the assessment stating '*I really enjoyed working on something that was more visual*' and '*it brought the topic to life and allowed us to explore it from a sport psychologists perspective . . .* ' More critically, questions regarding whether we have it right and if/how it can be improved are perhaps more pertinent points to consider and harder to answer.

While all of the students were enthusiastic about the task, we did inevitably have one or two groups who had problems in terms of group membership and working together. In each of these instances I met with each student individually and then the group collectively. The individual meetings were I think important, as students had time to express their concerns in a private forum and I was able to piece together where and why the group was not functioning productively. This information allowed me to develop a plan and structure for the group meeting and explore with the group how they were going to work cohesively on task while being aware of each other's needs I also believe that as the rubric was introduced with the actual assignment it raised student awareness that through their individual reflections on each group member's performance we had a method of monitoring group process. Monitoring in this manner through peer reporting might have been responsible for less social loafing and increased cooperation, and it could be that in the future peer monitoring could be incorporated into a component mark which reflects the actual group work of each member. This is an interesting avenue to think about given the higher education agenda of transferable skills and employability. Perhaps one of the challenges to this, however, would be that the honesty of reflections by the individuals on their group members would be reduced in the search for marks.

The students enjoyed the task and observing each other's presentations offered a further learning opportunity (Cartney, 2010), reinforcing for them different areas of the topics covered in an engaging manner. However, whether we really made the most of this is something I have continually reflected upon. Teater (2011) suggested that students need to be active participants in their own learning to maximise their potential while Cartney (2010) called for the active participation of students in their assessments. Although all students did complete the feedback crib sheets on each presentation, I believe that we could have used these more, both in terms of giving further feedback and engaging in a more detailed and in-depth post-assessment discussion. Adopting this approach would allow us to build the bridge between module assessment and assessment for continued learning. It may also reduce one of the continuing problems we face of how students perceive assessment with respect to the module they are taking. Quite often there is a tendency for students to divorce the assessment from the module once the task is completed; many do not see or embrace the continued learning that can be gained through assessment, instead many students see assessment as something to be done and then forgotten. Perhaps one way to address this would be to schedule a feedback review session with a 10-minute discussion on each presentation in terms of content led by another group, or return to the presentations during the final module summary.

Alternatively, rather than inter-group collaboration at the assessment point and building on the work of Cartney (2010) we could perhaps pair up groups so that one group becomes part of the assessment panel for another, completing a form of peer assessment (Orr, 2010). However, peer assessment within summative work is itself not without problems and caveats. Therefore, perhaps an interim stage would be to pair groups up for formative assessment on the task from which feedback could feed-forward (Carless, 2006) to the summative work. For example rather than me reviewing the clips with each group, the individual groups are paired up so that they can arrange a time to review each other's clip choice and comment on whether the analysis proposed is appropriate; in essence a peer member check approach. This could be supported with feedback sheets which would need to be submitted to the module leader. This feedback sheet would act as a monitoring mechanism for engagement with this stage and could be used to highlight any discrepancies between the groups' analysis of each other's clips. If discrepancies were highlighted then the teaching team could review the pro-posed clip.

During the actual assessment presentations one issue that we had was related to the playing of the clip. Where students had used a DVD they were able to find and play it relatively easily with little delay with respect to timings. However, where the clip was sourced from either the internet or YouTube we encountered buffering and downloading problems which meant that we over-ran on the scheduled timings. While the obvious solution is to mandate that all clips must be shown from a DVD this could mean that students might have to purchase it. Although DVDs can be sourced relatively cheaply from the internet I am not inclined to do this as I do not believe that students should incur any financial costs for assessment. At present I am contemplating two differing approaches to this problem. The first being to get the students to 'rip' the clips into their presentation and the second being to build in time for buffering because generally once the clip had been through it subsequently played perfectly. The films chosen by students completing this assignment often fall into one of two genres: fictional or those based on a true story. To date we have not legislated as to which genre students should use as we do not consider there to be any advantage to true story over fiction or indeed vice versa. It could be argued that pure fiction is more prone to exaggeration and the actions and reactions of the characters bear no resemblance to individuals in the real sporting world. In contrast, those based on a true story could be considered to be more 'true to life'; however, as the central characters even in these movies are actors their behaviours thoughts and actions may deviate from those of the sports player at the critical moment.

In thinking about this type of assignment I am conscious that one of the problems that could be encountered is that the groups or individuals become engrossed in film watching as opposed to film analysis. In both of the examples discussed I gave students the freedom to choose their own clip. Giving freedom of choice does mean however that we have a responsibility to make sure groups move forward with the task. They must be regularly reminded that no marks are awarded for the clip per se but for the analysis of the chosen clip. This raises the question of whether there are merits to clip pre-selection by the tutor or the presentation of a film list from which groups select a film. In certain situations lecturers may find this approach works better, for example, if using the technique with Level 4 or 5 students or where there are time limits on the assessment process or where the assessment is focused on one particular area of the course.

Reflecting on this assessment approach and having reviewed the benefits, possible issues and areas for development I also think that it is important to review the impact of the assessment on myself as the tutor and module leader. Working with students on a piece of work which is unique to a particular group is both interesting and increases student–tutor interaction. It is fascinating to see how students approach the task, to explore their film choices with them, and the subsequent conversations mediated by the clip are possibly at a deeper level than when students are approaching an essay title. I find this form of assessment stimulating, interesting and rewarding. The ability of the students to discuss what they are seeing exemplifies that they have absorbed the course information and have a depth of knowledge that at times they do not realise.

I believe that there are still ways we can develop this assessment to maximise the potential learning experiences for the students. Finding ways to increase their interaction and engagement with other groups' presentations will allow us to maximise the benefits of group work including the fact that it can promote deep and active learning (Davies, 2009), placing assessment as a central component of learning and not just as a task to be completed (Cartney, 2010).

Conclusion

Incorporating feature films into teaching and assessment presents us with a new dimension for engaging students' interest, stimulating discussion and fostering knowledge development. At the beginning of this chapter I highlighted one reason for exploring and examining the use of film was to find ways and methods for creating more 'theory in action' experiences and to move away from the more traditional 'unidimensional' sources of information often used in exemplars (e.g., narratives, vignettes and case studies). The use of film clips provides students with a multi-sensory experience which helps them think in terms of actions and reactions, emotions, behaviours and social relationships. The examples presented in this chapter introduce two ways of using feature films in terms of seminar/ formative assessment and summative assessment. Although the examples given relate to a specific discipline, the process and technique is malleable to numerous areas of social science. For anyone thinking of adopting this approach the Figure 5.2 flow chart provides a framework to follow based upon my experiences and reflections and the pedagogical literature. While there are caveats to using films,

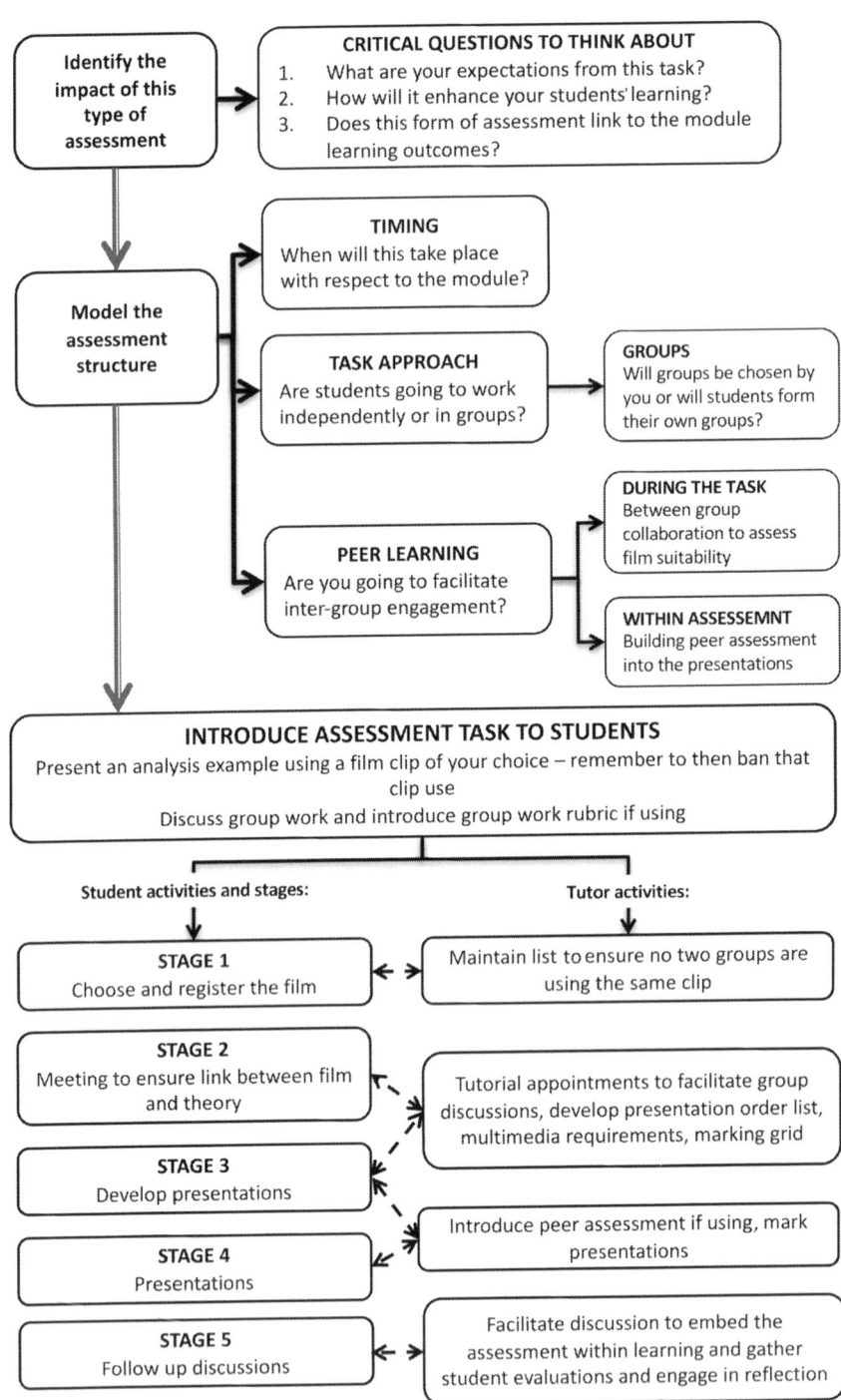

FIGURE 5.2 A flowchart of key stages in using feature films for assessment.

not least always being aware of the fiction–theory divide, evidence so far suggests that students enjoy using films in this manner and the clips serve as capstones and anchor points for the development of critical analysis skills.

REFLECTIVE ACTIVITIES

The following reflective activities are designed to make you think about using films within your own discipline and by working through each in turn you will be able to reflect on whether films would be a useful medium for you to use and develop strategies for some challenges which can arise.

1   To help you think about the availability of suitable films for your own discipline imagine that you have to recommend five feature films that exemplified topics covered in a core module. What would they be and why?

2   Offering differing forms of assessment can often be viewed negatively by colleagues more used to traditional essay-based approaches. What would be your key arguments for the introduction of a feature film assessment within your discipline?

3   A group of four students comes to you with a dilemma over film choice. They have two clips and the group is divided over which clip to use. Two students are adamant they should use clip A and two clip B. You have several options, meet with the group and have an open discussion, suggest that they find a clip they can all agree on or select a clip for them. Each of these options has consequences, think through them with respect to your own situation and formulate an action plan of how you would approach this situation.

4   Imagine that you had set up a feature film assessment and one of the groups had chosen a clip which might offend or distress other students due to its dramatic nature. You do not want to stop the group using the clip as their analysis and rationale have been justified. How might you manage the situation?

General note

Portions of this chapter have previously been published in the *Sport and Exercise Psychology Review*: Lafferty, M. E. (2013). Using feature films in the teaching and assessment of sport psychology. *Sport and Exercise Psychology Review*, 9(2), 74–82. Copyright of this article through the British Psychological Society allows for the use in whole or part.

Suggested reading

Berk, R.A. (2009). Multimedia teaching with video clips: TV, movies, YouTube, and mtvU in the college classroom. *International Journal of Technology in Teaching and Learning*, *5*, 1–21.

Edwards, J. (2010). Teaching and learning about psychoanalysis: film as a teaching tool, with reference to a particular film, *Morvern Caller. British Journal of Psychotherapy*, *26*, 80–99.

Gardner, R. and Davidson, R. (2010). Hypothesis testing using the films of the three stooges. *Teaching Statistics*, *32*, 49–53.

Ventura, S. and Onsman, A. (2009). The use of popular movies during lectures to aid the teaching and learning of undergraduate pharmacology. *Medical Teacher*, *31*, 662–4.

References

Akram, A., O'Brien, A., O'Neill, A. and Latham, R. (2009). Crossing the line: learning psychiatry at the movies. *International Review of Psychiatry*, *21*, 267–8.

Alexander, M., Hall, M. and Pettice, Y. (1994). Cinemeducation: an innovative approach to teaching psychosocial medical care. *Family Medicine*, *26*, 430–3.

Anderson, D.D. (1992). Using feature films as tools for analysis in a psychology and law course. *Teaching of Psychology*, *19*, 155–8.

Armstrong, S.A. and Berg, R.C. (2005). Demonstrating group process using *12 Angry Men*. *The Journal for Specialists in Group Work*, *30*, 135–44.

Berk, R.A. (2009). Multimedia teaching with video clips: TV, movies, YouTube, and mtvU in the college classroom. *International Journal of Technology in Teaching and Learning*, *5*, 1–21.

Bhugra, D. (2003). Teaching psychiatry through cinema. *Psychiatric Bulletin*, *27*, 429–30.

Blumer, M.L.C. (2010). And action! Teaching and learning through film. *Journal of Feminist Family Therapy*, *22*, 225–35.

Carless, D. (2006). Differing perceptions in the feedback process. *Studies in Higher Education*, *31*, 219–33.

Cartney, P. (2010). Exploring the use of peer assessment as a vehicle for closing the gap between feedback given and feedback used. *Assessment & Evaluation in Higher Education*, *35*, 551–64.

Casper, W.J., Champoux, J.E., Watt, J.D., Bachiochi, P.D., Schleicher, D.J. and Bordeaux, C. (2003). Feature film as a resource in teaching I-O psychology. *The Industrial-Organizational Psychologist*, *41*, 83–95.

Conner, D.B. (1996). From *Monty Python* to *Total Recall*: a feature film activity for the cognitive psychology course. *Teaching of Psychology*, *23*, 33–35.

Datta, V. (2009). Madness and the movies: an undergraduate module for medical students. *International Review of Psychiatry*, *21*, 261–6.

Dave, S. and Tandon, K. (2011). Cinemeducation in psychiatry. *Advances in Psychiatric Treatment*, *17*, 301–8.

Davies, W.M. (2009). Groupwork as a form of assessment: common problems and recommended solutions. *Higher Education*, *58*, 563–84.

Edwards, J. (2010). Teaching and learning about psychoanalysis: film as a teaching tool, with reference to a particular film, *Morvern Caller. British Journal of Psychotherapy*, *26*, 80–99.

Gardner, R. and Davidson, R. (2010) Hypothesis testing using the films of the three stooges. *Teaching Statistics*, *32*, 49–53.

Gilbourne, D., Triggs, C. and Merkin, R. (2006). 'Your Breath in the Air'. 2nd International Qualitative Conference in Sport and Exercise. Unity Theatre Liverpool 16th–19th May. Performance and Reflective Symposium.

Greenberg, H.R. (2009). Caveat actor, caveat emptor: some notes on some hazards of Tinseltown teaching. *International Review of Psychiatry*, *21*, 241–4.

Hemenover, S.H., Caster, J.B. and Mizumoto, A. (1999). Combining the use of progressive writing techniques and popular movies in introductory psychology. *Teaching of Psychology*, *26*, 196–8.

Higgins, J.A. and Dermer, S. (2001). The use of film in marriage and family counselor education. *Counselor Education and Supervision*, *40*, 182–92.

Jayawickreme, E. and Forgeard, M.C. (2011). Insight or data: using non-scientific sources to teach positive psychology. *The Journal of Positive Psychology: Dedicated to Furthering Research and Promoting Good Practice*, *6*, 499–505.

Norton, L. (2007). Using assessment to promote quality learning in higher education. In A. Campbell and L. Norton (eds), *Learning, teaching and assessing in higher education. Developing reflective practice* (pp. 92–101). Exeter: Learning Matters.

Orr, S. (2010). Collaborating or fighting for the marks? Students' experiences of group work assessment in the creative arts. *Assessment and Evaluation in Higher Education*, *35*, 301–13.

Paddock, J.R., Terranova, S. and Giles, L. (2001). SASB goes hollywood: teaching personality theories through movies. *Teaching Psychology*, *28*, 117–21.

Scherer, R. F. and Baker, B. (1999). Exploring social institutions through the films of Frederick Wiseman. *Journal of Management Education*, *23*, 143–53.

Sharp, S. (2006). Deriving individual student marks from a tutor's assessment of group work. *Assessment & Evaluation in Higher Education*, *31*, 329–43.

Teater, B.A. (2011). Maximizing student learning: a case example of applying teaching and learning theory in social work education. *Social Work Education: The International Journal*, *30*, 571–85.

Ventura, S. and Onsman, A. (2009). The use of popular movies during lectures to aid the teaching and learning of undergraduate pharmacology. *Medical Teacher*, *31*, 662–4.

Wrobbel, E.D. (2003). The interactional construction of self-revelation: Creating an 'Aha' moment. In P. Glenn, C. LeBaron and J. Mandelbaum (eds), *Studies in language and social interaction* (pp. 353–62). Mahwah, NJ: LEA Publishers.

6

DRAWING

A visual method as an expressive data collection technique

Edd Pitt

Introduction

The focus of this chapter introduces the reader to drawing as a creative and engaging method of data collection that can easily transfer to the classroom. Like photography, video and film, drawing holds immense potential as a visual communication tool that can be utilised within a qualitatively participatory research and teaching framework. As a technique, drawing affords insight into lived experience and opportunity to articulate the minutiae and nuances of everyday life in a mutually supportive and constructive environment. Based on my own pedagogical research that employed drawing as a method of self-expression, students were encouraged to explore their understanding and perceptions of assessment and feedback, this chapter will unpack how drawing can empower and enable students to critically and creatively reflect on their learning experiences. Beyond pedagogic research, I will advocate the usefulness and creativity of including drawing as a means of data collection in curricula; one that students find engaging and which embeds reflective and reflexive processes so necessary in qualitative research methods.

Background to using drawing: A pedagogic exploration into assessment and feedback

Pedagogically I wanted to explore students' experiences of assessment and feedback and based on their experiences, crucially, to further understand how these experiences potentially affected future assessment-related behaviours. In particular, I wanted to gain such insight by collecting data that reflected participants' emotional experiences across their academic studies. The use of visual methods as a medium for collecting such data affords the opportunity to place participants in an alternative environment rather than one that they are necessarily used to. When asked direct questions about how they feel in different or difficult situations people can tend to find it either problematic to articulate a response, or reject or divert the question, erecting an imaginary wall that avoids their inner feelings being exposed. I was very conscious of this fact and as such, considered drawing would help in circumventing this issue. The period for carrying out the drawings was neither time constrained nor prescribed. The participant was in control of what they drew and the extent of their drawing. The important part of the activity was affording the participant thinking time in which they could gather their thoughts and reflect upon their experience before putting pen to paper.

Participant-generated drawings seemed a logical and creative method that afforded the students the opportunity to visually explore and depict their experiences of assessment and feedback. The design of my research and the tasks asked of the students will be unpacked further in the chapter but for now it is enough to say in addition to the students' drawings, they also engaged in one-to-one interviews whereby the student's drawing later acted as stimulus from which to explore and articulate their experiences.

Drawing as a research tool: A review of the literature

Conceptually, visual methods can provide opportunity for reflective moments that can be employed and be useful for teachers, researchers, participants and, in this case, students in furthering their experience of research methods. In this regard, Literat (2013) has argued that visual methods are playful, not dependent upon linguistic expertise and therefore lend themselves to working with many different population groups. Visual methods thus are 'non-textual ways of knowing' that activate the 'performative dimensions' of image making (Singhal and Rattine-Flaherty, 2006, p. 327). In a sense, the participants' accounts that were previously ignored, rejected or suppressed can be articulated through visual methods. Supporters of, for example, drawing as a research or teaching method, generally argue that it is a fun, expressive activity that has the potential to transform an investigation into an enjoyable experience for all involved. I would argue that it also becomes a learning experience for participants if one considers that many of us learn by making or doing things. As such, a creative drawing experience provided opportunity for my students to engage in pedagogical research but at the same time assimilate drawing as a method within their research-training toolkit.

Drawing, however, is not without its critics. Stiles (2004) has argued that the accepted view within academia is that images are personal and unconventional therefore rendering them inferior in comparison to the spoken word or numbers all of which make the possibility of cross comparison more difficult to achieve. Conversely, it could be argued that the very nature of data derived based upon participants' lived experiences by definition is subjective, personal and therefore more representative of real life.

More recently literature on drawing-based research seems to be increasing and can be found across the social sciences. For example, within psychology and psychotherapy, the participatory nature of photo-elicitation has been further utilised to understand an individual's interpretations of their world (Gauntlett, 2007; Reavey, 2011). Researchers who have worked with child participants are the main adopters of drawings as a visual method. Such studies have concentrated upon children's understanding of health and illness (Oakley, Bendlow, Barnes, Buchanan and Husain, 1995; Williams and Bendelow, 2000; Radley and Taylor, 2003), representation of children in their own social world (Mercier, Barron and O'Connor, 2006) and experiences of childhood (Wang and Burris, 1997; Rasmussen, 2004; Wang, 2007). Within clinical psychology, stages of intellectual development have been identified from work undertaken with young children (Marzolf and Kirchner, 1973; Prytula, Phelps and Morrissey, 1978). However, within such research the focus is upon analysing the drawings produced in order to assess an individual's personality traits and psychological well-being. My initial enthusiasm for using drawings as a research tool became somewhat dampened after reading literature relating to this. The focus of my research and the students' participation was not to analyse their drawings. Instead, it was to investigate the efficacy of drawing as an effective method that promoted a deeper level of engagement with the students and served as a mechanism to stimulate reflective conversation during the subsequent one-to-one interviews. The work of Harper (2002; 2004; 2005) and Pink (2003; 2004) suggests that visual methods may be much richer than the written or oral word alone because it encompasses the context, processes, events and people within the situation under discussion thus helping researchers to frame a social reality. It was this element of drawing which really excited me and allowed me to explore the participants' drawings alongside their lived experiences in follow-up one-to-one interviews.

Participant-generated drawings

Benefits of drawings

The majority of the studies discussed within the literature share a commonality that the researcher and not the participants themselves generate the visual artefacts. Prosser and Loxley (2008) argued that a shift towards more collaborative research would suggest that participants have agreed to become involved in the study and more importantly generated the data themselves. Such suggestions infer connotations relating to equity in terms of power and knowledge distribution exists between participant and researcher. I was very mindful of this power relationship, given that I myself was a practitioner and was asking my students to engage in the research process. Following the participant-generated drawings the students retained an element of control within the power relationship because it was they who were responsible for bringing the drawings to life through subsequent discursive interview conversation. Adopting this method ensured rigour and reliability within the data collection. Psychoanalysing the contents of the drawings was not the focus of the research and students were reminded of this during the one-to-one follow-up interviews. Throughout the interviews, researcher interpretation of the oral accounts was verified alongside the meaning the students attributed to their drawings.

The tools utilised within this research are generally referred to as non-digital mechanical tools. In principle the drawing method is very much a simplistic method requiring very little equipment or indeed skill on the part of the participants. However, visual representations afford participants the ability to depict space and time in a more unregulated fashion. That is, participants can utilise a method such as drawing to represent concepts, emotions and information, which is not always possible through writing or oral diction, which by definition are bound by temporal logic. The participant-generated images act as a graphical metaphor, which represents the often-unseen experience of the individual. However, a cautionary note is needed here and I would argue that a certain level of developed maturity is needed on the part of the participants. What I mean here is that asking people to draw can be daunting for some people and expose weaknesses that they may not want to expose to relative strangers. Further, conceptions of ability in relation to drawing may generate undesirable and maladaptive feelings or behaviour if, for example, participants have a latent dislike for drawing. Therefore, the maturity level of the participant needs to be taken into consideration if participants are being asked to step outside of their comfort zone. I was therefore very aware that some of the undergraduates might have struggled with visually depicting their experience if they perceived the actual physical act of drawing to be a barrier. Throughout it was crucial to remind the students that I was not interested in their drawing ability but instead how their drawing helped them to conceptualise and express their social reality in framing and understanding their assessment and feedback experiences.

Drawing to elicit emotional response

So far in this chapter I have outlined my experiences of using the drawing method within research, but inherent within that was the focus on investigating how students responded to drawing, its potential usefulness as a tool that would engage students and one that could have direct application on informing HE curricula and more generally, learning and teaching practice. Expressing oneself creatively can hold immense potential for participants to elicit thoughts and feelings that are often not explored. The students were asked to explore their emotional experiences of feedback at various points across the academic calendar, especially those points reported as stressful or upsetting. In particular students were asked to discuss their feelings during high-stakes assessment periods and later their thoughts when receiving feedback from their lecturers. It is important for all practitioners to understand the inherent effect feedback can have on students' engagement with their studies and ultimately their propensity to succeed. Owing to the overriding effect high stakes assessment has on a student's final degree classification, I perceived these situations as ones that could potentially be stressful to those interviewed. As such, I predicted that many students when asked to talk about this would find it hard to express such emotional responses in oral form. I therefore concluded that drawing activities could offer a more insightful way to unlock student experiences. Drawing has the power to do this and encourages students to be reflective as part of their learning journey. Bryans and Mavin's (2006) research found that doctoral students became more aware of their own thoughts, opinions and emotions following a reflective drawing experience. More importantly, the students reflected that the drawing process had better enabled them to discuss their experiences with the researcher. This has applied implications for practitioners too, especially given the recent drive within the literature to increase feedback-related dialogue between lecturers and students (Carless, 2015). Exposing students to opportunities where they can articulate their thoughts and feelings could enhance the feedback-related dialogue to a level where both lecturer and student understand each other and therefore enhance the learning experience. Concerning my own research, I utilised drawing because it afforded research participants the opportunity to remember and, articulate implicit emotional and relational aspects about assessment and feedback which might otherwise have been overlooked had more conventional research methods been used alone. Logically following this argument, it also created time and a space where students could engage with the reflective process potentially enhancing the learning experience.

Drawing in conjunction with interviews

I was conscious that drawings alone would not afford full understanding regarding the complexities of individual experience and the logical addition of interviews would facilitate deeper insight. Gauntlett (2005) contends that participant-generated images can be ambiguous; therefore conducting interviews alongside the constructed artefact allows the researcher to address this. The majority of Gauntlett's research is carried out with children who often have abstract and imaginative interpretations. This can make it difficult for researchers to draw confirmatory conclusions. Banks (2001) suggests that informal interviews allow a child to express the meaning behind their visual depiction. Similarly, Mitchell (2006) states that

> Drawings are not a substitute for children's voices and the absence or muting or fragmentation of children's talk about their images means researchers need to be particularly cautious about over-interpreting their images.
>
> (p. 69)

However, regardless of age or experience, participants need to explain their drawings in order to reduce misinterpretations by the researcher. Interviews can take the form of a reflective discussion or informal interview. In order to ensure that the students reliably represented their experiences rather than imposing my interpretation, I adopted a more reflective style of conversation or discussion whereby participants revisited specific examples depicted in their drawings and described what was happening to them at that moment in time. These follow-up one-to-one interviews revealed a rich tapestry of experience that through student elaboration demonstrated the sometimes abstract nature of participant-generated images and the representations that the drawing method revealed.

In the majority of cases, drawing alongside interviews is favoured within literature because it serves as an opener or icebreaker to interviews although this may seem like a rather simplistic interpretation of the drawing process itself. In what I would regard as a more developed understanding of the drawing process, Gauntlett (2007) argues that drawing encourages active conceptualisation and contemplation. However, Rattine-Flaherty and Singhal (2007) contend that from a psychological point of view drawing can unlock subconscious emotions. As such, adopting this method allows more time for participants to really understand and formalise their responses. This was a major consideration for my research. I really wanted the participants to have time to reflect upon their experience and to begin to formulate their own understanding of what they had experienced within their studies. Further, as interviews can be a pressurised situation for many individuals, the length of the drawing time in my study was not prescribed. This enabled participants the time and space to contemplate more insightful responses during the subsequent one-to-one interviews. In essence then, a combination of the individual's visually generated interpretation of their experience and a subsequent verbal affirmation of the experience (through a one-to-one interview) forms the basis of the generated data in this study. Such an approach would also work very well for practitioners who wish to ascertain their students' thoughts and feelings about their experiences within the classroom for example.

Pedagogical research: Drawing with students

Warming up: The need to pilot

Before commencing the research with my students, it was essential to pilot the use of drawing as a method of data collection to ensure that the students would engage with the process and, importantly, to ensure that in doing so the process was a comfortable one. Three warm-up tasks were designed to ensure students engaged with the requirements of the drawing task. Stiles (2004) argued that a minimum of two warm-up tasks are necessary for successful drawing because this allows participants to move into a cognitive process of thinking in visual terms. I was conscious that many of the participants in my study might not have drawn since primary school. Therefore, the warm-up tasks allowed the students a low-stakes way to reengage with the act of drawing. The warm-up tasks gave students an opportunity to become comfortable with drawing purely as an act of free expression.

Pilot rationale: Who, what and how

The majority of the students who I planned to interview for the main research study studied some element of sport studies during their degree. For the pilot and the first warm-up task, three students who similarly studied an aspect of sport, completed a drawing based on how they felt when their sport team won. The objective was to elicit positive feelings that were more likely to have naturally occurred. The second warm-up task asked students to draw how they felt when their team lost. The final warm-up task then asked the students to imagine how they would feel if they won the lottery.

As a concept, winning the lottery afforded the students the opportunity to express their wants and desires pictorially. To avoid the potential pressures associated with a one-to-one situation, all three students carried out the drawing task in the same room at the same time and no time restraints were imposed. In order to avoid student concerns about drawing ability, it was explained that thoughts and feelings could, for example, be expressed through emoticons or by drawing 'stick' people.

The objective of the warm-up tasks in adjusting the students' mindsets towards the visual element was highly successful and put the students at ease for the main drawing task. In the main drawing task, the students visually represented their thoughts and feelings regarding their assessment and feedback experiences in higher education. Further, they reflected and drew how they thought their studies were progressing. There were no time restraints and in practice, the main drawing task took approximately 30 minutes to complete. Following the drawing tasks, the students participated in a 10-minute one-to-one interview which explored the underlying meaning of the final drawing. This allowed me to gain insight into how the students described their drawings and allowed me opportunity to ask related questions.

Tutor reflections: From piloting to the classroom

Piloting drawing as a method of data collection allowed me to evaluate its appropriateness when working with students and, further, whether the drawings could then serve as stimulus for subsequent conversation. Importantly, I was also able to ascertain whether the warm-up tasks were successful in waylaying student concern regarding drawing or artistic ability. At the end of the one-to-one student interviews, students commented on how they felt about engaging in the drawing tasks and whether they thought their drawing had been useful in expressing themselves. The students' feedback was unanimously positive commenting that both the method and conversation had afforded them time to reflect openly and honestly on their experience of assessment and feedback in higher education.

However, while expectation did not require students to be proficient at drawing, I was concerned that the drawings might potentially be so basic that it might stifle expression and/or hamper later explorative discussion. It was clear that the students in the pilot study enjoyed the process and as expected, their drawings were diverse in content and ability. In both respects, I was very aware that the unpredictable nature of a student's final drawing might have an effect on later discursive exploration holding the potential to help, hinder or disrupt a student's ability to disclose or discuss their emotional experiences of assessment and feedback. Contingently in case of discussion lulls and prior to the one-to-one interviews, an interview schedule was constructed. As it happened in the main study, the student-generated drawings were of a standard that found this precaution unnecessary. However, as a precautionary measure it was there to ensure student ease and comfort if conversation became difficult.

Drawing with students is a method that I would recommend to those who are keen to explore it within their teaching; students tend to find it engaging and are receptive to it, but more than that, it raises our students' awareness and understanding of how creative methods such as drawing, can be used within the researcher's toolbox. However, trying a new method with students for the first time can be a somewhat daunting prospect, particularly creative methods such as drawing where what a student might produce is a great unknown. In deploying drawing in the classroom, the first consideration in achieving a receptive reaction from students is in understanding what teachable moment you want the method to enhance. The second step is identifying and articulating to students what they will gain from engaging in the drawing activity. Finally, it is essential to trial the activity with a pilot audience. I would suggest colleagues supportive in the development of innovative teaching methods may be of help here in alleviating practitioner concerns. Based on my own experience you can see from Figure 6.1 that embedding drawing as a method of data collection within curricula and through to assessment need not be a daunting prospect but one that simply needs careful thought and planning.

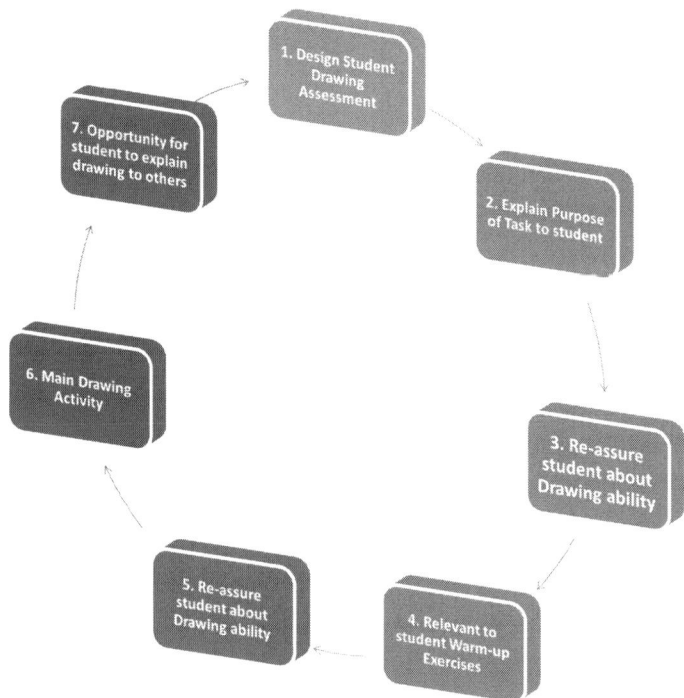

FIGURE 6.1 Implementing drawing in an assessment task.

Drawing: A pedagogic research study

As discussed previously in the pilot study, the aim of the study was to investigate how students experience assessment and feedback in higher education. In total twenty participants took part in the drawing activity. Based on the same design as the pilot study the student participants took part in three warm-up drawing tasks followed by a short one-to-one interview. The purpose of the drawing activity was to provide a creative mechanism from which students could later critically reflect thoughts and feelings associated with their assessment and feedback experiences in a one-to-one interview. All the interviews were conducted within 1 hour of the student completing their drawing. As the students retained their drawings until the interview, I had no prior sight of what they had drawn until we started talking. This precautionary measure ensured that any pre-conceived ideas or personal interpretations were avoided. Instead, this threw the focus squarely on the student voice and their reflections of assessment and feedback experiences. As with any other qualitative method, articulating to students the need for accurate representation alongside associated ethical concerns must be a priority for any practitioner who may be considering teaching drawing as a method for data collection.

Ethical approval for this pedagogical research was granted by my home university and student duty of care complied with BPS ethical criteria. Students gave full and informed consent based on the understanding that their identity would be, anonymised by means of a pseudonym; that all data would be stored confidentially; that they could withdraw from the study at any time and finally, that the data may be used for future publication. Concerned that some students might worry about their drawing ability, the students were reminded throughout the study that drawing ability was not the focus of the study but served simply as a creative mechanism to help them to reflect on their assessment and feedback experiences.

The process

Students were given two pieces of A2 flip chart paper and a selection of coloured marker pens for the drawing tasks and were informed that there were no time restraints on them and that they could take as much or as little time as they needed. The students then undertook the same drawing tasks as those outlined in the pilot study. It is particularly important to locate drawing tasks within the students' world or lived reality. The students in this study all studied an aspect of sport. Students were asked to draw how they would feel if their sport team won or lost; how they would feel if they won the lottery and finally they drew their reflections on assessment and feedback experiences in higher education and how they perceived their studies were progressing. Students were interviewed within 1 hour of completing the final task.

The student-generated drawings

The focus of this section is not to unpack the students' critical reflections of their assessment and feedback experiences but, instead, to illustrate some of the student drawings, how they engaged with drawing as an activity and, finally, to illustrate its usefulness in gathering student data. The visual quality and depth of the drawings produced varied greatly. Some students embraced the creative process and as anticipated, possessed a developed drawing ability than was evident in others. The drawing illustrated in Figure 6.2 is reflective of many different experiences and was the most expressive of those interviewed. However, despite the many different coloured pens available, the majority of the students chose only to use one pen. I had anticipated that by the final task the students would be more comfortable in expressing themselves and that this would be expressed more colourfully in their drawings.

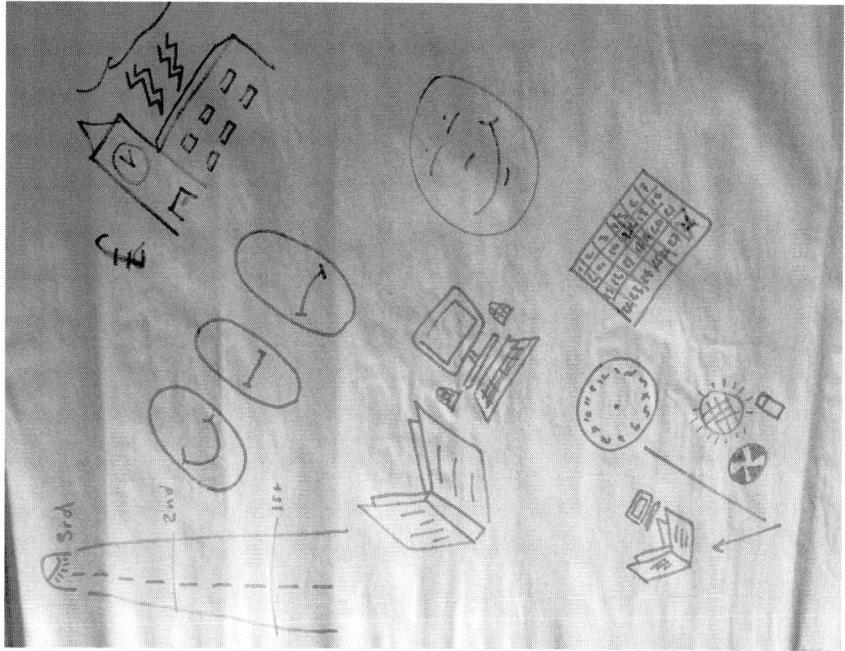

FIGURE 6.2 Student-generated drawing.

Figure 6.3 represents the drawings of a student who was unsure about their drawing ability and it is interesting to note that alongside the facial drawings supplementary words are included to indicate the different moods being drawn upon. This would seem to suggest a lack of confidence on the student's part and a way of qualifying meaning.

FIGURE 6.3 Student-generated drawing.

Finally, Figure 6.4 represents the work of a student whose drawing is more abstract in expressing experience. The use of a globe and a differentiation of each side of the page was a powerful way of describing their somewhat variable experience. Again, this was a demonstration of more confidence in drawing ability and suggested that drawing ability did often mediate the quality of the drawings produced but maybe not the quality of thoughts or expressions behind the drawings. However, as I have pointed out throughout this chapter, what is inside a participant's mind may not always come through in their drawings. As such, I would always advocate that if drawing is to be utilised, it is advisable to triangulate alongside another method, for example a follow-up interview where the content of a drawing can act as stimulus for further discussion. In the case of practitioners wishing to use drawing as part of an assessment, careful design needs to ensure that students have an opportunity or medium in which they can articulate the meanings behind their drawing. One way that this could be achieved is through an assessment that requires the student to generate a drawing relating to their experience and then to explain it in a group-based poster event. This would not only allow students to articulate their experience or interpretation of their drawing but also for students to understand their peer's experiences too.

FIGURE 6.4 Student-generated drawing.

Participant feedback relating to the drawing activity

At the end of each interview, I asked the student participants to reflect upon the drawing method and to explain what they thought about it as a way of exploring their experiences of assessment and feedback and its usefulness in stimulating later interview discussion. The students responded in a variety of ways and the following summarises their key thoughts.

The warm-up tasks were viewed positively because they introduced the participant to the activity and gave them time to practice before the main drawing activity:

> *Keith on the first two warm-up tasks* – 'It helped me in like cos I am not a very creative person in terms of drawing so it helped me, cos obviously you had the positive sides of your team winning and the negative side and everything and I could incorporate that into all the different types of assessment and which ones I preferred to the ones that I didn't, so yeah it definitely helped.'

> *Martha on the final warm-up activity and the main activity* – 'I think the one with the millionaire where you won the lottery. I think when you start thinking about that it gives you like happy thoughts. Like when it come to this one

I think your mind's a lot more flowing if you like. So you are just into that.
I think if I'd of started this first I don't think I would of got as many pictures
as I did.'

Some of the participants felt that the process gave them time to think about
what they wanted to draw and then articulate, rather than just having questions
sprung upon them:

> *Jennie on having time to reflect* – 'It was strange at first but once you got into
> it. I think it makes you think more because you've got to draw it so you've
> got to think of a picture that conveys your emotion.'

> *James on having time to reflect* – 'It would have taken a while for me to think
> of an example or whatever. Cos to have the questions sprung on you from
> like four years ago or something, but I have already had the time to think
> or evaluate all my experiences and put them all down already in the drawing.'

Some students however were not as positive about the process. One student in
particular reflected that he would have preferred the option to write down a list
of words instead of drawing, while another student felt, that her inability to draw
was a barrier:

> *Michael on preferring to write than draw* – 'I think personally because I'm no
> good at drawing, I'd of liked it if you'd have said to write down words instead
> of drawing if you'd said something like write down a list of words that you
> relate to in terms of winning, I think words I'd of found easier than drawing
> because I'm not creative but it definitely helped.'

> *Imelda on her lack of drawing ability* – 'I found it a bit weird because I can't,
> one I can't draw. When I sat down and started drawing there was feelings
> that I couldn't draw. Which kind of bugged me because I couldn't express
> everything I wanted to.'

Potential operational barriers

The use of drawing is certainly not without its critics or, indeed, resistance from
participants, which can sometimes be negative. The literature relating to visual
methods suggests that in order to fully understand participant resistance, research
should concentrate upon factors such as timings or the settings in which the drawing
tasks take place (Derry, 2002; Kearney and Hyle, 2003, 2004). Further explanations
regarding lack of engagement with the drawing process included those of both
Kearney and Hyle (2003) and Stiles (2004) who reported that perception of
drawing ability is often cited as a reason why participants may react negatively. This
was my experience with those who had not drawn for quite some time and for

others who felt their ability to draw was an issue. Similarly, it was problematic asking students to draw with whom I had had little previous social interaction. Utilising this method within one's teaching is not necessarily a major concern as long as there is a period of 'getting to know' the students beforehand. When a relationship of trust has been built up within the classroom, this results in far less resistance when requested to draw. It is obviously also good practice to overcome negative responses by offering words of encouragement regarding the focus of the drawing task. In my study, it was simply a case of reminding the students that drawing ability was not the focus of the study but that the drawing provided stimulus for conversation in the subsequent one-to-one interview. Once reassured, all the participants in my study eventually engaged in the drawing activities and, as far as one can tell, overcame their initial worries and concerns. However, these operational barriers should be carefully considered by a practitioner; in my experience students are very perceptive and generally tend to respond to requests to carry out tasks which are unfamiliar by questioning why they are being asked to do these. So understanding this and designing tasks that are overtly open and honest and of some benefit that a student will engage with, is essential. Careful planning and design can then ensure smooth running of a study or classroom activity or assessment.

The academic research world has demonstrated some resistance or reluctance to the use of drawing as a data collection tool. Bryans and Mavin (2006) report that the main reasons underlying this reluctance are, among others, subjectivity in interpretation, extreme variations in drawing ability, technical difficulties in getting published and uncertainties about the medium. My experience of this process indicates that although some participants held a perception that they were not able to draw or that their drawings were not of a suitable standard, their concerns soon evaporated when they engaged in the first drawing task. The crucial factor or potential obstacle is actually getting the students to begin the task, once this is achieved and the students are warmed up they tend to realise that it is not a scary activity that necessitates a precise drawing ability and become far more comfortable with the situation or the tasks being asked of them. While I raise some of these concerns and implications relating to the application of this method for practitioners, my experience also demonstrates that, when students are given a chance to try something new out, the practitioner has a far greater chance of successfully using the drawing method within their teaching.

Conclusion

The process of using participant-generated drawings in my research was an extremely transformative experience for me as a higher education researcher and practitioner. When designing my study I did have some initial reservations about the efficacy of drawing as a method of data collection with student participants. However, these proved to be relatively unfounded and the eventual results of the drawing activity produced excellent artefacts which generated discussion with the students regarding their assessment and feedback experience. Reflecting on the lessons I learned from using the drawings, I feel that in particular one must always ensure that participants know who the audience of their drawings will be. If possible, it is highly advantageous to have some form of developed social and working relationship with the participants beforehand particularly when those participants are our students because this makes the request to draw a much easier prospect. Furthermore, as I discovered during the pilot study and the subsequent main study, having participant relevant warm-up tasks allows the participant to be highly familiar with the process and produces more engagement with the activity. I believe these activities are the key to a successful outcome and make the experience far more comfortable for the participants. The students that took part in my study reflected that they found drawing difficult at first and affirmed that the warm-up activities helped them to settle down and come to terms with the tasks requested of them. Further, the complexity of the students' drawings developed between the warm-up and the final activity. A key consideration for researchers and practitioners wishing to use this method is to ensure that they offer reassurance throughout the whole drawing process. Participants with this kind of activity will tend to experience doubt regarding their ability to draw, to articulate their thoughts and feelings about their drawing and sometimes lack clarity regarding the underpinning subject of their drawing; such is the nature and fluidity of reflection. Finally, in bringing all these points together, the degree of planning needed to utilise this method is crucial. This is particularly relevant to practitioners planning an assessment that incorporates student-generated drawings. As practitioners, careful planning is key in ensuring that students can engage in drawing as an assessment point, that our curricula hold the potential to explore underpinning meaning and that students can successfully meet set learning outcomes.

REFLECTIVE ACTIVITIES

1   The drawing method allowed me to discuss participants' emotional experiences. In your teaching are students' emotions important and if so could this method help you to better understand your students?

2   The concerns relating to drawing ability and subsequent generated drawings were very apparent within my research; how could one overcome this in future research or teaching situations?

3   I have used the drawing method here, but this is not the only visual method available to us. Could a combination of methods such as photos, videos and drawings foster a deeper level of engagement and a richer visual description of experience?

4   Drawing alongside a follow-up one-to-one interview worked for me, but could this method be operated with groups of students who collaboratively generate a drawing and then take part in a follow-up focus group? Would this produce a richer description of the collective experience?

Suggested reading

Bryans, P. and Mavin, S. (2006). Visual images: a technique for surfacing conceptions of research and researchers. *Qualitative Research in Organizations and Management: An International Journal*, *1*(2), 113–28.

Kearney, K. S. and Hyle, A.E. (2004). Drawing out emotions: the use of participant-produced drawings in qualitative inquiry. *Qualitative Research*, *4*, 361–82.

Literat, I. (2013). A pencil for your thoughts: participatory drawing as a visual research method with children and youth. *International Journal of Qualitative Methods*, *12*, 84–98.

Stiles, D.R. (2004). Pictorial representation. In C. Cassell and G. Symon (eds), *Essential guide to qualitative methods in organizational research* (pp. 123–39). London: Sage.

References

Banks, M. (2001). *Visual methods in social research*. London: Sage.

Bryans, P. and Mavin, S. (2006). Visual images: a technique for surfacing conceptions of research and researchers. *Qualitative Research in Organizations and Management: An International Journal*, *1*(2), 113–28.

Carless, D. (2015). *Excellence in university assessment: learning from award-winning practice*. London: Routledge.

Derry, C. (2002). More than words can say? The value of drawings in qualitative research. Paper presented as part of the symposium, Using visual images in research: Methodological issues and innovations, at the annual meeting of the American Educational Research Association, New Orleans, LA.

Gauntlett, D. (2005). Using creative visual research methods to understand media audiences. *Medien Pädagogik*, *4*(1).

Gauntlett, D. (2007). *Creative explorations: new approaches to identities and audiences*. London: Routledge.

Harper, D. (2002). Talking about pictures: a case for photo elicitation. *Visual Studies*, *17*(1), 13–26.

Harper, D. (2004). Photography as social science data. In U. Flick, E. Von Kardorff and I. Steinke (eds), *A companion to qualitative research*. London: Sage.

Harper, D. (2005). What's new visually. In N.K. Denzin and Y.S. Lincoln (eds), *The SAGE handbook of qualitative research* (3rd edn). London: Sage Publications.

Kearney, K.S. and Hyle, A.E. (2003). Drawing out emotions in organizations: the use of participant-produced drawings in qualitative inquiry. Paper presented as Drawing out emotions: participant/researcher revelations, at the annual meeting of the American Educational Research Association, division: Qualitative Research Methods. 1–33.

Kearney, K.S. and Hyle, A.E. (2004) Drawing out emotions: the use of participant produced drawings in qualitative inquiry. *Qualitative Research*, *4*, 361–82.

Literat, I. (2013). A pencil for your thoughts: participatory drawing as a visual research method with children and youth. *International Journal of Qualitative Methods*, *12*, 84–98.

Marzolf, S.S. and Kirchner, J.H. (1973) Personality traits and colour choices for house-tree person drawings. *Journal of Clinical Psychology*, *29*, 240–45.

Mercier, E.M., Barron, B. and O'Connor, K.M. (2006). Images of self and others as computer users: The role of gender and experience. *Journal of Computer Assisted Learning*, *22*, 335–48.

Mitchell, L. (2006). Child-centred? thinking critically about children's drawings as a visual research method. *Visual Anthropology Review*, *22*(1), 60–73.

Oakley, A., Bendelow, G., Barnes, J., Buchanan, M. and Husain, O. (1995). Health and cancer prevention: knowledge and beliefs of children and young people. *British Medical Journal*, *310*(6986), 1029–33.

Pink, S. (2003). *Visual research, encyclopaedia of social science research methods*. London: Sage.

Pink, S. (2004). Performance, self-representation and narrative: Interviewing with video. In Seeing is believing? In C. Pole (ed.), *Approaches to visual research*. Amsterdam: Elsevier.

Prosser, J. and Loxley, A. (2008). Introducing visual methods. National Centre for Research Methods Review Paper 010. Available at www.ncrm.ac.uk

Prytula, R.E., Phelps, M.R. and Morrissey, E.F. (1978). Figure drawing size as a reflection of self-concept or self-esteem. *Journal of Clinical Psychology*, *34*(1), 207–14.

Radley, A. and Taylor, D. (2003). Remembering one's stay in hospital: A study in photography, recovery and forgetting. *Health: An Interdisciplinary Journal for the Social Study of Health, Illness and Medicine*, *7*(2), 129–59.

Rasmussen, K. (2004). Places for children, children's places. *Childhood - A Global Journal of Child Research*, *11*, 155–73.

Rattine-Flaherty, E. and Singhal, A. (2007). Method and marginalization: Revealing the feminist orientation of participatory communication research. Paper presented at the annual meeting of the NCA 93rd Annual Convention, Chicago, IL.

Reavey, P. (2011). Back to experience: psychology and the visual. In P. Reavey (ed.), *Visual methods in psychology: using and interpreting images in qualitative research* (pp. 1–13). New York, NY: Routledge.

Singhal, A. and Rattine-Flaherty, E. (2006). Pencils and photos as tools of communicative research and praxis: Analyzing Minga Peru's quest for social justice in the Amazon. *Gazette*, *68*(4), 313–0.

Stiles, D.R. (2004). Pictorial representation. In C. Cassell and G. Symon (eds), *Essential guide to qualitative methods in organizational research* (pp. 123–39). London: Sage.

Wang, C. (2007). Youth participation in photo voice as a strategy for community change. *Journal of Community Practice*, *14*(1/2), 47–161.

Wang, C. and Burris, M.A. (1997). Photovoice: concept, methodology, and use for participatory needs assessment. *Health Education and Behaviour*, *24*, 369–387.

Williams, S. and Bendelow, G.B. (2000). Recalcitrant bodies? Children, cancer and the transgression of corporeal boundaries. *Health*, *4*(1), 51–71.

7

BRICOLAGE

Visual and creative arts in the design of applied psychology assessments

Julie Taylor

Introduction

This chapter focuses on the use of visual creative arts within undergraduate teaching and assessment, drawing on a range of techniques associated with intervention design and evaluation research. As part of an applied psychology course, students were required to design a methodologically robust while creative intervention and/or evaluation targeted at a specific community population. The students produced a body of theoretically situated creative interventions including board games and theatrical interpretations. The chapter explores the challenges faced by both the students and staff. The impact of the project is discussed in the context of student participation, achievement and the development of graduate employability skills.

Background to using bricolage in teaching

Bricolage refers to the act of combining methods. In this project the bricolage metaphor was co-opted with the express intention of helping students to approach design in ways that promote thoughtful responsivity to community issues. Consequently the bricolage metaphor provided a means to bring creativity in without compromising on academic rigour. The concept of bricolage was introduced by Levi-Strauss (1966) who used it to refer to the act of using whatever is available to create new 'objects' from existing materials. This is an activity that involves the re-appropriation and combining of elements to form novel outcomes. This endeavour resonates with the identified need of practitioners. It is not about casting out the traditional; it is about modifying, combining and augmenting traditional techniques by drawing upon whatever else is available at the time that is compatible with the practice context. The re-appropriation of the traditional conforms

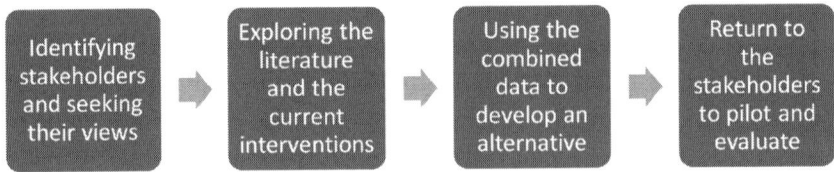

FIGURE 7.1 Examples of steps in intervention design.

to a gestalt principle; '*the whole becomes other than the sum of its parts*' (Koffka, 1935, p. 11). It is not a case of simply reframing a questionnaire to accommodate those with low literacy; it is about creating a way of answering the same questions by presenting them in a different way, a way that does not reinforce the low literacy but instead draws upon the strengths of the individual. It is undoubtedly time consuming and naturally invites service users to be the experts in their own experiences, thus centralising the participation agenda. It has genuine potential to draw upon the 'experts by experience' discourse (Skilton, 2011). Including participants in the design may not always be feasible in an undergraduate context but putting this possibility firmly on the agenda was designed to raise their awareness for future practice.

Levi-Strauss adopted the term bricolage to explain the way humans strive to make meaning; subsequent advocates have elucidated this theme and so supported its operationalisation. Kincheloe (2001) arrogated the metaphor and extended the task of bricolage to subsume a form of research triangulation, by advocating the exploration of a problem from a variety of different perspectives. In the case of intervention design, see Figure 7.1 regarding what this may include.

Bricolage as described by Kincheloe conforms to Cresswell's (2003) description of transformative triangulation. Transformative designs are associated with research questions that seek to promote social action and combat social injustice. Therefore the idea is to co-produce interventions and associated evaluations that enable and empower service users and providers. While the investment of time and the range of ethical challenges involved in designing interventions using bricolage are considerable, the resultant exchange is authentic, meaningful interventions that potentially yield robust evaluation data. Moreover, if the participants are part of the design, then researchers whose '*frames of reference*' are by definition distinct (Rogers, 1959) are more likely to start asking questions that have currency for those experiencing the issues in the world.

The pedagogical drive to incorporate the concept of bricolage in the curriculum was rooted in pragmatism as opposed to philosophy; the task was to provide appropriate foundational breadth in a way that maintained the balance between theory and method and promoted a social action agenda. Indeed, the traditional techniques while undoubtedly essential can be a poor fit with the needs of vulnerable or marginalised groups in particular. Psychometric tests for example are common tools in both research and practice settings; these often require comprehension of instructions, focused and sustained attention within a formal environment and literacy or listening comprehension skills. Thus, while meeting the needs of the many, they may if used in their original format be accused of reinforcing the marginal status of the few (Francis, *et al.*, 2005). Similarly, Nind (2009) explained that many of the techniques associated with the qualitative paradigm can make it difficult for people with learning disabilities to engage. Therefore, understanding how to apply methods to the diverse needs of community populations is a key skill for an applied practitioner and thus its role within contemporary curriculum is justified.

The project described here was an attempt to encourage students to consider the diverse needs of service users and how these needs might be met. This need has become increasingly visible with the inception of the service user involvement agenda (Public Administration Select Committee, 2008). In order to embrace a participatory agenda and eschew tokenism, practitioners at all levels need the skills and knowledge required to facilitate engagement and co-construct solutions with those who are experts by experience (Mee, 2012). A service user involvement agenda may be unsatisfactorily served by an over-reliance upon the more traditional approaches to eliciting phenomenological accounts and so a series of novel creative alternatives may be necessary (The Social Care Institute for Excellence, 2007). Bricolage seemed to be an opportunity to realise the ambition to juxtapose creative and traditional methods. The bricolage technique involves '*combining methods from the social sciences, humanities and hard sciences to derive a suitable model of inquiry*' (Yee and Bremner, 2011, p. 2). The rationale therefore for embedding flexible, responsive and creative approaches within the psychology curriculum is founded upon inclusion, service user participation, employability and ethical practice.

Identifying the conceptual and logistical fit of bricolage within the existing provision required some thought. As a foundational knowledge of a range of qualitative and quantitative methods was required in preparation, it seemed sensible to peruse the final-year modules for an appropriate place to situate the project. A module with a community psychology orientation was co-opted to serve as the vehicle. The module content, as written, was ideal because as the name implies it is about applying psychology to complex developmental settings. In having identified an extant module whose congruity with the programme was not in question, the task was to subtly reshape it so that the theoretical content was retained but an emphasis placed on equality and diversity in practice.

My main concern with regard to delivery was that the more traditional lecture-seminar model might unintentionally stifle the students' creativity because my penchants and experiences may dominate, consciously or otherwise. The lecture topics selected and the seminar paper choices may have inadvertently closed down as opposed to opened up the learning experience and so positioned too much of the power with me. A problem-based model seemed to provide an opportunity to share the power more equitably among all participants.

Problem-based learning

Notwithstanding the mixed reviews problem-based learning (PBL) approaches have received in terms of enhancing student performance (e.g., Schmidt, Rotgans and Yew, 2011), a problem-based approach seemed at the very least to provide an opportunity to open up the opportunities and directions taken by the students. PBL expects the facilitator or module lead to initially define the problem but this is then further defined and re-positioned by the student. PBL has been variously defined but three main approaches are described in the literature:

> PBL as a 'process of inquiry'; PBL as 'learning to learn', and PBL as a 'cognitive constructivist' approach, . . . all three perspectives concur on the following, that the defining characteristics of PBL are: (i) problems are used as a trigger for learning; (ii) students collaborate in small groups for part of the time; (iii) learning takes place under the guidance of a tutor; (iv) the curriculum includes a limited number of lectures; (v) learning is student-initiated, and (vi) the curriculum includes ample time for self-study.
>
> (Schmidt *et al.*, 2011; p. 792)

While the type of PBL itself was not really considered at the point of the original module design, subsequent musings and reflections have situated the goal of brico-lage within the cognitive constructivist domain. The goal was for the students' current knowledge to be supplemented and challenged, for a series of existing mental models to be activated and then reconstructed. The reconstruction needed to en-courage students to critically engage with the available theory and become cognisant of current evidence and practice. This evaluation would incorporate the students' own reflections and the reflections of their peers; it would also be contingent upon the interpretation of the evidence, the problem and the feedback (Alfieri, Brooks, Aldrich and Tenenbaum, 2011). In particular the problem needed to be constructed in a way that encouraged students to examine and reflect upon their preconceptions about the psychologist's role and their own value base. It also posed questions with respect to the situated nature of research; how for example the socio-political context may influence the design, execution and evaluation of an intervention.

It rapidly became obvious that this could not simply be a case of writing a problem and handing it over. While it was important not to restrict the direction of travel, working in a way that encouraged engagement with what were, in some respects, implicit goals was critical if students were going to be able to access the top bands of the marking scheme. Moreover, as Alfieri *et al.'s* (2011) meta-analyses demonstrated, the facilitator's role is important in terms of scaffolding and feeding back. PBL is not a detached hands-off option: Quite the reverse. The tutor needs to be in the room both literally and metaphorically following each group's progress, prompting, scaffolding and supporting positive group work practices.

Reflection on the PBL evidence base implied a number of important design principles which required attention: The task itself needed to comply with a number of good practice guidelines and the marking criteria needed to be well defined and focused. While producing clear, focused criteria was a priority, the impetus became to make the criteria a focal point in a way that meant that the student groups regarded engagement with them as fundamental to success. This hurdle was negotiated by attributing marks to engagement with the assessment process: In order to access 10 of the 100 marks available, the students needed to self-assess, peer-assess and discuss any resultant discrepancies with examiners directly. Where differences exceeded 5 marks then students needed to discuss their thinking with tutors in a formal while relaxed context. Positive engagement with this process was deemed to justify an allocation of marks because effective engagement displayed an ability to negotiate, to realistically self-appraise and equitably judge the performance of others.

The bricolage metaphor

In having established that PBL was an appropriate mode of delivery, the focus could be shifted to the content. PBL involves producing an authentic challenge that is highly relevant to practice or work within the field. In order to acknowledge the many and varied roles open to psychologists, both research and applied fields needed to be accessible from the brief (see Figure 7.2). The problem had to be written in a manner that enabled inductive reasoning in order to access deeper learning (Allen, Donham and Bernhardt, 2011). The relevance of the problem also needed to be explicit so that students could relate to the issues and access existing knowledge. Cognitive dissonance should be anticipated and welcomed because it is intended to promote discussion and further evidence searching (Festinger, 1957). If the problem is context relevant then the likelihood of retention and future application is proposed to be increased (Norman and Schmidt, 1992). The problem needed to be sufficiently complex so that the process of solution seeking requires the analysis, synthesis and creation of new knowledge. Moreover, meta-cognitive processing needs to be integral to the development of a meaningful solution (Wood, 2003).

The problem and task needed to be constructed in a way that encouraged small-group rather than individual learning. The argument is that collaboration, managing conflict and seeking effective constructive problem resolution are important cognitive, personal, social and workplace skills (Schmidt *et al.* 2011). For the work to embrace bricolage the students needed to:

1 identify and redefine the problem;
2 undertake a systematic review of the relevant theory and evidence drawing on literature from across relevant psychological fields and across disciplines where relevant;
3 critically consider the methods used to elicit evaluation data or to implement interventions, with a focus on their accessibility to the population of interest, for example, do wellbeing initiatives for children include children with a range of needs or are they focused on a normative population?

4   reflect on their own values and how these may impact on decision making and demonstrate regard for ethical and professional body guidelines relating to intervention design;

5   critically consider a range of methods to justify the design of the intervention and the subsequent tools for evaluation. This may include interviewing service users/providers, literature and evidence searching, questionnaires, deliberative inquiry, photo-voice, discourse analysis, thematic analysis of web-based forums, posing discussion questions online. The key was to gather data from a range of sources using techniques that are best suited to each source then work to make a meaningful intervention and evaluation package to reflect this process;

6   present and defend the intervention and evaluation process proposed;

7   work in a team and keep professional records of their practice;

8   self- and peer-assess in a criteria-focused and equitable manner.

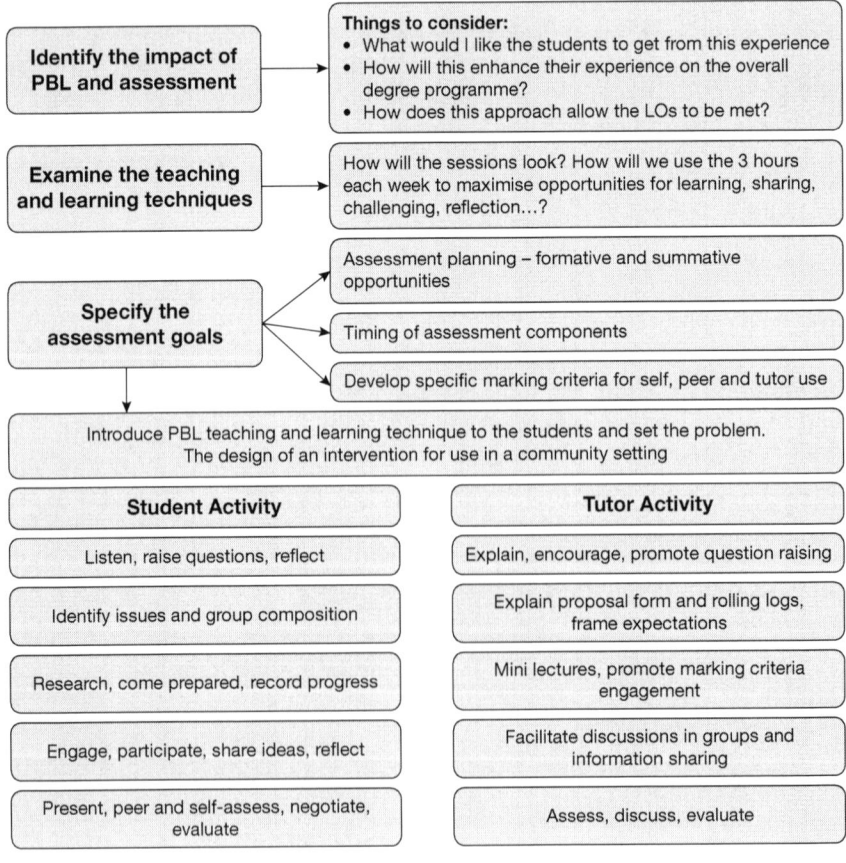

FIGURE 7.2 A flowchart of key stages in using bricolage as a creative approach to teaching and learning.

TABLE 7.1 Week-by-week summary of key student and facilitator tasks

Week/s	Student task	Facilitator task
One	Identify issues that interest you and fit the remit. Share ideas and start forming working groups.	Introduce the overarching problem and situate it within the context of equality, diversity, service user participation. Introduce PBL.
Two/Three	Research and discuss ideas for targeted interventions.	Short lectures on topical issues, e.g., cyber bullying, disability, poverty, abjection, child sexual exploitation, teenage pregnancy, sexually harmful behaviour, self-harm. Hand out the *proposal form* and explain that it is needed for Week Four.
Four	Share progress, concerns, discuss ideas and challenge each other appropriately.	Assess the proposals and encourage groups who have not yet completed them to do so, through elaboration, responding to issues and worries. Start the *rolling log* with each group, explain the role of it in the submission.
Five–Seven	Share research and implications. Gather data.	Introduce a range of intervention styles, design principles and good practice guidelines, identifying stakeholders, considering finance and feasibility, pilot runs, sampling issues.
Eight–Ten	Share ideas about intervention techniques and critically consider what these could add to the current body of work.	Examine evaluation techniques, advantages and disadvantages, practitioner needs and pragmatic concerns.
Eleven	Attend tutorial ready to ask questions and check your own progress against the marking criteria.	Work with each group to support the final phase and prepare them for presenting their work.
Twelve	Group work.	Support flexibly as required.
Thirteen	Present and assess.	Assess.

TABLE 7.2 Proposal form for permission to proceed to product design

Intervention and Evaluation Proposal Form (no more than 250 words)	
Names:	
Date:	
PROPOSAL	
Proposed title:	
Proposed area of child/adolescent psychology (e.g., sexual exploitation, bullying, mental health, substance misuse, domestic violence)	
Brief summary of the issues you wish to include in your intervention	
Brief rationale, why do we need this intervention, does the literature suggest a gap in provision?	
Who is the intervention aimed at?	
Assessment presentation style, e.g., workshop, game, web pages	
Why have you elected to use that presentation style?	
How do you intend to evaluate the success of your intervention?	
Tutor signed:	

Operational issues

The brief was revealed in stages with the broadest level of the problem introduced in Week One: 'the task is to design an intervention to tackle a contemporary problem in society that has potential to impact child and/or adolescent development and wellbeing. In addition to the intervention itself you need to consider an appropriate way to evaluate the success of your intervention.'

This broad level promoted excitement within the group; the level of autonomy, the possible problems available to explore and the implicit suggestion that they could competently intervene empowered the students. Table 7.1 provides a broad week-by-week view of the main tasks for the students and the facilitator.

The students were given a proposal form at the end of Week Two (see Table 7.2). The proposal form was designed to serve as a progress review and permission document. It was intended to guide students with respect to appropriate content but also to encourage full engagement with the task from the outset. Students could not gather data until the form was signed.

TABLE 7.3 Rolling log – action progress planning

Goal	Theory/evidence underpinning goal	Application How can the evidence be translated into practice with your population?	Who will action?	Review date

Cognitive dissonance

Week Three ended with a feedback and progress review which was the point at which some groups were starting to display cognitive dissonance. This stage was quite a challenge to negotiate with some anxiety being evident. It was interesting to see that about half the group were fully engaged, excited and focused while the other half were anxious, uncertain and reported feeling lost. To try and ameliorate this, I asked the half who were making progress to explain what they were doing, how it fits in with the literature and evidence, and how their plans were moving forward. They did this group by group and it seemed to have the desired effect, that is, making the task seem achievable and exciting again.

Another tool that was used to facilitate the smooth running of the task was a *formal rolling log* so that each week the groups could record their progress and their conceptual shifts could be plotted (see Table 7.3). The minutes in the form of the rolling log were a requirement of the submission; the act of seeking minutes seemed to reduce the potential for social loafing and any emergent in-group conflict. The log meant that group members were very clear of what was expected of them. Moreover, they had each been part of the negotiations and so had readily agreed their roles and the associated timeframe.

Identifying challenges formed the main emphasis of the later sessions, considering power, ethics and even the financial constraints that might underpin a 'one size fits all' package approach, with students self-reflecting on their own proposed solutions. The sessions ended up following a cyclical process of presentation, challenge, evidence gathering and wider group discussion, reflection and conceptual revision.

Dialogue

The practical and analytical implications generated levels of cognitive dissonance that temporarily unsteadied a large proportion of the student group. The students have, after all, spent two years being enculturated into a largely positivist paradigm, where scientist practitioners are constructed to be value free, transcending politics and treating everyone with equal regard. To oppose these fundamental assumptions naturally disrupts some core beliefs and starts conversations about power, status and social structure. Bringing social structure into the dialogue invited discussions around the relationship between structure, agency and choice. Choice escalated discussions around access, participation and social, cultural and human capital (Baron, Field and Schuller, 2000). Ability, disability, equality and inclusion rapidly provoked debate around how data are collected and so the different ways methods can be appropriated, combined and transformed took centre stage. At this point the bricolage concept was animated: how could we engage service users using photo-elicitation, video-diaries, easy read picture cued instructions, games, storyboards, life narratives, case studies, kinaesthetic activities, technology assisted activities? The list has snowballed with each iteration of the module.

The learning experience

The students were tasked with finding out about different methods that resonated with the problem they were seeking to solve and each week would present their findings to each other. Throughout the discussions the word robust was central, for example: 'Robust evidence is more likely to attract funding and ongoing support for the intervention.' It was marvellous to observe the engagement and excitement that groups were clearly experiencing when sharing their accounts of methods and how these might be used in practice and why this method may work with 'x' problem or 'y' group. The often almost tangible excitement around learning was contagious and many classes ran over time; fortunately the classes were time-tabled at the end of the day and so did not disrupt other groups.

It was interesting to note that the role of fiscal matters such as attracting funding was not at the outset recognised as particularly relevant. As the module progressed and the discussions exploded, a number of previously held beliefs and expectations, those founded on idealism, became tempered with pragmatism. It was somewhat alarming to realise how the academic and practical are often divorced. However, in times of austerity the need for employees to be creative on a budget comes increasingly to the fore. These sorts of discussions have no obvious place in other parts of the curriculum except as passing observations. The relevance of finance was drawn into sharp focus when seeking to design a sustainable community intervention. There were a number of epiphanies during the presentation of this module that demonstrated how implicit knowledge needs an opportunity to be made explicit if we expect our students to understand how politics and policy impact on the services we seek to provide.

Another practical concern for students revolved around the evidence-based nature of the work. It was critical that the intervention and its evaluation were designed to meet the stringent criteria associated with good design. The criteria against which robust research is assessed were held up as design reminders, in particular, Lincoln and Guba's (2000) evaluative criteria and the concepts associated with reliability and validity in quantitative techniques. We also drew upon Craig, *et al.'s* (2008) paper exploring the Medical Research Council's guidance for the design of complex interventions. As the weeks passed, the problem and associated challenges became increasingly complex and the difficulty of effective intervention design and evaluation progressively evident. The students were not expected to produce a publishable intervention; rather the marks were awarded for the cognitive processes that had led to the intervention and evaluation choices they had made. The evidence-based justification was the most prized element of the assignment.

Assessment principles and practices

The marking criteria were relatively straightforward presumably because of the high level of detail and planning required. The planning had already identified and defined the problem and been very specific about the reasons why bricolage had been embedded and the socio-political and methodological discourses that this had generated. The learning outcomes were few and generalist which was also helpful under the circumstances. For example, in order to produce an intervention a critical review of the literature around child and adolescent development would be pre-requisite. The requirement to produce an intervention evinces a need to engage with a range of theoretical approaches to the problem and finally an evaluation of the theory. The evaluation of the theory was simply extended to include an analysis of the practical and policy-based implications. Clearly to create criteria that stretch students and make clear statements about what is required, a grading grid is helpful (see Table 7.4). In this instance a grading grid was particularly necessary because the students needed to be able to mark themselves and others. The problem-based method meant that the criteria needed to include access and inclusivity issues, and the range and nature of the methods the students considered in their evaluation meant each group had a bespoke range of abilities and population characteristics to consider. Thinking about the intervention design and the evaluation of the intervention raised a range political and ethical challenges which again lent themselves to assessment in the context of the arguments made to justify, situate and explicate the decision-making processes. The justification and explanation of their design choice had to be rooted in a pragmatic account of the fiscal and policy implications. Implicit in the above were eight clear criteria upon which the work could be assessed. The marking grid also included a space for additional comments and grade agreement.

TABLE 7.4 Part of the marking criteria style as an example

Grade / Criteria	70+	60–69	50–59	40–49	0–39
Professional values and ethics	An excellent review of the values that underpin the work, engagement with the stakeholders or those working with the population of interest. A very thorough review of the ethical challenges.	A clearly articulated review of the values that underpin the work, engagement with the work, stakeholders or those working with the population of interest. A thorough review of the ethical challenges.	A reasonable review of the values that underpin the work, engagement with the stakeholders or those working with the population of interest. A reasonable review of the ethical challenges.	Little evidence of consideration of the professional values or the ethical challenges associated with intervention design.	No evidence that professional values or ethical challenges have been considered.
Design and evaluation justification for choices made	Outstanding and creative approach to the identified problem. The choices made have been very clearly articulated and the rationale is robust.	A positive approach to the identified problem. The choices made have been clearly articulated and the rationale is robust.	A reasonable approach to the identified problem. The choices made have mostly been articulated and the rationale is reasonably robust.	There is a weak relationship explained between the choices made and little in the way of justification.	The link between decision making and evidence is missing or poor.
Presenting the work and selecting the medium to present the findings	The medium selected was excellent for the problem identified and the audience were clearly engaged throughout. Generated lots of questions that were developmental.	The medium selected was a reasonably good one for the problem identified but the audience did appear to get lost in details at times. The questions were a mixture of trying to understand the content and thinking about the concepts in a developmental way.	The medium selected was not ideal but worked to some extent, the audience did appear lost or disengaged for a significant part of the presentation and this was reflected in the questions.	The medium selected was not appropriate for the problem identified. The audience were not guided or included and although they did generate some good questions these questions were to help them understand rather than develop their knowledge further.	The medium has not been considered and the audience were clearly confused. Questions were not raised and the audience were disengaged.
Self-assessment including discussion skills with tutor	Excellent application of the scheme, preparedness to appreciate areas for development and a consensus agreed through full and appropriate discussion using the mark scheme and criteria.	Very good application of the scheme, some preparedness to appreciate areas for development and a consensus agreed through discussion using the mark scheme and criteria.	Good application of the scheme, some preparedness to appreciate areas for development and a consensus agreed but with some hesitation on the part of the team who were a little reluctant to discuss areas for development wishing only to focus on strengths.	Poor application of the scheme, elements avoided, developmental focus is solely on justifying why the work should get a good score. Resorts to disputational talk throughout.	No attempt to link discussion with mark scheme. The mark cannot be rationalised by the team. No evidence of engagement.

Formative and summative assessment

The formative assessment was a short proposal, orally presented, outlining what the group intended to do and their current rationale. This was designed to be assessed in class against the criteria and so gaps in thinking were identified at this early stage. Moreover, it served as a valuable opportunity to engage everyone in the use of the assessment criteria.

The formative assessment was scheduled in week four and the final assessment in weeks twelve and thirteen. The PBL approach meant that feedback and scaffolding were ongoing; however, the organic nature of the process meant the final products were evolving each week and so the final presentation sessions retained a degree of mystery. The summative assessment required the students to present and evidence team meeting minutes, self- and peer-assessment forms, an intervention plan or package, and a rationale for the intervention and a means to evaluate its efficacy.

The range of responses was astounding, and some examples are shown below:

1   a board game to tackle the problems of teen pregnancy;
2   therapeutic drama activities to explore self-harm and suicidal ideation (see Figure 7.3);
3   interactive classroom IT packages to support victims of school bullying;
4   bereavement toolkits for schools to use in primary school settings;
5   an interactive board game to address homophobic attitudes in youth group settings;
6   wildlife activities for child victims of domestic abuse.

The discussions around creativity and bricolage had influenced the intervention design as well as the planned evaluation of their efficacy. The groups generally advocated multiple evidence sources, each using bespoke methods and often including visual and kinesthetic strategies, the criteria for robust evidence was clearly embedded in design as was the recognition that equality means different and not better or worse. As a result rather than take a questionnaire and write it in simple words with a few pictures or smiley faces, the students acknowledged the role of the participant as an expert in their experience. Consequently, the proposed techniques were typically based on service user involvement and the identification of ways that draw on people's strengths. The module outcomes and aims had not just been met, the module had engaged students on a variety of levels: Meta-Cognitive, political, ethical, humanitarian and reflective. Moreover, they had critically engaged at depths that had rarely been observed previously; they challenged the assumptions of theorists, the accessibility of current provision and the ontological and epistemological position of mainstream psychology.

There were many more interventions where the evaluations used included photoelicitation with service users and deliberative inquiries with all stakeholders, alongside traditional techniques such as questionnaires, interviews and psychometric tests.

SCENE 6 – THE BASSET'S   **7.7**
LIVING ROOM

PROPS.....................
COUCH
CHAIR
TELEVISON
TELEVISION REMOTE
CONTROL
DINING TABLE
FOUR DINING CHAIRS
LAPTOP
BRIEFCASE
DAD'S JACKET
CANS OF LAGER
WASTEPAPER BIN
CUSHION

CHARACTERS.........
LAURA BASSETT
JULIE BASSETT
DAVID BASSET

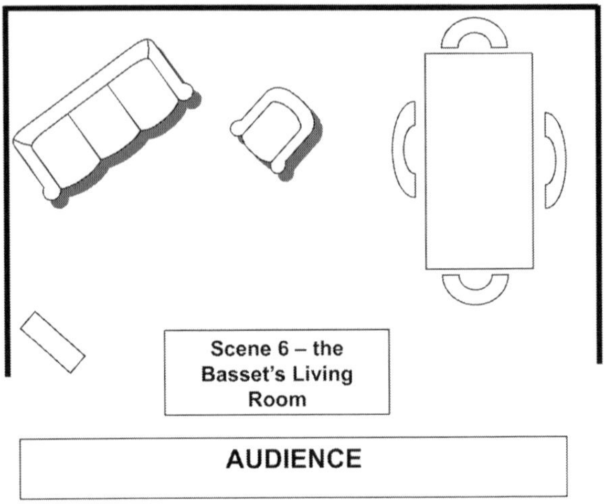

Scene 6 – the
Basset's Living
Room

AUDIENCE

FIGURE 7.3 Example page from the suicide play script and teacher pack developed for use with adolescents within a school setting.

Student evaluation

Student feedback was sought weekly but more formally at the end of the module. Formal feedback is typically gathered using module evaluation forms; I decided to do this prior to the release of any marks. These standard forms seek feedback on the teaching, learning and assessment and pursue reflection on what students would change and what they would encourage more of. In some respects the feedback was unhelpful because it was so positive that no areas for development were proposed, except that one student suggested that as a teaching technique it should be used earlier in the programme. While at the time of reading the evaluation such positivity is delightful it did make me revisit the reflections and pick up on the underlying issues and concerns and interrogate some of the experiences and practicalities more thoroughly. Moreover, it is only after iteration three that I have really appreciated the centrality of the concept of bricolage and the need to include an introductory session on bricolage and making this concept explicit to the students. One of the students, when I sought feedback to write this chapter had not realised that the process of making meaning by re-appropriating and reconstructing existing knowledge and tools was called *bricolage*, and that it could be used in research as well as design contexts. Therefore, while the reviews were positive there is clearly further work for me to do.

In terms of student feedback, unanimously they expressed their enjoyment of the module and its delivery, albeit this was juxtaposed by the students feeling some anxiety by being out of their comfort zone and what they perceived as task vagueness. For example, Rachel said, I thoroughly enjoyed the module – probably due to the relaxed and informal way in which it was delivered. However, when it came to the assignment I thought I had probably chosen the wrong module. How was I going to produce an 'intervention' when I was so much more used to spending the early hours putting together an essay to aim for a 'first'?

While students identified creatively with the task, they were acutely aware of the sensitivity required and their responsibility in acting appropriately:

> We were able to be creative with our approach so that we could help children deal with the pressures of bereavement. I found some parts of the research very upsetting as it is a very raw and a neglected topic that so many children go through.
>
> (Lizzie)

However, the students used the group work element of the project to gain greater understanding of the requirements and logistics of the work. For example, Libby said,

> I really enjoyed the opportunities for group discussion, being able to feed off each other's ideas, interests and enthusiasm. I found combining the vast amount of relevant research on our topic into a concise yet comprehensive resource for primary schools challenging. It was very daunting at first as it was nothing like I had had to do before. But once we knew what 'area' and topic we wanted to do I really enjoyed it. It was empowering, it felt good to get the experience of actually putting theory into practice so to say.

Many of the students aligned the projects with their own experiences, thus enhancing the perceived value of the work:

> Spending the summer completing a bereavement module which was independent to the degree course, coupled with trying to help two children who were recently very suddenly bereaved of both of their grandparents, I realised that there was very little available to assist adults in helping children cope with bereavement – and so the 'Bereavement Package' was born. It was a project which working collaboratively drew on all our strengths, thus producing the finished intervention.
>
> (Rachel)

The students also demonstrated meaningful engagement with the projects, and the power of the experience is highlighted through their insightful comments. For example, Trudy points out,

> It was quite bizarre but genuinely empowering, I was being charged with a professional task, to design an intervention for what some would describe as a hard to reach group. I realised they were only hard to reach because the methods we were traditionally using did not respect and value their needs and strengths ... I loved it, I cried more and worked harder on this assignment than any other but I am really proud of what I produced and it made me feel I could be a psychologist.

The external examiner identified the module as an example of good practice and stated that 'here, there was some creative and innovative work which equates to the very best in the field' (July, 2013).

Tutor reflections

Bricolage does not necessarily include visual methods but there is a strong steer for students to think of evaluation techniques that are inclusive and participant oriented. Photo-elicitation, deliberative inquiry, video diaries are all tools that can be usefully employed alongside traditional techniques to provide an effective evaluation. It was a pleasure to observe the student journey and progression through this module, the emotional responses to the lack of access, the abject status of many of our client groups and the possible impact of occupying the margins on health, wellbeing and sense of self and others (Tyler, 2013). The engagement with the political and methodological and the appreciation of so many practical and ethical dilemmas was extremely rewarding to observe. Students used words like *'inspirational, thought provoking, empowering, useful, exciting and positively challenging'* to reflect on their personal journey through the module, which was precisely the response hoped for. The sheer range of skills honed and concepts challenged in the course of this module made it a learning experience for all.

Recommendations for future iterations

The module was positively received by the students, the assessors and the external examiners. Reflection on the process of teaching and learning, hearing the student feedback, examining the student performance and comparing it across modules all suggested that the current approach is both effective and engaging. However, these positive reports and indicators are about process and module structure as opposed to content and one of the exciting aspects of working with methods is the sheer range of techniques that can be drawn upon to respond to the challenges associated with working with human beings.

Consequently there are a number of possible elements that can be introduced in future iterations. Semiology for example holds particular appeal. Semiology is a method that can be applied to visual data and involves extricating the visuals and the texts of the visual media work being explored and the process of developing a narrative around how, when combined, they convey meaning. This method while involving a vocabulary of its own may, using simple visuals and interviews, enable service user experiences to be explored in a unique but effective way. One of the biggest barriers is seeing the world through the eyes of the experiencer, and sometimes just asking questions is not enough, because the questions asked reflect the interests and perspective of the researcher rather than the service user. Audio methods may also be a valuable addition for the future, when working with the visually impaired for example. There are a host of exciting methodologies which if carefully combined with traditional techniques and assessed against the criteria for robust research may extend the undergraduate skill set and actively promote inclusive, creative ways of working.

On a more structural note, in future iterations the students will share the responsibility of creating the marking criteria. Given the centrality of the criteria to the process, helping the students understand how criteria are developed and empowering them to contribute to this process may be a worthwhile venture. Finally, I need to include an explicit session based on student feedback and experiences of bricolage, whereas my emphasis to date has been on explaining PBL.

REFLECTIVE ACTIVITIES

1   Reflect on how equality and diversity are addressed within your curriculum. Do you encourage students to consider the concept of constrained choices and the implications this may have on how we intervene?

2   Compare the range of skills, concepts and methods that are accessed within this module with one that you typically teach. How do they compare? Then reflect on your programme's aims about employability skills. Are you teaching skills and methods from a normative population perspective?

3   What is your ontological and epistemological position? Does social action resonate with your approach to psychological research? If not, is this something that you might wish to embed within your programme?

4   Reflect on the role the bricolage metaphor could play in your curriculum and consider how it might augment the student experience.

Suggested reading

Denzin, N.K. and Lincoln, Y.S. (eds). (2011). *The SAGE handbook of qualitative research*. London: Sage.

Hodge, S. (2005). Participation, discourse and power: a case study in service user involvement. *Critical Social Policy*, 25(2), 164–79.

Ritchie, J., Lewis, J., Nicholls, C.M. and Ormston, R. (eds). (2013). *Qualitative research practice: a guide for social science students and researchers*. London: Sage.

Rose, G. (2012). *Visual Methodologies: an introduction to researching with visual materials*. London: Sage.

References

Alfieri, L., Brooks, P.J., Aldrich, N.J. and Tenenbaum, H.R. (2011). Does discovery-based instruction enhance learning? *Journal of Educational Psychology*, *103*(1), 1.

Allen, D.E., Donham, R.S. and Bernhardt, S.A. (2011). Problem-based learning. *New Directions for Teaching and Learning*, *128*, 21–29.

Baron, S., Field, J. and Schuller, T. (eds). (2000). *Social capital: critical perspectives: critical perspectives*. Oxford: Oxford University Press.

Craig, P., Dieppe, P., Macintyre, S., Michie, S., Nazareth, I. and Petticrew, M. (2008). Developing and evaluating complex interventions: the new Medical Research Council guidance. *British Medical Journal (BMJ)*, *337*. DOI: 10.1136/bmj.a1655

Creswell, J.W. (2003). *Research design: qualitative, quantitative, and mixed methods approaches* (2nd edn). Thousand Oaks, CA: Sage.

Denzin, N.K. and Lincoln, Y.S. (eds). (2011). *The SAGE handbook of qualitative research*. London: Sage.

Festinger, L. (1957). *A theory of cognitive dissonance*. California: Stanford University Press.

Francis, D.J., Fletcher, J.M., Stuebing, K.K., Lyon, G.R., Shaywitz, B.A. and Shaywitz, S.E. (2005). Psychometric approaches to the identification of LD: IQ and achievement scores are not sufficient. *Journal of Learning Disabilities*, *38*(2), 98–108.

Hodge, S. (2005). Participation, discourse and power: a case study in service user involvement. *Critical Social Policy*, *25*(2), 164–79.

Kincheloe, J.L. (2001). Describing the bricolage: conceptualizing a new rigor in qualitative research. *Qualitative Inquiry*, *7*(6), 679–92.

Koffka, K. (1935). *Principles of gestalt psychology*. New York: Harcourt, Brace, and World.

Levi-Strauss, C. (1966). *The savage mind*. Chicago: University of Chicago Press.

Lincoln, Y.S. and Guba, E.G. (2000). The only generalization is: there is no generalization. *Case study method*, 27–44.

Mee, S. (2012). *Valuing people with a learning disability*. Keswick, M and K Update Ltd.

Nind, M. (2009). Conducting qualitative research with people with learning, communication and other disabilities: methodological challenges. ESRC National Centre for Research Methods Review Paper. *NCRM/012* http://eprints.ncrm.ac.uk/491/

Norman, G. R. and Schmidt, H.G. (1992). The psychological basis of problem-based learning: a review of the evidence. *Academic Medicine*, *67*(9), 557–65.

Public Administration Select Committee (PASC). (2008). www.publications.parliament.uk/pa/cm200708/cmselect/cmpubadm/998/998.pdf

Ritchie, J., Lewis, J., Nicholls, C.M. and Ormston, R. (eds). (2013). *Qualitative research practice: a guide for social science students and researchers*. London: Sage.

Rogers, C. (1959). A theory of therapy, personality and interpersonal relationships as developed in the client-centered framework. In S. Koch (ed.), *Psychology: a study of a science: formulations of the person and the social context*. New York: McGraw Hill.

Rose, G. (2012). *Visual methodologies: an introduction to the interpretation of visual material* (3rd edn). London: Sage.

Schmidt, H.G., Rotgans, J.I. and Yew, E.H. (2011). The process of problem-based learning: what works and why. *Medical Education*, *45*(8), 792–806.

The Social Care Institute for Excellence (SCIE). (2007). Practice guide: the participation of adult service users, including older people, in developing social care. www.scie.org.uk/publications/guides/guide17/files/guide17.pdf

Skilton, C.J. (2011). Involving experts by experience in assessing students' readiness to practise: the value of experiential learning in student reflection and preparation for practice. *Social Work Education*, *30*(3), 299–311.

Tyler, I. (2013). *Revolting subjects: social abjection and resistance in neoliberal Britain.* London: Zed Books.

Wood, D.F. (2003). Problem based learning. *British Medical Journal (BMJ), 326*(7384), 328–30.

Yee, J. and Bremner, C. (2011) Methodological bricolage: What does it tell us about design? In Doctoral Design Education Conference, 23–25 May 2011, Hong Kong Polytechnic, Hong Kong. Retrieved from http://nrl.northumbria.ac.uk/8822/

Case studies

Different student populations

8

STUDENTS

Examining photo-ethnography and documentary film as an unorthodox learning and teaching strategy

Joel Rookwood

Introduction

The unprecedented development of sporting cultures and industries during the last half century has helped generate an increase in focused educational provision in institutions of the Global North. This both reflects and informs sporting application, understanding, production and consumption. Academics in higher education contexts responsible for devising related social science curricula should include within their courses exploratory and critical analysis of relevant contemporary issues that matter to significant portions of populations. 'Problem-solving' educational approaches to sport and related social science curricula increasingly focus on some of the significant challenges facing communities, including perceived and indisputable threats to peace, health, poverty and development (Sugden, 2010). Sport is being employed, for instance, as a vehicle to build peace in fractured communities, to address health objectives and agendas, to help stimulate financial growth in emerging economies and to promote social development in unstable environments. However, sport can also be manipulated in socially deconstructive contexts, often with damaging consequences. Exploitative practices have emerged in sporting forms in relation to spectator disorder, drug abuse, organised crime and violations of human rights, for instance. Elements of these have been evidenced, culminating in proportionate prosecutions in courts of law; however in many cases such behaviours are thought to persist as uncovered realities, or remain as mere accusations of illegality and immorality, including allegations of bribery, financial mismanagement or political malpractice (Pielke, 2013). It is important that those studying related degree programmes are exposed to critical examinations of such problems, while exploring potential forms of response.

This chapter explores the impact of film and photography employed as visual teaching methods within the specified sport-based social science provision in a British higher education context. The work illuminates relevant reflective accounts offered by the author and a range of students at the second and third levels of an undergraduate programme, primarily during the 2014–15 academic year. From this perspective all four educational contexts included here are international in focus, namely: Continental Europe, South America, sub-Saharan Africa and Western Asia. It is necessary first to frame a detailed rationalisation of the contextual approach, as the employment and impact of visual methods make little sense without an understanding of the educational settings to which they are applied. The chapter continues with an outline of the visual methods adopted and a justification for their inclusion in such undergraduate teaching provision, and then proceeds to examine the perceived impact of these processes on student learning and assessment. This work gives voice to student reflections of their engagement and experience, and also details the educator's deliberations pertaining to the perceived effectiveness of this educational model in relation to the associated assessment expectations and student engagement and experience. The chapter concludes with some suggestions for higher education practitioners, drawing the reader's attention to specific relevant readings and reflective activities.

As the learning and teaching focus adopted here centres on various international engagements spanning four continents, it was not plausible to take the entire student body to the respective locations. Consequently, the visual methods utilised offered an alternative means of exposing the student population to the various localities and associated issues, essentially serving as connected attempts to 'bring the world' to the classroom. Each example was one in which the author personally led projects and/or conducted interviews, and collected, analysed and represented visual forms of 'data' from the respective locations, which informed the subsequent teaching approach. The context centres on three key areas of focus, namely conflict, development and peacebuilding. The first pertains to Bulgarian perspectives of the phenomenon of football hooliganism in the Balkans in November 2014. The second relates both to Brazilian perceptions of the impact of hosting a sport mega-event (the FIFA World Cup in June 2014) on an emerging economy, and to representations of a sport-based education project staged in Malawi in September 2014. The third features insights into a multi-ethnic peacebuilding sport-for-development project that I was involved in between July 2006 and September 2014.

Conflict, development and peacebuilding: Context and challenges

Football grounds have in some cases become sites of conflict and violent disorder. Increased numbers of away supporters altered the dynamics of fandom from the 1960s, and the subsequent segregation of partisan supporters in stadiums helped control elements of the emerging phenomenon of football hooliganism (Goldblatt, 2008). However, this also sharpened distinctions and enhanced hostilities between fans. Due largely to the structure of grounds and the behaviour and control of supporters, football violence produced injuries and fatalities, and caused property damage both inside and outside of stadiums. Broadcasting football disorder (including sensationalist media coverage) effectively advertised football grounds as sites to engage in violence (Redhead, 2012), with those disinclined from hooliganism often dissuaded from attending matches. This exacerbated the problem, and concentrated the demographic of support. In the UK, the last three decades have seen legislative responses and policing methods revamped, enabling stiffer penalties and banning orders to deter and penalise hooligan conduct (Hopkins, 2013). Simultaneously, elite clubs have attempted to attract new supporter types to increase revenues and alienate or enforce behavioural change among violent fans (Rookwood, 2014).

In South America and Eastern Europe however, football hooliganism has remained particularly problematic. In the Balkans for example, the disintegration of Yugoslavia and the emergence of various independent states before, during and following the Bosnian War (1992–95) was thought to have been instigated by violent incidents at a football match in Zagreb between Dinamo Zagreb and Red

FIGURE 8.1 *The Animals* football hooligan documentary.

Star Belgrade in May 1990 (Brentin, 2013). Groups of disorderly supporters connected to clubs formed paramilitary organisations responsible for rape and murder
of thousands in the protracted conflict that followed (Vrcan and Lalić, 1999). Given
the prevailing intensity of ethnic and nationalist sentiments and violence in the
Balkans and the contemporary importance of football in this region, this peninsula
offers a natural laboratory for exploring the associations between sport, conflict,
ethnicity, religion and nationalism (Sterchele, 2013). I travelled to Bulgaria in
November 2014 and made a film (Figure 8.1) on the 'Animals' hooligan group of
CSKA Sofia (a club whose hooligan supporters are allied with those of fellow Balkan
clubs Partizan Belgrade and Steaua Bucharest).

The film *The Animals* which is published on YouTube focuses on the context
of the club's support, the forms of violence evident, fan relationships with the club
and the police, and attitudes towards nationalism, immigration, homophobia,
racism, segregation and the media. The film was shown to groups of students in
January 2015.

Sports mega-events (SMEs) have experienced considerable growth in the last
few decades. This partly reflects the assumed and substantiated sporting, financial
and political benefits of hosting such competitions, facilitating growth in trade,
tourism and influence (Grix, 2012). SMEs are often critiqued relative to attendance
figures, sponsorships, broadcasting contracts and television audiences (Millward,
2011); the perceived legacy and sustainability of infrastructural investments and
the long-term use of facilities (re)constructed for SMEs (Coates and Depken, 2011);
and the socio-economic impact on the host community (Briedenhann, 2011).
The 2014 World Cup in Brazil was subject to mass protest, with over a million
Brazilians mobilised in objection to World Cup organisers FIFA and the Brazilian
government. Protestors cited alleged corruption, violence, civil rights violations,
and the prioritised expenditure of public finance on the World Cup over demanded
developments in health, education, housing and infrastructure (Holston, 2014).

I travelled to four Brazilian cities during the World Cup and made a film showcasing a snapshot of life in Rio. The film, *Rio: Football and Favelas,* was published
on Vimeo. The film (Figure 8.2) centres on Rocinha, Brazil's largest favela, and
explores many central themes of the protests. The documentary was used in teaching
sessions from September 2014 to January 2015.

Football emerged as a codified sport in Britain in the nineteenth century during
a period of behavioural reform. The characteristics, behaviours, beliefs and
'morality' of players were emphasised in conjunction with their physical health,
as a manifestation of 'Muscular Christianity' (Rookwood, 2012). Football spread
through institutions, trade and colonisation, and was variously received. Internationally, such receptions included assimilation, imitation, adaption and resistance
(Haxall, 2015). Although football's diffusion came to represent opportunities
for protest against imperialism, the perceived developmental and 'pacifist potential' (Stidder and Sugden, 2003, p. 135) of football is still evident through some
contemporary sport-for-development initiatives. Non-governmental organisations (NGOs), sports agencies and educational institutions have employed sport as

FIGURE 8.2 *Rio: Football and Favelas* documentary.

a means by which processes might be initiated, messages communicated, relation-ships improved, development facilitated and peace promoted. Given the focus on higher education in this book, the remaining contexts stem from related university commitments.

Liverpool Hope University for example, has been involved in international educational development since 1982, underpinned by social justice, partnership and learning (Kenyon and Rookwood, 2009). Under its current branding, 'Global Hope' has delivered sport-based initiatives, including the sport, physical activity and education project staged in Malawi in September 2014. Malawian public health and economic activity have proven persistent causes for concern (Wachira and Ruger, 2011), and the IMF ranked Malawi's 2014 GDP one hundred and fifty fourth of 187 countries graded. The Global Hope project was based at an SOS Children's Village in Lilongwe, where staff and students ran educational workshops and sport coaching clinics for teachers and pupils at the school attached to the orphanage (Figure 8.3). Lessons in English, physical education, maths and geography all adopted 'physical components' as attempts to make transnational connections across linguistic, educational, socio-political and sporting divides. I led the project and produced a documentary showcasing the approach, challenges and impact of this sport-for-development initiative. A version was formed for educational purposes, which was shown to groups of students between October 2014 and January 2015.

FIGURE 8.3 The Malawi sport and physical education project.

The final context of peacebuilding is represented here through the Football for Peace (F4P) project that has been staged annually in Israel since 2001, predominantly led by the University of Brighton. F4P is a collaboratively designed, inter-ethnic youth programme which aims to facilitate peaceful integration within splintered Jewish and Arab communities (Sugden, 2010). This fractious relationship is deeply rooted in history, with complex and widespread contemporary manifestations, notably: Protracted armed conflicts, territorial disputes, human rights violations and claims for political recognition and representation (Rookwood and Wassong, 2010). F4P coaches partake in comprehensive training programmes before travelling to various locations in Israel to lead the youth football project, supported by local personnel, who provide practical and linguistic support. The project is underpinned by values, as demonstrated in Table 8.1 below. These are introduced through 'teachable moments' (Lambert, 2007, p. 20). Each project culminates in a tournament festival day, where teams of mixed identities compete. Players are encouraged to co-operate to achieve common objectives on the field, lessons which it is hoped might be adopted in life (Rookwood, 2012). As one of the F4P coaches, I took various photographs representing different versions of the project, which were employed as visual teaching methods in educational contexts between January 2007 and January 2015.

TABLE 8.1 The F4P values (adopted from the F4P training manual)

Value	Application
Neutrality	4P is a politics-free zone. Those who participate in F4P – players, coaches, parents, administrators – leave their political views and ideological positions outside. This does not mean changing political and ideological standpoints, but such positions are not expressed in and around the F4P experience.
Equity and inclusion	The appreciation of one's own individuality and the value of others in a context of social diversity. Respect for: Oneself, team mates, opponents, coaches, parents, the laws of the game and those that administer them are essential features of F4P.
Respect	The appreciation of one's own individuality and the value of others in a context of social diversity. Respect, for oneself, respect for team mates and opponents, respect for coaches and parents, and respect for the laws of the game and those that administer them are essential features of F4P.
Trust	Players that trust one another play well together. Learning to have faith in the capacities of others to carry out their roles and responsibilities dutifully and mutually, in ways that also contribute to the well-being of team mates, is an essential ingredient of good sportsmanship.
Responsibility	With trust comes responsibility: Understanding that individual behaviour in practice sessions and in games influences and impacts upon the performance and experience of others. Working with and for others are key aspects of F4P projects. Success in sport, particularly team sport, relies upon mutual aid and self-sacrifice.

FIGURE 8.4 Working together 4P

Film and photography as visual methods

Developments in social, journalistic and educational representations of events, processes and experiences have often featured alterations in the ratio between employed textual and visual components, especially in newer forms of social media. Such accounts help shape the way people communicate and understand the social world. Images and videos can be recognised as important mediums in such contexts, to emphasise an argument, encourage an interpretation or even sensationalise a message. However, higher education teachers and particularly scholarly researchers have often been comparatively reluctant to adopt such visual methods. In many disciplines these processes remain marginal and unorthodox. As with popular, ethnographic and journalistic equivalents, the 'visual educator' often encourages students to engage with a photograph or video differently. There is a common suggestion or supposition that pictures can tell a story or impart richness beyond mere words, potentially stimulating (mis)interpretation (Furman, Szto and Langer, 2008). Alternatively, perhaps a given image carries no inherent meaning, but serves as an object to be deployed in different means: 'Images are used in very diverse ways. They are created, shared, pirated, broadcast, narrowcast, copied, mashed and otherwise circulated; they work to record things, to represent things, to argue and to create affect' (Rose, 2014, p. 38).

This chapter is a reflection on the use of images (photography/photo-ethnography) and film (documentary) in higher education. Photo-ethnography was used in this educational context because it was considered to be an effective means of encouraging a student body to address, interpret and respond to some of the complex theoretical, experiential and contextual realities experienced in and presented across different locations from the field. This approach was deemed appropriate because technological advancements, notably the widespread educational application of programmes such as Microsoft PowerPoint and Prezi, have provided an established platform for visual components in lectures and classes for certain disciplines. Images were selected from the author's photographic catalogue as it was felt that they could offer insight into peacebuilding through interpreted experiences of the F4P project over several years. Students were exposed to these specific images to encourage them to consider the socio-political context, approach, challenges and limitations of the initiative.

Reflecting the nature, complexity and demands of the medium, video technology has perhaps proven less influential than photography in many educational contexts. However, technological advancements have enabled video websites like Vimeo and particularly YouTube to become part of the mainstream media landscape. Despite the interjection of corporate involvement, YouTube still orientates many of its services towards community-generated, consumer co-creation and content sharing (Rose, 2014). It serves as a high-volume website, media archive, broadcast platform and social network (Potts *et al.*, 2008). It is a representation of participatory culture and public imagination, with a diverse range of producers and consumers, who have grown accustomed to creating, disseminating and sharing videographic messages (Burgess and Green, 2009). Video analysis has become an established educational and applied tool across various disciplines beyond those directly related to media and communications, such as sports performance, forensic psychology and occupational therapy. Although the medium remains marginal in some disciplines, the use of video footage, including factual programming, dramatisation and documentary, now feature in some aspect of most subjects taught in higher education.

In recent years advancements in mainstream technologies and software have increased the accessibility and usability of the medium for creators and consumers. Indeed, while all the images employed in the educational provision under scrutiny were photographed on various mid-range digital cameras, the equivalent video footage was captured on an Apple iPhone 5s and edited using iMovie. The 'conflict' football hooliganism documentary (Bulgaria – 34 minutes), together with 'development' SME (Brazil – 12 minutes) and sport project (Malawi – 51 minutes) versions all adopted Doyle's approach, who fittingly suggested this sequence in reference to the F4P programme in Israel about which he made a series of documentaries: 'Researchable footage can be edited, combined sequentially into a narrative and merged observational-style with interpretive reflexivity' (2007, p. 157). Each film made for the current educational project was unscripted but semi-structured, with footage captured reflecting the theoretical, contextual and thematic constructs relevant to the respective subjects explored in the previous section. All films were published on YouTube or Vimeo to enable open access to the films, particularly for the student population.

The impact of visual methods on student learning and assessment

The objectives of modern university courses can reveal tension between principles and pragmatism. The advancing focus on employability has swung the pendulum towards the latter in many cases, inspiring reassessments of these objectives. Boud, Cohen, and Sampson (1999, p. 415) refer to a 'new emphasis on generic learning outcomes' in this context, which remains evident today, focusing on broad skills, key competencies, communication beyond specialisation and transferable skills; fostering peer-assisted, self-directed and lifelong learning through reflective practice and critical self-awareness. In 2011, Liverpool Hope University introduced an integrated curriculum for all levels of undergraduate study. In theory, this transfer from a modular system allows for a greater degree of change (configurationally) under a broad framework, without course revalidation. Consequently, the emphasis on necessarily generic learning outcomes in this context remains firmly intact.

There are a number of aims and learning objectives for the university's sport and physical education course at second and third year (with greater emphasis on critique in the latter). Collectively, these include references to:

*   applying critical research and analytical skills;
*   evaluating and applying knowledge and understanding of the multi-disciplinary aspects of sport in appropriate contexts;

- critical evaluation of how sport-related policies shape individual and collective engagement across population groups;
- developing a broad appreciation of theoretical and applied sport-related issues from a critical knowledge base;
- critical evaluation of the development and enhancement of sports participation and performance through a multidisciplinary approach;
- developing communication skills that enable the delivery of information to a variety of audiences using different media;
- and finally, critical exploration and positioning of sport in the context of relevant communities and professions.

The learning outcomes for individual sessions reflect a contextualised focus on a number of these overlapping objectives.

In light of these learning outcomes, photo-ethnography and documentary were employed in contexts already explored within the course, but in different ways. *The Animals* football hooliganism documentary facilitated examinations of conflict and its relationship with mitigation, social identity, politics and discrimination. The short film *Rio: Football and Favelas* produced at the World Cup in Brazil allowed for connections to be examined between hosting and experiencing SMEs and development, protests, economics and politics. The documentary *Malawi – The Warm Heart of Africa* supported analysis of the approach, context, challenges and impact of sport-for-development projects. The photographs of the F4P project in Israel encouraged critique of the socio-political context, value-based approach, limitations and possibilities associated with using sport as a tool for peacebuilding in fractured communities.

In the case of the three documentaries, the students were introduced to some relevant theories, frameworks, literature, approaches and challenges before watching the films. After the respective viewings, the students partook in conversational critical reflection, exploring issues such as sporting engagement and participation across population groups. For instance, in relation to the Malawi project, students made reference to the local environment, equipment, language and culture in comparison with western countries. Unorthodox forms of sporting participation proved another focus of student reflection. For example, the film about football disorder stimulated one very interesting debate about whether hooliganism can be conceived of as a sport in itself, which led to explorations of the essence and meaning of sport, and the prevalence of and response to sporting violence in other cultures. The students also examined the role of communities and the impact of sports policies regarding SMEs in Brazil. Many of them then offered comparisons to their own experiences and perspectives of London's 2012 Olympic Games in this respect.

In relation to peacebuilding, some photographs used were embedded in the PowerPoint presentations to introduce key thematic issues. Students were then assigned to small groups with each given various enlarged prints of pictures. Here participants were tasked with forming comparisons with other disciplines of sport

FIGURE 8.5 The F4P project.

(such as history, politics, development, psychology) to analyse and interpret the photographs in relation to sports participation, performance and communities, for instance. Students then took turns to lead discussions of the meanings gauged from the images. Figure 8.5 is an example.

Each component formed part of the teaching provision, subsequently featuring in particular student assessments. For instance, some students were tasked with giving group presentations or student-led sessions on SMEs and sport-for-development, following taught sessions which included applied visual methods. Furthermore, the F4P project has regularly featured in the assessment of undergraduate students in essays, examinations and presentations. In this respect students have been asked to reflect on visual and textual teaching and research methods to explore war and peace in the Middle East, complications of cross-ethnic integration, modes of developing and embedding values in sport, and the challenges of employing sport as a means of contributing to attitude and behavioural change in post-colonial and splintered communities.

Student reflections

To allow for in-depth reflection, all students in classes subject to these visual methods were tasked with writing and submitting a reflection after the taught session, and where applicable after the related assessment. They were encouraged to reflect on

CASE STUDY – USING DOCUMENTARIES

First, it is important to review the learning outcomes for the session or module. When producing a documentary, it might be useful to select a relevant context that is difficult to teach without visual components, and where a video might make a contribution in terms of enhancing student understanding. The next stage involves researching locations and personnel and if relevant, devising interview questions. Such processes are often simplified if the film is based on an existing project. The videographer then travels to the location and captures the footage. It is useful to download the footage at various intervals onto whatever computer system will be used to produce the film, and inspect it on a larger screen. Depending on the nature of the documentary, a camcorder is recommended to capture footage. This is not essential, however, as technological advancements are facilitating alternatives, rendering the process of amateur filmmaking increasingly accessible. When using the film in a teaching session, it may be useful to introduce students to some relevant theories, literature, themes and challenges beforehand. After the students watch the film, they should be encouraged to critique the film, through informal conversations and then structured analysis. They might explore relevant issues and consider comparisons to other contexts, for instance. It is useful for students to write and anonymously submit a reflection after the taught session, and where applicable after the related assessment. This feedback can be used to analyse the pedagogic approach, and determine whether or how to improve such practice in the future (see Figure 8.6).

issues including what they had learned, enjoyed or disliked about the session and the method employed. Students were asked to type up their anonymous response (under the headings of 'session type', 'class title' and 'visual method'), with a student volunteer from each class collecting and submitting these to the lecturer within a week of the respective session. A thematic analysis was then undertaken in relation to the dominant themes of process, engagement, context, learning and assessment.

In terms of the use of these visual processes, student reflections were mixed. One student argued:

> Using just text can be seen as boring and less effective than videos and when discussing various different cultures, activities and experiences through the use of media it can become more engaging for the learner.

Another student claimed:

> When a lecturer throws a random video on from YouTube, I'm usually a bit cynical. Unless it's really relevant or interesting at least, you can think of

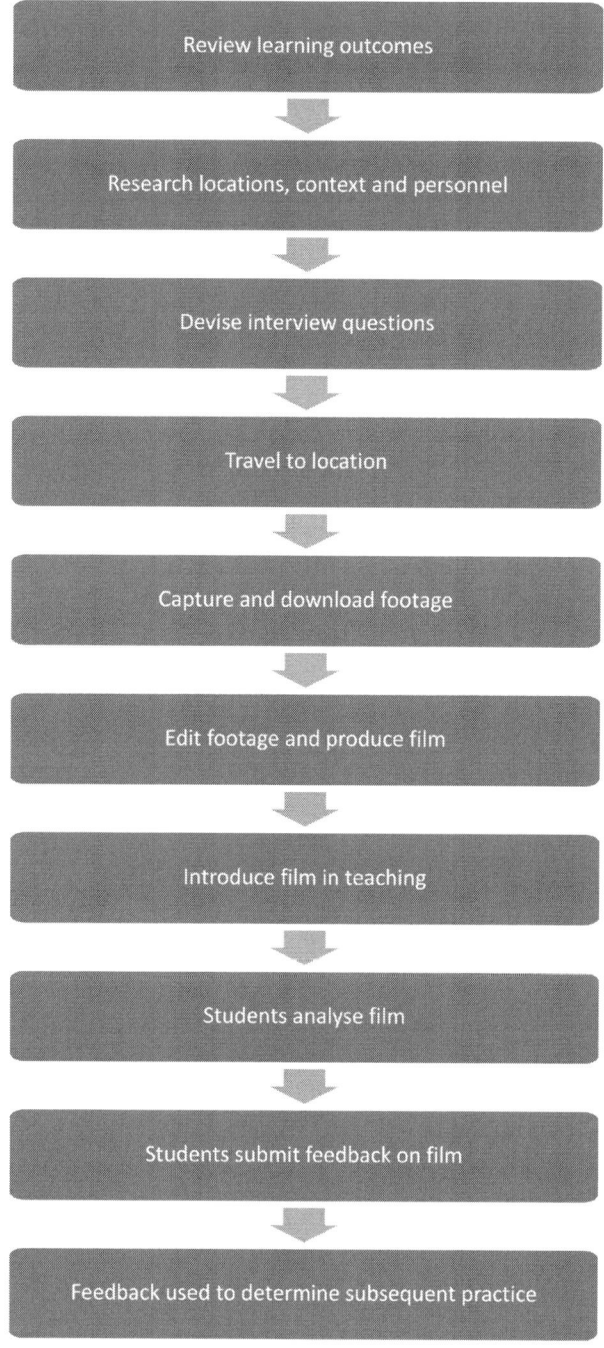

FIGURE 8.6 A flow chart of the process of using a documentary as a visual teaching method.

it as a bit of a time-filler for them. It's a bit lazy. But if the lecturer has actually made them you appreciate the effort.

Meanwhile as the respondent below suggested, such visual methods can impact on student engagement:

> Some subjects are just so theoretical it's hard to see the point in them. If you switch off you're lost. And some of the political issues we look at are from places you've never been and can't visualise. But the videos bring the places to life, which helps us see the problems and talk about possible solutions. I guess the films shape your imagination.

Additionally, various students made reference to how the films have influenced their contextual understanding. For example:

> We all know that hooliganism used to be rife in England, and how it's changed with the policing and laws and new grounds, but although you hear reports of trouble in Eastern Europe, you don't really know what it's like. Joel's film on Bulgaria showed the attitudes towards homophobia and racism and violence. The film helps you see what the police have to deal with and how policies should be shaped. It helped me understand how hard it is to combat hooliganism.

In a developmental context, another respondent claimed: 'None of us in the class had been to Africa, so the Malawi film gave us an idea of what life is like and what sport means to the people.' Furthermore, another participant argued: 'The film helped me structure the presentation we had to do.'

Other students also focused their reflections on experiences of related assessments. In relation to the Brazil SME film for instance, one respondent wrote:

> We managed to gain a local perspective towards the city hosting the mega-event. This is a very useful and dynamic way of teaching. I have now started to include brief clips during my [assessed] student-led sessions. This teaching style has inspired my interest in short films.

Other participants suggested they had learned from engaging in these visual processes:

> I remember in my exam last year we were asked about sport and peace-building in the Middle East, and the picture of the Arab and Jewish lads came to mind, doing the problem solving activities. It helped me write about values and conflict and peace. Pictures speak a thousand words, but an image can stay with you too.

Therefore, many students clearly considered such visual components of taught sessions useful. The videos and pictures shown in lectures were found to have inspired student interest in their subject, facilitated their engagement, helped them visualise contextual nuances, and promoted their understanding of different perspectives. Some students also suggested that visual teaching methods inspired more creative and effective approaches to assessment. However, such methods were only valued subject to certain conditions. Videos in particular have to be perceived as dynamic and specifically relevant supplements of lectures in order to be considered valuable.

A teacher's reflections

My reflections are structured relative to Gibbs' (1988) six-stage reflective model (Figure 8.7). 'Descriptions' of practice have been well documented in this chapter, and the embedded focus therefore centres more on feelings, evaluation, analysis,

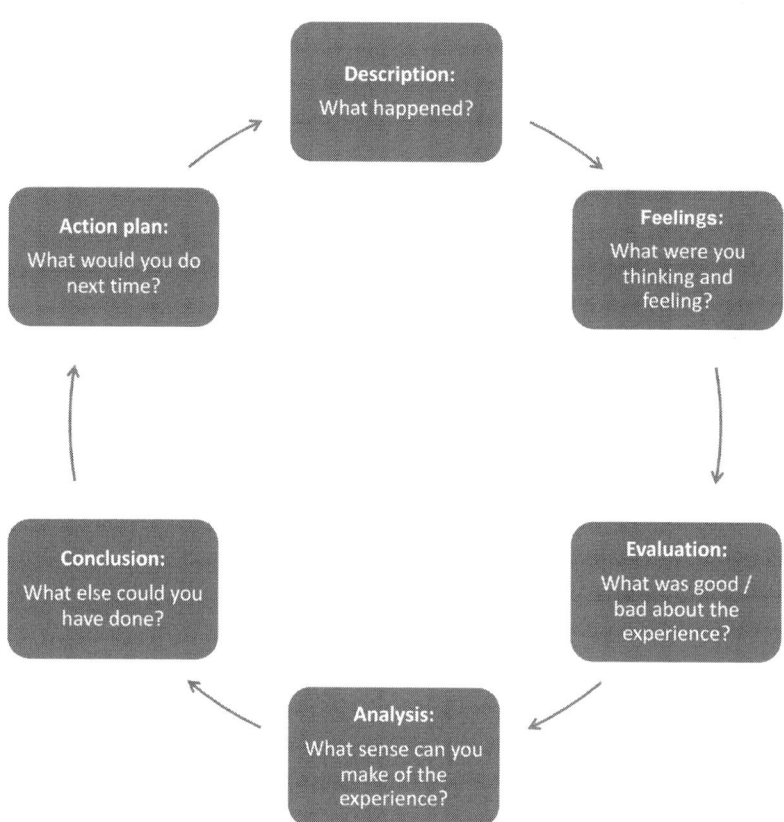

FIGURE 8.7 Gibbs' (1988) six-stage reflective model.

conclusion and action. After having taught theoretical and applied approaches to sport-based peacebuilding without visual methods, the subsequent inclusion of related images seemed to have an additional impact. The student engagement and depth of focus in assessed presentations and examinations increased as a consequence. However, introducing photographic analysis did not prove immediately successful, as the students did not respond immediately to the tasks. The levels of improvement in student interaction, engagement and attainment seemed proportionate to my degree of familiarity with the process. Important lessons have been learned about reflection, persistence and modification.

Forms of new media have become saturated with both images and videos, aiding their respective transferability and acceptance in educational contexts. My approach was as a beneficiary of this development. The type of film and process of analysis the students were exposed to here, however, was perhaps less familiar. For 'non-visual disciplines' such as sport (as opposed to media for instance), documentary analysis often proves an unorthodox, marginal educational vehicle, relative to more established techniques. The resultant novelty can be used to the lecturer's advantage. Through this process I have learned to use only selected videos and to employ the method intermittently, to prevent students becoming immune to their impact. The unfamiliarity of the process can help make the associated lessons more memorable and effective.

On reflection, it is clearly important to select appropriate films for classroom activities, particularly if assessment is linked to related exercises. Publishing films before using them in class offers a potential gauge of their effectiveness. For example, the Balkan football hooligan documentary had 16,000 views by the time the video was shown in class. However, if some students consider the 'random' insertion of YouTube videos in lectures to be potentially 'lazy', it is important that educators counter this damaging perception by avoiding this practice. I have learned the importance of explaining the rationale for the use of such unorthodox methods. Also, using documentaries I had created meant I had intricate knowledge of them, and could offer detail about what underpinned them. This contributed to their reception. However, as with referencing a scholar's written publications, I am now more mindful about the implications of using the visual artistry of another in this regard.

My employment of photo-ethnographic techniques is more established than my use of documentaries. Although I have been making films for a decade, I have only started using them in class relatively recently. Given the aforementioned shortcomings of this research, I now recognise the importance of analysing and reflecting on their impact longitudinally and laterally, notably regarding the curriculum, learning outcomes and student assessment. This will become the next step on my reflective journey, incorporating focus groups and interviews. Pending the outcome of the succeeding analysis, I may make more films focusing on different curricula constructs such as coaching practice and sports management, in conjunction with alternative versions on subsequent developmental, peacebuilding and SME contexts.

Conclusion: Using visual imagery in higher education

Conflict, development and peacebuilding are difficult subjects to teach. The decision to make research-informed documentaries, capturing footage and images from the field, was a reflection of a decade of writing and lecturing on complicated international sporting issues in the UK alongside the development and investigation of numerous international projects. For readers responsible for the delivery of sociological and sporting degree programmes in higher education institutions, the thematic disciplinary focus of this chapter might prove familiar, even if the contexts do not. However, for those involved in teaching other disciplines or levels, there are various applicable and transferable lessons pertaining to process, application and reflection.

Teaching higher education students about complex transnational issues requires creative pedagogical approaches. Theoretical and philosophical underpinnings of constructs might call for traditional textual procedures, but using (and if possible creating) visual forms can prove useful supplements for contextual and concentrated investigations. Curricula should be designed with investigative activities and assessment tasks aligned with learning outcomes, to facilitate depth of scholarship while maximising academic performance. Finding imaginative ways of combining textual and visual educational forms may become as beneficial and as inevitable as the recent blending of online and face-to-face approaches, reflecting changes in how people learn. Contemporary educational practices should maximise the resources available to the teacher and enhance the depth, rate and efficiency of student learning.

Regardless of the teaching or investigative techniques adopted, one should acknowledge their bias and limitations. Visual approaches should involve consideration of ethical and logistical considerations including piracy and selectivity. The former is of central significance to visual methods, but was not covered in this chapter because the film and documentary content was created by the author. In many cases, neither photographer nor filmmaker can capture 'the whole scene' and the resultant selectivity infers an inevitable bias. Ironically, in the case of the F4P project, this may fracture assertions of neutrality, on which the programme is partly based. Nevertheless, visual techniques can evoke a more nuanced understanding of how social actors experience their lived reality, revealing that which might otherwise remain hidden or taken for granted. Visual methods can also help mitigate some of the limitations set by the linearity of verbal narrative (Mannay, 2013). Language, like culture, is not static, but changes relative to contemporary conditions, events and experiences. Similarly, however, the meanings attached to visual materials can prove provisional, unstable and fluid. Educational analysis of visual artefacts and media therefore should focus not simply on relative meanings, but also on their origins, uses and appropriations (Rose, 2014).

Reflective activities

The process of considering each of the four teaching scenarios suggested here should begin with a review of the learning objectives for the respective course. After determining the relevant learning outcomes and the remit or context of the session, the following hypothetical activities should then be considered. These essentially involve interpreting images, taking photographs, analysing documentaries and producing films.

1   Photo elicitation: The teacher presents the students with a series of 'relevant' printed images. The students then caption and attribute meaning and value to the pictures, and each person takes turns to facilitate a discussion of how the images might be interpreted. Consideration should be given to content, composition, focus, connection and context. If the images are well known, attention could focus on their respective origins and appropriations (Rose, 2014).

2   Photographic autodriving: Students are either loaned a digital camera, use their own or use the camera on their mobile telephone, and pictographically document their activities for a given time period when undertaking tasks relevant to their course. If the students are on a placement, field trip or international project, for example, they could capture and visually represent their experience, remaining conscious of the approach and rationale of each image. Students then offer visual displays of their pictures, as a poster, photographic exhibition or PowerPoint presentation. The lecturer could even suggest the students follow the PechaKucha 20X20 format, where twenty images are shown for 20 seconds each, the images advancing automatically as the presenter talks along to the images (Levin and Peterson, 2013).

3   Documentary analysis: After selecting relevant films of appropriate duration (to be determined by the educator, depending on the length and type of session), the students should be led in a structured examination or critique of the film. This might focus on semiotic analysis (signs and relations), philosophical underpinnings, ideological assumptions, political motivations, or contextual intricacies. Berger's (2014) work on media analysis techniques offers a useful framework in this regard.

4   Film production: Students are responsible for writing, directing, producing, editing and presenting a documentary themselves. Students should be trained in the process in relation to preparation, location, focus, production and editing. Clevé's (2014) text on the management of film production offers some useful insights and advice. The students should then present their films and produce a reflective account of the experience, documenting the process and rationalising their approach.

Suggested reading

Burgess, J. and Green, J. (2009). *YouTube: online video and participatory culture*. Cambridge: Polity Press.

Doyle, J. (2007). The neutral lens: constructing a visual critique of football for peace. In J. Sugden and J. Wallis (eds), *Football for peace? the challenges of using sport for co-existence in Israel* (pp. 155–71). Oxford: Meyer and Meyer.

Rookwood, J. and Palmer, C. (2009). A photo-ethnography: a picture-story-board of experiences at an NGO football project in Liberia. *Journal of Qualitative Research in Sports Studies, 3*(1), 161–210.

Rose, G. (2014). On the relation between 'visual research methods' and contemporary visual culture. *The Sociological Review, 62*(1), 24–46.

Shell, L. (2014). Photo-elicitation with autodriving in research with individuals with mild to moderate Alzheimer's disease: advantages and challenges. *International Journal of Qualitative Methods, 13*, 170–84.

References

Berger, A. (2014). *Media analysis techniques*. London: Sage.

Boud, D., Cohen, R. and Sampson, J. (1999). Peer learning and assessment. *Assessment and Evaluation in Higher Education, 24*(4), 413–26.

Brentin, D. (2013). A lofty battle for the nation: the social roles of sport in Tudjman's Croatia. *Sport in Society, 16*(8), 993–1008.

Briedenhann, J. (2011). Economic and tourism expectations of the 2010 FIFA World Cup – a resident perspective. *Journal of Sport and Tourism, 16*(1), 5–32.

Burgess, J. and Green, J. (2009). *YouTube: online video and participatory culture*. Cambridge: Polity Press.

Coates, D. and Depken. C.A. (2011). Mega-events: is Baylor football to Waco what the Super Bowl is to Houston? *Journal of Sports Economics, 12*(6), 599–620.

Clevé, B. (2014). *Film production management*. Abingdon, Oxon: Focal Press.

Doyle, J. (2007). The neutral lens: constructing a visual critique of football for peace. In J. Sugden and J. Wallis (eds), *Football for peace? the challenges of using sport for co-existence in Israel* (pp. 155–71). Oxford: Meyer and Meyer.

Furman, R., Szto, P. and Langer, C. (2008). Using poetry and photography as qualitative data: a study of a psychiatric hospital in China. *Journal of Poetry Therapy, 21*(1), 23–37.

Gibbs, G. (1988). *Learning by doing: a guide to teaching and learning methods*. Oxford: Oxford Polytechnic.

Goldblatt, D. (2008). *The Ball is Round: A Global History of Soccer*. New York: Riverhead Books.

Grix, J. (2012). 'Image' leveraging and sports mega events: Germany and the 2006 FIFA world cup. *Journal of Sport and Tourism, 17*(4), 289–312.

Haxall, D. (2015). Pitch invasion: football, contemporary art and the African diaspora. *Soccer and Society, 16*(2–3), 259–81.

Holston, J. (2014). Come to the street! Urban protest, Brazil 2013. *Anthropological Quarterly, 87*(3), 887–900.

Hopkins, M. (2013). Ten seasons of the football banning order: police officer narratives on the operation of banning orders and the impact on the behaviour of 'risk supporters'. *Policing and Society, 24*(3), 285–301.

Kenyon, J. and Rookwood, J. (2009). Sporting education – a global hope? Examining a sport development educational initiative at a Tibetan SOS children's village in northern India. *Journal of Qualitative Research in Sports Studies, 3*(1), 105–26.

Lambert, J. (2007). A values-based approach to coaching sport in divided societies: the football for peace coaching manual. In J. Sugden and J. Wallis (eds), *Football for peace? the challenges of using sport for co-existence in Israel* (pp. 13–34). Oxford: Meyer and Meyer.

Levin, M.A. and Peterson, L.T. (2013). Use of Pecha Kucha in marketing students' presentations. *Marketing Education Review, 23*(1), 59–64.

Mannay, D. (2013). Who put that on there . . . why why why?' Power games and participatory techniques of visual data production. *Visual Studies, 28*(2), 136–46.

Millward, P. (2011). *The global football league: transnational networks, social movements and sport in the new media age.* Basingstoke, UK: Palgrave.

Pielke, R. (2013). How can FIFA be held accountable? *Sport Management Review, 16*(3), 255–67.

Potts, J.D., Hartley, J., Banks, J.A., Burgess, J.E., Cobcroft, R.S., Cunningham, S.D. and Montgomery, L. (2008). Consumer co-creation and situated creativity. *Industry and Innovation, 15*(5), 459–74.

Redhead, S. (2012). Soccer casuals: a slight return of youth culture. *International Journal of Child, Youth and Family Studies, 3*(1), 65–82.

Rookwood, J. (2012). Constructing peace and fostering social integration through sport and play in Azerbaijan. In B. Segaert, M. Theeboom, C. Timmerman and B. Vanreusel (eds), *Sports, governance, development and corporate responsibility* (pp. 30–43). New York: Routledge.

Rookwood, J. (2014). Hooliganism. In H. Copes and C. Forsyth (eds), *Encyclopaedia of Social Deviance* (pp. 347–51). Thousand Oaks, CA: Sage.

Rookwood, J. and Wassong, S. (2010). NGOs – using sport to promote peace and integration infractured societies. In N. Ferguson (ed.), *Conflict and the reconstruction of civil society* (pp. 32–50). Newcastle: Cambridge Scholars Publishing.

Rose, G. (2014). On the relation between 'visual research methods' and contemporary visual culture. *The Sociological Review, 62*(1), 24–46.

Shell, L. (2014). Photo-elicitation with autodriving in research with individuals with mild to moderate Alzheimer's disease: advantages and challenges. *International Journal of Qualitative Methods, 13,* 170–84.

Sterchele, D. (2013). Fertile land or mined filed? Peace-building and ethnic tensions in post war Bosnian football. *Sport in Society, 16*(8), 211–24.

Stidder G. and Sugden, J. (2003). Sport and social inclusion across religious and ethnic divisions. A case of football in Israel. In S. Hayes and G. Stidder (eds), *Equity and inclusion in physical education* (pp. 135–51). London: Routledge.

Sugden, J. (2010). Critical left-realism and sport interventions in divided societies. *International Review for the Sociology of Sport, 45*(3), 258–72.

Vrcan, S. and Lalić, D. (1999). From ends to trenches and back: football in the former Yugoslavia. In G. Armstrong and R. Giulianotti (eds), *Football cultures and identities* (pp. 176–85). London: Palgrave.

Wachira, C. and Ruger, J.P. (2011). National poverty reduction strategies and HIV/AIDS governance in Malawi: a preliminary study of shared health governance. *Social Science and Medicine, 72*(12), 1956–64.

9

FIELDWORK

Using visual methods as a tool for field data collection

Janet Speake

Introduction

This chapter focuses on curriculum design and especially the related pedagogic, practical and ethical issues of using visual techniques while undertaking fieldwork with students. In particular, focus will be on how students selectively identify a particular phenomenon or location to frame in respect of field photographs and will explore the subjective nature of such framing. Specific attention will be paid to the positive and rich experiences that students subsequently report when given the opportunity to incorporate visual methods when collecting field data.

Fieldwork and visual methods

The approach to students' visual methods learning described in this chapter has been developed within the geographical domain with its strong and traditional focus on the practices of data collection in the field and underlining spatiality. It is, however, not discipline specific as it clearly draws on research conducted beyond the geographical academy and is resonant with, and has potential application in, the many areas of the social sciences and beyond that also place strong emphasis on the development of visual methods and field research techniques.

The use of visual methods in general and of photographic images in particular, is an integral part of the field research toolkit and is almost universally accepted, especially within the geographic academy. There is also an extensive literature on the fundamental role that fieldwork experience plays in the development of students' academic and transferable skills (e.g., Fuller, Edmondson, France, Higgitt and Ratinen, 2006; Wall and Speake, 2012; Fuller and France, 2015). Singly and taken together, these provide strong validation for the inclusion of visual methods in students' field-based research. It is therefore not surprising that there are many published case studies which present individual examples of field-based visual methods learning and research activities for students (e.g., Latham and McCormack, 2007; Sanders, 2007; Hall, 2015) and wider overviews of the role of photographs as a research tool for students (see Rose, 2008; Hall, 2009). However, what is perhaps surprising is the lack of published material on *pedagogic* facets of the development of students' skills in field-based visual methods research. Hence the specific contribution made by this chapter is its exemplification of curriculum design and learning frameworks that can facilitate and enhance the development of under-graduate students' visual methods field-based research skills.

Commenting on the application of photographic approaches to student field-work data collection in Berlin, Latham and McCormack (2007) saw a visual approach as the conception and enactment of fieldwork as a set of experiences distributed across a number of sites. Furthermore, Sanders (2007) explored ways of developing geographers through the use of photography. After a subsequent lull in publications there has recently been a resurgence of interest in geography about the use of visual imagery in student learning environments such as fieldwork (e.g., Welsh, France, Whalley and Park, 2012; Dando and Chadwick, 2014; Hunt, 2014; Lemmons, Brannstrom and Hurd, 2014). A similar pattern has occurred in cognate disciplines with a recent rise in published materials on the use of photographic imagery in field and other contexts, for example, 'So much for snapshots: The material relations of tourists as cultural dupes' (Picken, 2014) and 'Capturing neighbourhood images through photography' (Schoepfer, 2014). Both articles highlight the importance of developing skills in understanding the over-arching and more nuanced facets of the application of visual research methods and the interpretation of the resultant findings.

It is also the case that since the last major focus on the use of photographic images in geography fieldwork (e.g., Rose, 2007; 2008; Hall, 2009), there have been substantial technological advances in recording and transmitting visual imagery that little by little are being reflected in the literature. The emergent ubiquity of digital spatial technologies is generating a world in which the types and forms of engagements between people and places is transforming rapidly. This opens up new opportunities for individual and collective exploration, observation and interpretation of city space(s) and city place(s). People's visual, spatial and social interactions at the interface of the real-world/real-time and virtual digital world are now frequently (albeit often unknowingly) created and mediated through (generally) accessible and pervasive digital technologies such as GPS-based navigation and Google Street View (see Elwood and Mitchell, 2015).

The visual and other lenses through which people view the world, and in turn are viewed, change as these technologies evolve, develop and present other facets of the 'visual turn' (Spencer, 2011, p. 2). The transformative capabilities of the current wave of digital technological innovation, including spatial media, in changing knowledge of and relationships with places and spaces are substantial and are part of people's (particularly young people's) everyday engagements with the world. Yet across the disciplines, these transformative technological capabilities and their impacts are still largely under-researched and reported (Speake and Axon, 2012).

This chapter therefore reports on ways in which undergraduate students' engagement with visual research methods and photographic images can be encouraged in the learning context of field-based investigation and research. It includes students' comments, observations and evaluations that are woven into the author's own narration and reflections. Both report on how the development and enhancement of student field skills in the application of critical visual methods in city settings may be approached in terms of pedagogy, curriculum development and assessment.

Developing critical visual methods in students' urban field research

As an urban, social and economic geographer based in Liverpool UK, I am intrigued by the processes and practices of urban change and I have grappled with ways of enhancing pedagogic practice to best engage undergraduate and postgraduate students in geography and more widely across the social sciences, with urban transitions and transformations. For geography students I work with, Liverpool's rapid economic, cultural and social post-industrial restructuring provides a readily accessible local 'observatory' for the practical development of research skills. Other opportunities for students to explore urban change as part of academic courses have been created during fieldwork in Berlin, Bucharest and Malta. In all these instances, meaningful, varied and effective ways to promote students' in-depth understandings of cities' kaleidoscopic urban environments have been sought.

The academic and pedagogical approaches used are multi-faceted and have included the development of critical visual research methods. Theoretical framing incorporates the interpretation of cityscapes as text, explorations of the semiotics and symbolism of the visual and material representations of urban life. This has been achieved through the use of photographic images and associated visualisations of urban space and place. It also includes exploration of the ways in which the new spatial technologies impact on how people engage with, represent and navigate city environments in a context of neo-geographies. That is, the blurring of the distinctions between producer, communicator and consumer of geographic information (Goodchild, 2009), and the associated popularisation and democratisation of image/map creation and use (see e.g., Welsh *et al.*, 2012; Leszczynski, 2014; Speake, 2015).

The academic approach taken is grounded on the premise that images are everywhere and that image 'matters' (e.g., Rose, 2007; Sturken and Cartwright, 2001, 2009; Spencer, 2011). The pedagogic delivery accords with the progressive mainstreaming of visual studies teaching and the development of critical research methodologies, which are frequently situated in the spatial settings of cities (e.g., Latham and McCormack, 2007; Sanders, 2007; Spencer, 2011). The city is an appropriate context for the application of critical visual methodologies (see Tormey, 2013) since it provides a dynamic setting for thinking about the impacts and influences of visual objects and also for an individual's explorations of their own way(s) of looking at, seeing and interpreting such objects.

For students honing their skills in using visual/photographic images for data collection, the development of reflexivity in their considerations of what images mean is fundamental. This allows them to engage with the ideas that the photographic image is constructed by the maker and the viewer (Pink, 2007) and that it is important to learn about 'what' is seen/viewed and 'how' it is seen/viewed.

Developing students' awareness of ethical issues and the use of visual data collection methods

The study of ethical issues provides a further dimension in raising students' critical awareness of the use of visual images as a means of data gathering and the development of the reflexive research process. Ethical considerations are wide-ranging (Kearns, Le Heron and Romaniuk, 1998; Rose, 2008) and include, for example, the use of photographs of people overtly and/or covertly, without granting specific permission to do so, or images where there are copyright issues. Overall, however, as Rose (2014) reports, official guidance is limited although she does refer to some guidance proffered by the British Sociological Association (2006) and Papademas and the International Visual Sociology Association (2009). In the geography subject area, most discussion has tended to focus on independent student research projects (e.g., Vujakovic and Bullard, 2001; Boyd *et al.*, 2008) and recently on ethical issues associated with Geographical Information Systems (GIS) (e.g., Davis, 2014).

Within the geography curriculum that colleagues and I have devised and developed, the raising of undergraduate students' knowledge and understanding of the ethical dimensions to research is embedded throughout the students' learning experiences across all levels of study. This enables students to enhance their competencies in ethical visual methods research and in the completion of the requisite ethics documentation which students undertake before field-based data collection.

Introducing and developing visual methods approaches to data collection in urban settings

The use of critical visual methodologies in urban fieldwork learning and researching spaces described here suggests some learning approaches that initiate and enhance students' knowledge, understanding and application of them. It is also situated broadly in the development of the four 'r's of visual research:

- Research-found visual data
- Research created visual data
- Respondent generated visual data and
- Representation and visual research (Prosser, 1998).

TABLE 9.1 Exemplar schema for critical research methods in undergraduate urban fieldwork

---

Year 1 Undergraduate
- Developing the proto-researcher in field-based visual methods
- Work focused on exploring underpinning principles of visual and image interpretation in local Liverpool settings

Curriculum context: Introduction to cultural, economic and social urban contexts

Assessment: Local fieldwork presentation (G) and Fieldwork poster (G)

Year 2 Undergraduate
- Skilling the emergent undergraduate researcher in field-based visual methods
- Work has emphasis on reflexivity, positionality and intertextuality, the development of qualitative research skills, including visual methodologies, again in local environments

Curriculum context: Explorations in cultural, economic and social urban contexts

Assessment: Local fieldwork presentation (G) and Fieldwork report (I)

Year 3 Undergraduate
- Enhancing undergraduate researcher skills in field-based visual methods
- Work on the development of more sophisticated, higher level approaches to field data collection and increased student researcher autonomy, practised in a range of local and international city settings

Curriculum context: Advanced studies in transforming geographies – urban specialism

Assessment: International fieldwork report (I) and Dissertation (I)

(G) = Group assessment (I) = Individual assessment

The following critical visual methodology examples are taken from a 3-year undergraduate programme in geography. In line with the university's practice, the programme is delivered not through discrete modules but through an integrated curriculum that comprises elements contributing to undergraduate courses at UK Levels 4 (first year), 5 (second year) and 6 (third year). Class and field-based activities are able to be built-in and delivered relatively flexibly within delivery modes of a combination of lectures, seminars and tutorials, and vertical curriculum structures informed by the principles of spiral and scaffolded learning, as defined in Table 9.1.

Developing the proto-researcher in field-based visual methods

Year 1: Task 1

As proto-researchers (i.e., early/new researchers), first-year undergraduate students are encouraged to draw on their own experiences of creating and taking photographs and being critical of them, and to start to become aware of the role(s) of the viewed and viewer, that is, to view through 'the eyes of the enlightened witness' (hooks, 1997). Initial class and field-based activities encourage students to take photographic images and reflect on when, why and how they were chosen and what meanings they have. They are encouraged to interpret and critique, and also become aware of the development of the nature of informed criticality. For example, during their first urban fieldwork activity, students work in small groups, following a published town trail of the rapidly regenerating area of Ropewalks in Liverpool City Centre (Speake and Fox, 2006). This enables them to record and reflect on the processes of culture-led regeneration as the area transitions from a former warehousing area for the neighbouring south docks to a vibrant mixed-use residential and commercial area dominated by bars and clubs.

Students are asked to observe and interpret the cityscape to promote their engagement with both the visual and material dimensions to urban change. Their observations are recorded both in narrative and photographic form. Students are not directed about the photographs they might take. After the fieldwork the students choose one of their photographs and then present their chosen image to the class, with a 5-minute oral presentation about where and when they took this photograph, and also answering the questions 'Why *this* photograph?' and 'What does it mean to you?' The following section narrates responses from students who undertook this activity in 2014.

Students remarked on the variety of images chosen and were fascinated by the explanations given about why they were chosen. Although initially reflecting on the image as 'documentary' data, for example, what it shows, such as architectural styles, street furniture, the morphology of street configuration, they started to look beyond the buildings and became engrossed by the subjective nature of the image taking suggested interpretations such as 'the area is more run-down than expected' and '[I] like how it [a streetscape in Chinatown] shows both cultural unity and diversity . . . and how they come together'. When asked if they were to do the field research activity again what they would do differently, common responses were to 'prepare more'; 'take more pictures'; 'take pictures of the same place in the day and in the night to see the difference'. Three students also indicated that in future they would make sure that their phone was fully charged-up so that they could use GPS-based locational technology to locate themselves when taking photos and geo-tag them. The students have a chance to apply these 'improvements' in subsequent field activities at Level 6.

From a tutor perspective, creating curiosity-generated questions regarding the discursive and reflexive character of the urban image among the students paves the way for future investigation, raising issues such as:

- the immediacy of capturing an image;
- the need (or not) for its contextualisation with words;
- that images can be questioned and interrogated;
- that asking questions of images reveals as much about the questioner as it does about the cityscape and the image being questioned.

The activity also raises students' awareness of the multiplicity of interpretations of the same image and introduces notions of audiencing (Rose, 2007, p. 261). Essentially, at the end of this activity, students were introduced to the three sites at which the meanings of photographic images are made:

- site of production (how an image is made),
- site of the image (what it looks like) and
- site of its audiencing (how it is seen).

(Rose, 2007, p. 257)

They were asked to reflect on each of these aspects with respect to their own chosen image and the others presented.

Typically students' reflections are descriptive regarding these three sites at which images are made. However, application of the behavioural (action), cognitive (knowledge and understanding) and affective (emotion and feeling) framework revealed different forms of engagement with each of them. First, in the case of site of production, responses revealed largely behavioural engagement with the technical artefact used to make the chosen image (in most cases a smartphone and what was 'great' or 'not so great' about its technical capabilities). Second, student remarks about the site of image for the photograph chosen showed mostly cognitive and (occasionally) affective engagement with what it looks like and is indicative of, as in 'the photograph demonstrates the changes to Liverpool over the years'. Third, comments on the site of audiencing showed affective or affective-cognitive engagement, for example, in relation to others' images, 'the pictures triggered personal reflections' and were a 'visual clue for the memory'.

The activity sometimes activates students' questioning of ethical dimensions in visual methods research, for example as implied in comments such as 'we're not used to taking photos of streetscapes and are not sure when we should or not'. Others stated that they were more used to taking 'touristy photos' and that they had 'taken loads more pictures' on other fieldwork at a beach location.

Year 1: Task 2

To maintain student engagement with the visual and links between the visual and material, further practice in the use of critical visual methodologies for first-year students also takes place during residential fieldwork in Snowdonia, North Wales. Assessment of this work is an academic poster, incorporating photographs. Throughout the field visit, the students not only, create, compose, make, take and present photographic images, but also participate in discourse about the reflexive character of their own, and others', engagements with landscape. As illustration, student reflections revealed that that they thought that the use of photos had given them 'an overall sense of place from the start' and an 'awareness of the different emotions connected to different findings as to how they relate to society'.

Such comments indicate recognition of the key roles of landscape observation and interpretation and the creation and use of photographic images. In their reflections about the inclusion of photos in posters some students clearly displayed that they were progressing beyond regarding photos as 'just' documentary records to beginning to think about (self-)identity, positionality and intertextuality. For example, the students stated that photographs can be 'very different to other people' that they generate 'different opinions among the group' and that 'images can be misleading'. In reflection about the use of photography in their studies across the year students observed that they had been surprised 'how accurate they [photos] can be – how much more memorable everything is'; 'how much more aware you are walking through the landscape'; 'that it's so basic, but very useful' and 'you are much more aware and alert for details of your fieldwork'.

When asked about how their knowledge of visual research methods changed over the year, students responded positively, explaining that 'it takes more time to look at the area', but that there was an understanding regarding the importance of it as 'data and visual cues'. As one student commented, 'I have leaned towards visual research/observations before deeper evaluation, contrasting initial perceptions to findings'.

Skilling the emergent undergraduate researcher in field-based visual methods

Year 2: Task 1

At Level 5 (second year undergraduate), the development of visual methods includes more scrutinising of self and others with respect to visual imagery as a research tool. Throughout the year, the use of visual imagery provides a lens through which to consider, for example power and cultural meaning in landscape. Textual analysis techniques using images (including photographic images as text) are developed in conjunction with explorations of positionality and intertextuality.

The positionality of self and how it can be revealed are readily explored through the use of photographs. For example, in class sessions on identity and landscapes, students present a photographic image of a landscape that has particular meaning and resonance for them and explain why. Images of garden sheds and supermarket check-outs, cafés and skyscrapers have been among those chosen. Perspectives of the 'audience' are sought as they too engage with the images and in doing so reveal the various interpretations that an image can be subject to. In many respects these conversations between researcher/presenter and the audience demonstrate to students, often potently, that through the influences of positionality and inter-textuality 'we "read" the images in front of our eyes through the pictures we have in our heads' (Spencer, 2011, p. 19).

These and other similar discussions begin to immerse students in dialogue about the subjective nature of knowledge *and* the socially, ideologically and politically constructed nature of images. In the context of the visual interpretation of cityscape

FIGURE 9.1 Bold Street, Liverpool. The rapidly transforming and revitalised Bold Street, Liverpool provides an exemplar cityscape in which the use of photographic imagery elicits multiple readings and interpretations of its urban character and change.

Source: Janet Speake

these themes are expanded to include what is visible and also what is not visible. Students become familiarised with what Rose (2014) refers to as symbolic and communicative activities and are also encouraged to reflect on the assertion that 'seeing is never innocent' (Spencer, 2011, p. 34). Over several years, Bold Street, in Liverpool City Centre has been the locus of such learning activities.

During the past century Bold Street has transitioned from being Liverpool's leading up-market retail area, then through profound economic downturn in the 1980s to being more recently reinvigorated as an area of 'alternative', independent stores in a newly residential part of town. Students are encouraged to engage with its distinctive cityscape and life during a series of activities. For example, they are asked to create written and visual narratives of Bold Street as a 'streetscape of fear and hope' and to look beyond the visible to explore and record who and what is not visible and to comment on absence(s) and gaps. For the tutors it affords an opportunity to encourage students to think laterally and 'interrogate' the street. For the students it is a visual challenge that, with encouragement, they rise to. Over the years the activities have become more detailed, nuanced and demanding as it has become clear that students respond well to the challenge and learn practically, as they draw upon and develop their skills acquired at Level 4.

TABLE 9.2 Student reflections on the use of photography as a research tool at the end of their Year 2 undergraduate studies, 2015 ($n = 13$)

Question 1. What have you learned about the role of photography as a research tool?

Key themes identified
- It is as helpful as other research tools.
- It provides a useful visual methods research tool.
- It enables the visual recording of people and places.

Exemplar student observations

'Photography is useful as a research tool as it allows you to capture a place and time and allows you to evaluate what is going on. Why is it there? Why was this photo taken at this particular place? How can this photo be viewed by different people? Who is visible?'

'I have learnt a lot about using photography as a research method and it has helped me understand it more about surveillance and memoryscapes.'

Question 2. In your opinion what are the three most important positive aspects of using photographs in research?

Key themes identified
- Creates a photographic record that can be revisited later.
- Contributes to an understanding of what is viewed and not viewed.
- Allows for the expression of multiple interpretations.

Exemplar student observations

'Allows you to capture a place and time and evaluate it. Shows evidence of fieldwork. Shows evidence of how you can interpret it.'

'Photographs can be interpreted in different ways to which the photographer intended, therefore new interpretations and views of the image may be discovered.'

Question 3. In your opinion what are the three most important negative aspects of using photographs in research?

Key themes identified
- Provides just a snap shot which might miss the bigger picture.
- Lacks other embodied realities.
- Difficulties experienced in interpreting meanings behind the image.

Exemplar student observations

'A photograph only captures a moment in time and may not truly represent the area to its fullest.'

'. . . being 'read' differently may not necessarily be a good thing as the creator of the photograph may have created the image for a completely different reason as to how it has been interpreted.'

Question 4. How has the development of your skills in critical visual research methods contributed to your understanding of urban environments?

Key themes identified
- Through observation and interpretation skills of who and what is photographed.
- Developing deeper understanding of how the character of cities can be revealed in photographs.
- Being able to interrogate what is not visible as well as that which is visible and explore these in the context of 'difference'.

Exemplar student observations

'The development of my skills in critical visual methods has contributed to my understanding of urban environments as it has allowed me to observe and notice features and characteristics, and therefore interpret them, where otherwise I might have missed them.'

'My development through visual analysis of landscapes has helped as I can now see certain aspects of them that I never did [before]. How I view urban landscapes has been enhanced as I know what to look for and what goes on in this environment.'

In adopting a poststructuralist approach, students are asked to take a photograph that to them best encapsulates one of several themes and then present it to the rest of the class in a fieldwork follow-up seminar. At the end of the academic year students as part of their course evaluation are asked to reflect on four questions relating specifically to the development of their visual methods research skills. Key themes of the feedback from a group of students at the end of their Level 5 studies are shown in Table 9.2.

From a pedagogical stance, the principal outcome from the students' reflections is the evidence of their engagements with the construction, creation and viewing of images and that they are able to articulate their perspectives on the role of photography as a research tool. They can narrate how visual methods research skills have contributed to their understanding of urban environments. Students also show a keen awareness of the subjectivity of photograph generation and use – for some this is a truly positive attribute but others display cognitive-affective 'unease' with it (see Watt and Wakefield, 2014).

Enhancing undergraduate researcher skills in field-based visual methods

Year 3: Tasks 1 and 2

In their final year students prepare two research reports: a dissertation and a report. The latter is based on a week's field visit to Malta. Every year some students choose to base their research on photographs and include them as part of their data collection and analytical approach. In all cases, students who use visual methodologies in their data collection are encouraged to think carefully about how they want photographs to work for them, to reflect about the wider agency of photographic images (see Rose, 2007, p. 255) and what photographs add to knowledge and understanding of their chosen research areas. Examples of how students use photographs include:

* researcher created and interpreted images;
* researcher created images that are interpreted by others;
* images created by others that are interpreted by the researcher.

Student evaluations of chosen visual research methods are discussed in the following two sections about research dissertations and international fieldwork reports.

Research dissertations using visual methodologies

The research projects that use photographic methods have tended to hone in on landscape/cityscape analysis, for example users' landscape preferences and what particular landscapes mean to them. Some of the most insightful of these projects have been where the student researcher has asked participants to take a photograph of a place of meaning to them and asked them to articulate in the form of a vignette or short narrative, what that meaning is and why. This has then formed the basis for further analysis by the researcher. Students have often expressed surprise at the images chosen by the participants (i.e., they did not match their own) and the reasons for their choice but have sometimes been very inquisitive and motivated to explore underpinning conceptual contexts to better understand the photographer's and their own positions.

At best, in these instances, encouraging students to work through their own research discoveries themselves can be a very rewarding learning experience for both students and tutors which can become an exemplification of co-learning (Le Heron, Baker and McEwan, 2006). This is particularly so in the case of studies conducted over a number of months, during which time development of reflective and reflexive student learning is seen to evolve.

As an illustration, dissertations exploring senses of place through photographic images of cities, have produced results that have dramatically challenged the student researchers' pre-conceived ideas of what would be chosen, that is, well-known landmarks. However, participants tended to present 'everyday' urban landscapes that conveyed a special meaning to them rather than iconic views. Such observations have sparked engaged dialogue with participants and university tutors, not only about the reasons behind such image creation but also about appropriate and ethical ways to analyse, interpret, present and academically contextualise such personal images and written narratives.

Fieldwork research projects using visual methodologies during international fieldwork

The comparatively short length of the field visit by the UK-based students to Malta (usually 7 days) and the Maltese islands' largely urban character provides an appropriate context for the use of visual data collection methods by student researchers. To date, projects that have adopted critical visual approaches using photographs have been varied in theme and scope. The research studies listed below provide an indicative insight into the types and range of studies conducted by students:

- Remnant visual signs of British colonialism in the streetscapes of Valletta. Photographic images and interpretation conducted by student (i.e., photographs taken and interpreted by student researcher).
- Image versus reality in photographic postcards of Maltese cityscapes (i.e., images taken by others compared to images of the same viewpoint taken by student researcher).
- Representational meanings of frequently used photographic images of buildings and views in Malta and their meanings to various audiences, for example, visitors and local residents (i.e., images taken by student researcher but interpreted by others).

When students have used photographic research methodologies they have reported interesting insights into their engagements with technological, compositional and social modalities as illustrated below and in the case study that follows:

CASE STUDY

The smart city is a truly modern concept. It seeks to integrate technological infrastructure within the pre-existing physical, social and environmental infrastructures, creating sustainable growth and a 'smarter' way of living.

Smart cities are often seen as a utopian way of living, a dream-like state. This is due to their ability to meet and exceed living, health and economic needs through the implementation of technology. It was this dream view that was integral in the visual methods of analysis used within the research, the ability for the author and reader to visually interpret the smart city dream against its reality. This was done by matching visualised imagery (see Figure 9.2), 'the dream', against the observed visual experience 'the reality'.

The first comparison drawn was that between Figure 9.2 and Figure 9.3, with the smart city 'dream' (Figure 9.3) becoming the reality, with very little difference in vision and design. The use of visual methods of analysis allows the reader to experience the realisation of the dream. The smart city dream is further brought into reality with a focus on traditional Maltese architecture. Narrow street paths and open square design are used to channel air, providing cooling for the city during warmer days. Although slightly

FIGURE 9.2 SmartCity Malta: Visualisation

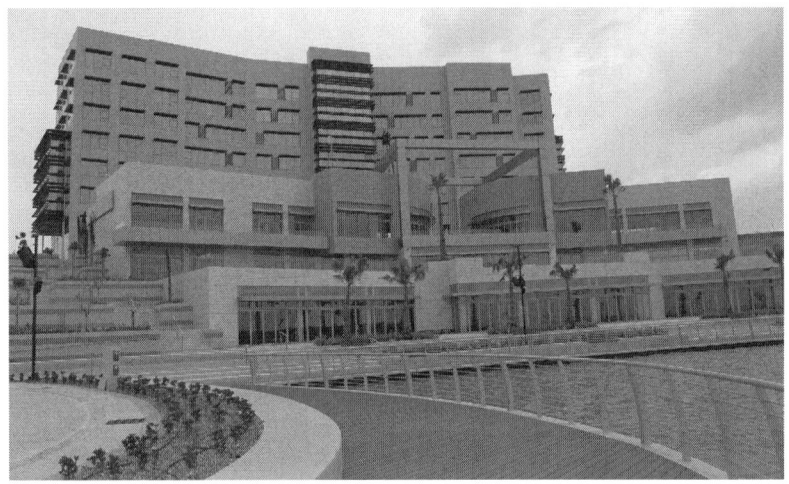

FIGURE 9.3 SmartCity Malta: Reality – SCM001 building

modified, the use of narrow streets and an open oval water feature are better suited to the needs of the city, thus making it 'smart'. The dream comes closer to reality by converging socio-cultural infrastructures with physical and technological infrastructures. Although the design includes traditional influences e.g. some building material, there is very little evidence of more tradition. Furthermore the SCM001 building stands in isolation, like a ship in a sea of desolation abandoned by its captain and crew. There is no life in the city. Life, from people and the buildings, is integral to the smart city success. The figures clearly show the current emptiness.

The use of a globigerina limestone facia is a distinctive feature to Maltese architecture. Figure 9.4 instantly draws attention, particularly when viewed from a cultural, economic and environmental perspective. It captures the macro scale of Malta and SmartCity within micro-scale boundaries. Stemming from Neolithic temples to present technological cities this represents the culture of Malta readily being embodied in the image. However the image presents the apparent frailty of the urban design. It is already damaged, even before the smart city has been opened. The urban building facia are in keeping with cultural designs but conflict with environmental and ultimately sustainable design practices. This is due to damage easily occurring, thus suggesting the facia already need replacing and the stresses of further quarrying and transporting limestone to the city on the Maltese environment. Consequentially this casts the sustainability 'dream' of smart cities into doubt because the 'reality', presented in the image, shows the very building blocks cannot live up to the 'dream'.

A visual methodology works best here due to the ability to draw an immediate conclusion on the benefits and limitations of urban design theories

FIGURE 9.4 Globigerina limestone facia

and models. The researcher is able to easily track developments of an area, particularly as it progresses through time. If the research was extended it would enable the researcher to have a clear chronology of development, detailing if the smart city dream becomes a reality. Visual methods are also a way of instantly engaging the reader into the research as their eye will be drawn towards images, allowing them to experience elements of the research and enabling them to interpret the data from their own perspective with ease. This is vital within subjects with an interdisciplinary approach in order to create debate and drive the subjects forward. The use of a statistics-based approach could be seen to lack emotion and may restrict some readers from drawing their own conclusions on the data.

Direct visual comparison of the smart city theory to the smart city reality works effectively: where the needs of the dream can be clearly seen to be met and where they have failed to achieve their target. This creates a basis for discussion, the driving force behind any research. The speed at which visual data can be loaded or printed and analysed allows the researcher to rapidly begin the discussion. The use of a statistical approach requires numerical input and analysis through programmes such as SPSS; slowing down the research and analysis: an important factor in such a fast moving environment.

Images co-created by Sean Molyneux and Stephen Torney
Critical Reflection by Sean Molyneux

- Narrative and critical commentary on photographic images of SmartCity Malta taken by the student photographer during its early construction phases (i.e., photographs taken and interpreted by student researcher). See Case Study for student observations and critical reflection on this project.

Over the years, several things have stood out in the work of the student researchers. Their projects enhanced their understanding of images as ways of 'seeing and viewing' and, 'being viewed'. Students also showed an appreciation of other people's cultures and the cultural, social and political framing of the photographs. Finally, they grasped the importance and contribution of the 'audience' as neatly expressed in the student observation:

> The audience is the ultimate contributor to the piece of visual research. If they cannot understand or see your argument then your research is not achieving its purpose. The power of visual methodology is to engage the audience on every level.

From the tutor's perspective, field-based visual methods used by students in international settings provide substantial pedagogical benefits in terms of working in unfamiliar environments and encountering/engaging with different social and cultural contexts. In this respect, the outcomes in terms of boosting generic and transferable skills conform to the positive impact reported regarding skills development during fieldwork and student responses to working in unfamiliar environments (e.g., Hawthorne, Solís, Terry, Price and Atchison, 2015).

Conclusion

This chapter has focused on curriculum design and especially the related pedagogic, practical and ethical issues of using visual techniques while undertaking geography fieldwork with students. It has reported on the teaching of visual research techniques, particularly photographic research and analytic techniques, can be built into and scaffolded throughout an undergraduate student's learning trajectory.

It shows, in the context of the distinctive pedagogical approach to the teaching of research methods reported here, that the use of critical visual methods offers opportunities for developing knowledge and understanding of the modes of looking at and creating photographic imagery. Visual methods are applied as a research tool in collecting data about urban transformation and the everyday spaces in which people in cities live, work and relax.

The curriculum structure and mode of delivery provide contexts in which students become critically aware of the constructed nature of image creation, image making and image critiquing. They are also enabled to develop as reflective and reflexive learners with respect to their own and others' engagements with visual research methodologies, photographic imagery *and* the urban world.

Through the spiral development of visual methods delivered during their 3 years of undergraduate study, students are given the learning space in which to develop the requisite skills to enable them to operate ethically as proto-researchers in the first year and later in their third year to conduct their own research projects using field-based, visual data collection techniques should they choose to do so. This planned, longitudinal approach to the framing of students' visual methods learning enables them to experience the 'slow release of meaning' advocated by Spencer (2011, p. 64) as their interpretation skills of photographic imagery are enhanced.

The approach to students' visual methods learning reported in this chapter has been devised and delivered in the geographic domain with its long-standing focus on the practices of field-based research and the underlining spatiality. It is, however, not discipline specific as it clearly draws on research conducted beyond the geography community. It is resonant with and has potential application in the many areas of the social sciences and beyond that also place strong emphasis on the development of visual methods and field research techniques in urban settings.

REFLECTIVE ACTIVITIES

The following reflective activities have been devised to encourage you to think about and reflect on some issues and challenges relating to the teaching of visual research methods through the use of photographic images in fieldwork settings.

1   In the context of a 'local' or 'international' fieldwork location conduct a SWOT (strengths, weaknesses, opportunities and threats) analysis of its potential for the development of student skills in critical visual research methods and then use it to identify the general and location-specific issues to be taken into consideration when planning and preparing for field-based activities there.

2   Reflect on the preliminary preparation that might be needed to encourage students to think about risk assessment and ethical issues associated with using visual methods research (a) in an urban location at 'home' and (b) in an international setting.

3   In terms of curriculum development reflect on different approaches to the use of photographs and then devise appropriate activities to illustrate each, for example, 'documentary photography'.

4   Reflect on the sorts of copyright issues that might need to be factored in to image creation (when taking) and also using images (e.g., street scenes containing pieces of art, pictures of shops, etc.). Where would you look for guidance?

5   Issues of 'audiencing' regularly surprise students – particularly how their own photographic images are interpreted by others. What issues are worth discussing with students *before* they view photographs and then *after* viewing?

Suggested reading

Hall, T. (2009). The camera never lies? Photographic research methods in human geography. *Journal of Geography in Higher Education*, *33*(3), 453–62.

Rose, G. (2008). Using photographs as illustrations in human geography. *Journal of Geography in Higher Education*, *32*(1), 151–60.

Rose, G. (2014). On the relation between 'visual research methods' and contemporary visual culture. *The Sociological Review*, *62*(1), 24–46.

Spencer, S. (2011). *Visual research methods in the social sciences: awakening visions*. London: Routledge.

References

Boyd, W.E., Healey, R,L., Hardwick, S.J., Haigh, M. with Klein, P., Doran, B., Trafford, J. and Bradbeer, J. (2008). 'None of us sets out to hurt people': The ethical geographer and geography curricula in higher education. *Journal of Geography in Higher Education*, *32*(1), 37–50.

British Sociological Association. (2006). Statement of ethical practices for the British Sociological Association. Available at www.visualsociology.org.uk/BSA_VS_ethicalstatement.pdf

Dando, C.E. and Chadwick, J.J. (2014). Enhancing geographic learning and literacy through filmmaking. *Journal of Geography*, *113*(2), 78–84.

Davis, M. (2014). What to consider when preparing a model core curriculum for GIS ethics: objectives, methods, and a sketch of content. *Journal of Geography in Higher Education*, *38*(4), 471–80.

Elwood, S. and Mitchell, K. (2015). Technology, memory, and collective knowing. *Cultural Geographies*, *22*(1), 147–54.

Fuller, I., Edmondson, S., France, D., Higgitt, D. and Ratinen, I. (2006). International perspectives on the effectiveness of geography fieldwork for learning. *Journal of Geography in Higher Education*, *30*(1), 89–101.

Fuller, I.C. and France, D. (2015). Securing field learning using a twenty-first century cook's tour. *Journal of Geography in Higher Education*, *39*(1), 158–72.

Goodchild, M. (2009). Neogeography and the nature of geographic expertise. *Journal of Location Based Services*, *3*(2), 82–96.

Hall, T. (2009). The camera never lies? Photographic research methods in human geography. *Journal of Geography in Higher Education*, *33*(3), 453–62.

Hall, T. (2015). Reframing photographic research methods in human geography: a long-term reflection. *Journal of Geography in Higher Education*, *39*(3), 328–42.

Hawthorne, T.L., Solís, P.,Terry, B., Price, M. and Atchison, C.L. (2015). Critical reflection mapping as hybrid methodology for examining sociospatial perceptions of new research sites. *Annals of the Association of American Geographers*, *105*(1), 22–47.

hooks, b. (1997). *Cultural criticism and transformation*, video produced and directed by Sut Jhally, Media Education Technology.

Hunt, M.A. (2014). Urban photography/cultural geography: spaces, objects, events. *Geography Compass*, *8*(3), 151–68.

Kearns, R., Le Heron, R. and Romaniuk, A. (1998). Interactive ethics: developing understanding of the social relations of research. *Journal of Geography in Higher Education*, *22*(3), 297–310.

Latham, A. and McCormack, D.P. (2007). Digital photography and web-based assignments in a urban field course: snapshots from Berlin. *Journal of Geography in Higher Education*, *31*(2), 241–56.

Le Heron, R., Baker, R. and McEwan, L. (2006). Co-learning: re-linking research and teaching in geography. *Journal of Geography in Higher Education, 30*, 77–87.

Lemmons, K.K., Brannstrom, C. and Hurd, D. (2014). Exposing students to repeat photography: increasing cultural understanding on a short-term study abroad. *Journal of Geography in Higher Education, 38*(1), 86–105.

Leszczynski, A. (2014). On the neo in neogeography. *Annals of the Association of American Geographers, 104*(1), 60–79.

Papademas, D. and International Visual Sociology Association (2009). IVSA – code of research ethics and guidelines. *Visual Studies, 24*(3), 250.

Picken (2014). So much for snapshots: the material relations of tourists as cultural dupes. *Tourist Studies, 14*(3), 246–60.

Pink, S. (2007). *Doing visual ethnography.* London: Sage Publications.

Prosser, J. (1998). *Image-based research: a sourcebook for qualitative researchers.* London: Falmer Press.

Rose, G. (2007). *Visual methodologies: an introduction to the interpretation of visual materials* (2nd edn). London: Sage Publications.

Rose, G. (2008). Using photographs as illustrations in human geography. *Journal of Geography in Higher Education, 32*(1), 151–60.

Rose, G. (2014). On the relation between 'visual research methods' and contemporary visual culture. *The Sociological Review, 62*(1), 24–46.

Sanders, R. (2007). Developing geographers through photography: enlarging concepts. *Journal of Geography in Higher Education, 31*, 181–95.

Schoepfer, I. (2014). Capturing neighbourhood images through photography. *Visual Ethnography, 3*(1), 3–34.

Speake, J. (2015). Navigating our way through the research–teaching nexus. *Journal of Geography in Higher Education, 39*(1), 131–42.

Speake, J. and Axon, S. (2012). 'I never use "maps" anymore': engaging with sat nav technologies and the implications for cartographic literacy and spatial awareness. *The Cartographic Journal, 49*(4), 326–36.

Speake, J. and Fox, V. (2006). Discovering cities: Liverpool. Sheffield: The Geographical Association.

Spencer, S. (2011). *Visual research methods in the social sciences: awakening visions.* London: Routledge.

Sturken, M. and Cartwright, L. (2001). *Practices of looking: an introduction to visual culture* (1st edn). Oxford: Oxford University Press.

Sturken, M. and Cartwright, L. (2009). *Practices of looking: an introduction to visual culture* (2nd edn). Oxford: Oxford University Press.

Tormey, J. (2013). *Cities and photography.* Abingdon: Routledge.

Vujakovic, P. and Bullard, J. (2001). The ethics minefield: issues of responsibility in learning and research. *Journal of Geography in Higher Education, 25*(2), 275–83.

Wall, G. P. and Speake, J. (2012). European geography higher education fieldwork and the skills agenda. *Journal of Geography in Higher Education, 36*(3), 421–35.

Watt, S. and Wakefield, C. (2014). Picture It! The use of visual methods in psychology teaching. *Psychology Teaching Review, 20*(1), 68–77.

Welsh, K.E., France, D., Whalley, W.B. and Park, J.R. (2012). Geotagging photographs in student fieldwork. *Journal of Geography in Higher Education, 36*(3), 469–80.

10

CROSSING OVER CULTURES

Using visual methods in a cross-cultural context for teaching and research

Simon J. Davies and Lorna J. Bourke

Introduction

This chapter documents the use of visual methods within the context of working beyond one's own culture and language, and includes a rationale for using visual methods to facilitate cross-cultural communication in teaching and research. The two methods outlined are photo-production/elicitation (Harper, 2002; Reavey, 2011) and an art-production/elicitation task (Katsiaficas, Futch, Fine and Sirin, 2011) using postcards developed through our own practice in communities within developing countries. These methods have been developed in conjunction with more typical verbal/textual-based techniques to inform our teaching and research (Leitch, 2006). We, our student teachers from the UK, and a group of Tibetan students we have worked closely with in recent years, reflect on how the methods were used, their effectiveness in relation to both developing confidence in interactions and gaining a broader understanding of different world views and perspectives (Smythe and McKenzie, 2010; Pink, 2012).

Background

The material presented in this chapter has originated from a series of international projects we have volunteered on for the last few years in a number of developing countries (e.g., Malawi, Sri Lanka and several locations in India). The projects have been for a UK-based educational charity hosted by Liverpool Hope University. While the main aim is to provide education to both students and teachers from the countries that we work in, another key objective is to afford home students and teachers the opportunity to gain a more in-depth critical appreciation of cross-cultural issues through active participation within different communities (Morais and Ogden, 2011; Bourke, Bamber and Lyons, 2012).

A typical project involves two or more staff members (HE lecturers) as well as several UK-based undergraduate students and trainee teachers. Most staff members have had experience working on such projects, but extensive training is given to all staff and students prior to departure. The nature of the projects differs depending on the skill set of the staff and students, whether the participants are children or adults, and is a direct response to the needs of the host organisation. An integral part of our provision is an on-going cycle of reflection on teaching practice and its effectiveness (Biggs and Tang, 2011). Owing to the diverse nature of the projects we engage in, this means that adjustments both during each project as well as at the end of each set of projects need to be made. The use of the multiple methods documented in this chapter is a direct response to this reflective practice.

Although each project is unique there are common challenges that all projects encounter from a teaching perspective. In particular, communicating with the host staff and students whose first language is not English, and working within a different cultural environment with different cultural expectations of what it means to be a student and what it means to be an educator (Entwistle, 2009). Consequently, apart from language barriers, there are also personal and cultural barriers and identities that need to be negotiated based on experience and expectation. In an attempt to bridge these factors and gain a greater insight into the processes that underpin them, we have started to regularly use visual methods in our teaching. The first attempt at using visual methods was with primary school-aged children in Sri Lanka in 2011. Feedback from that project led to their inclusion in projects in 2013 and 2014 with adult Tibetan university students living in India and are reported in more detail later in the chapter. The two visual methods we use (art-production/elicitation [art drawn onto a postcard piece of paper] and photo-production/elicitation) have subsequently become integral to the research conducted along with our international teaching projects.

Using visual methods for teaching in cross-cultural contexts

Increasingly, we began to view our work and that of the students we take with us as ethnographic. It involved lived, observable, naturalistic and interactive experiences in the host community as well as a bidirectional learning process. The notion of communication is not solely about linguistic comprehension, but also about developing a joint understanding of each participant's world view and sense of identity that occur in different teaching and social contexts (Hills, 2006). Without this shared perspective, much of the teaching delivered as well as received is wasted. One way to facilitate communication cross-culturally is to avoid using only verbal/textual-based tasks, at least in the initial teaching sessions. Ethnographic research includes visual methods of inquiry through which participant involvement provides a potential avenue to develop relationships between ourselves and our host community further (Pink, 2012). Through taking a more novel approach to our teaching we hoped this would lead to greater communication and greater confidence in the project, both for our student teachers as well as the participants. From this, we have also tried to create a more general interface between being involved in projects through teaching and formulating research questions and ideas.

Visual methods employed in general as a teaching method, and also in a cross-cultural context have several advantages over using traditional didactic delivery (Leitch, 2006; Harper, 2012; Watt and Wakefield, 2014). The first is simply that it does not require the participant to use words. Participants can fully engage in the task without the need to use a second language or indeed to try and verbally articulate their ideas to people with a different world view. The images produced can also transcend what may be less easy to convey in language and instead 'encourages the expression of multiple truths and the interaction of these truths to make new, individual and collective meanings' (Leitch, 2006, p. 553). As such, a secondary advantage is the development of a qualitatively different 'bigger' picture of the participants with whom we are working.

The task is also a creative process. The creative act of selecting the subject of drawings or photographs requires the participant to make personal decisions about what to draw and photograph. Beyond visually conveying the aim of the task (which in our case with the Tibetan students was to represent their identity, and for our Sri Lankan students was to convey what they like), participants were given a degree of freedom. This freedom and the lack of restrictions on what was photographed allowed the participants scope to incorporate a range of styles and means of expression (Leitch, 2006). For example, the use of colour for some communities is important. For our Tibetan students the colours of the Tibetan flag (predominantly blue, red and yellow) were frequently used in their drawings and photographs other than to represent the flag itself. Similarly, there are frequently symbols that are a shortcut to expressing a cultural idea or convention (e.g., the use of an apple rather than a heart to convey love for the Sri Lankan children; or the inclusion of some prayer beads in a photo for the Tibetan students to express a Buddhist identity).

Although visual methods are not viewed as being of greater benefit than verbal/textual methods in these circumstances, a requirement to include alternative more creative methods has been proposed to ensure the wider inclusion of the voices of more marginalised groups (e.g., Tibetan diaspora and children being looked after in the social care system in Sri Lanka) (Long and Carless, 2010). This may subsequently help teachers and researchers to think differently about the experiences that are being communicated by young people in those situations and thus reduce the distance between them and ourselves. When working on the projects with adults, English is normally embedded to some extent within the teaching process; when working with very young children this is often not possible, as was the case when we worked with primary school children in Sri Lanka in 2011. It was for this reason that we initially started using the 'postcard' task which later became integral to the projects with the Tibetan community in India in 2013 and 2014. For the Sri Lanka project we wanted to try a simple art-based task to explore the children's lives to allow us to understand their lived experience in greater depth, but also to provide a relevant teaching context for the children. This both helped our student teachers to form bonds with the children by engaging in a shared task, but also to help shape the delivery of teaching that was to follow.

The task was relatively uncomplicated and based around postcard sized pieces of art that the children produced in response to a given idea. One example was 'things or people we love' or 'things which make me happy'. These particular topics were chosen because we were also conducting a programme of learning with the children's teachers in Sri Lanka that included a focus on attachment issues and social-emotional intelligence. From the outset there were unexpected complications associated with our approach. For instance, we had intended to place a picture of a heart at the centre of each card to start the children's thinking. This was corrected by one of the Sri Lankan teachers who told us that an apple was the Sri Lankan symbol of love. When given a picture of an apple the children understood the nature of the task and quickly produced a range of other images that conveyed what made them feel happy. Their pictures were of the natural environment, more specifically, those aspects of the environment that they very much loved feeling connected to; for example, waterfalls, mountains, wild animals, sunshine, flowers (see Figure 10.1). This initial foray into using art as a way to break down barriers and start a 'conversation' led us to appreciate that all assumptions we had of our host communities really needed to be open until they were validated through experience. It also highlighted the potential to use visual narratives to explore issues related to the development of identity in different cultures (Frost, 2009; Graham and Kilpatrick, 2010; Harper, 2012).

Thus, the combination of visual and verbal approaches to understanding cultural, political and social identities has been recommended for research (e.g., photo-production/elicitation followed by interviews) (Buckingham, 2009; Frost, 2009; Phoenix, 2010; Reavey, 2011). Therefore, one of the established roles a visual narrative plays is not to just serve as a point of analysis in itself but to provide a basis of a prompt for later activities that involves elicitation by speaking and writing (Harper, 2012). In the case of the teaching projects we were involved in, speaking and writing was improved by communicating in English, which was undertaken as a focus of skill development requested by the host community. Although the production of such a small image as a postcard allowed a great deal of creative freedom, the end result is nevertheless one that is focused. When engaging the participant in a written or verbal activity based on the drawing or photograph, they then have a wealth of material to work with. The images tell some form of story or constructed narrative (Leitch, 2006) that has the beginnings of a coherent structure that the participant can use to organise their writing and ideas. In a sense, the pictures can act as a brainstorming activity without the restrictions of having to apply linguistic conventions for those who do not have English as a first language.

From a practical standpoint using a simple task such as art production also allows a teacher to engage with larger audiences; something common on our international projects. As the task is easy to explain, requires minimum materials and is not

FIGURE 10.1 Two postcard examples from Sri Lankan primary-aged school children responding to the cues of 'happy' and 'sad'.

complicated to do, it is a good way to get a larger group to work on a creative task to start the thinking process. The material can then instigate a secondary stage of teaching by acting as a 'gobbet' (Brown and Knight, 1994). This is a chunk of content that can be in any media format (e.g., pictures, written text, music, a diagram, etc.). Gobbets allow students to freely react to the material in a way that is personal to them. With a self-created gobbet such as the visual tasks that we use, the students are later responding to their own creative process and putting into words what their pictorial creations represent (e.g., postcards and photo-elicitation).

From teaching to research using visual methods

Following our Sri Lankan project we were approached by Liverpool Museums for help in contextualising Tibetan identity as part of a large exhibition of Tibetan contemporary and historical art. In conjunction with museum curators and based on our personal reflections, a multi-modal approach enabled the development of the wider picture the exhibition required (Reavey, 2011). A between-method triangulation (see Figure 10.2) allowed us to view the data from a number of different perspectives. It seems appropriate that in order to disentangle the multiple dimensions (e.g., social, political, historical and cultural) of participant narratives, several analytic techniques would be required (Frost, 2009). The primary advantage is not just that consistencies between perspectives could be derived but also where the expected contradictions for students who were part of the Tibetan diaspora in India might also lie from living within several different variations of identity construct (Moran-Ellis *et al.*, 2006).

Therefore, this and the following points affirmed the use of visual methods alongside interviews and observations to support the broad narrative. First, our experience in Sri Lanka taught us that our own views were probably wrong. Second, the economy of pictures in conveying complex feelings and perceptions (Leitch, 2006) meant in a short space of time we could get a substantial amount of data. Third, the narrative that was to be produced for the museum was to include visual artefacts, so some of the 'data' would end up directly representing the voices of the Tibetan contributors more directly. Finally, the methods themselves allowed a degree of freedom to depart from the constraints inherent in language.

When conducting research across cultures one needs to ensure that the research methods used transfer and offer valid data. There are well-established differences across cultures along a range of psychological dimensions. This is a well-known problem that is normally referred to as the WEIRD population of research participants; the acronym stands for Western Educated Industrialised Rich Democratic (Henrich, Heine and Norenzayan, 2010; see also Arnett, 2008). The essential argument is that much research exploring human personality, behavioural characteristics and identity has been conducted on students from universities in the developing world. Proponents of WEIRD suggest that using tools developed in WEIRD countries do not necessarily reflect the populations being researched. Henrich, Heine and Norenzayan (2010) explore a variety of areas in which cultural differences are evident for psychological processes that are assumed to be universal (e.g., personality traits). Apart from the methods used possibly being unsuitable, the understanding of what research is and what its data should 'look' like may also be perceived differently depending on one's cultural outlook.

One way to partially bypass this problem is to allow the participants themselves to explain how they feel in their own words (or pictures) without any structured researcher mediation. In this sense, our research became semi-ethnographic, as the data we collected were not subject to pre-existing hypotheses or coded with any existing coding method. The postcard task and subsequent short essays allowed the participants to creatively express themselves in how they saw their lives and their world with minimal interference from the researchers. The analysis performed on the data was then largely inductive and participant driven (Heisley and Levy, 1991).

An inductive process is an ideal way to accrue the research data we needed. The narrative we are helping to create to express Tibetan identity and lived experience needs to be independent of the views from outside of the community itself. To further assist in this independence we utilised four methods to form a triangulated approach (Johnson, Onwuegbuzie and Turner, 2008; Katsiaficas *et al.*, 2011) to help confirm any inductive conclusions we would arrive at through later analyses. The postcard task was accompanied by a photo-production/elicitation

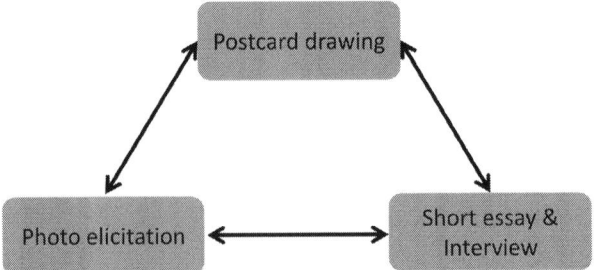

FIGURE 10.2 Triangulation of methods.

task (see following sections), and also verbal and text-based tasks (a short essay and a verbal interview). The order of the presentation of the tasks was dictated through the relationship we built up with the Tibetan students. Therefore, to build confidence in the initial stages, the postcard task was chosen. The task instructions were closely aligned to those developed from prompts in previous research for the construction of hand-drawn identity maps (Katsiaficas *et al.*, 2011). From this the Tibetan students were encouraged to write in English about a topic they were very familiar with. As the relationship built, a number of students were keen to volunteer to take photographs and then participate in interviews. During the interviews all the material from the previous tasks was included as discussion points. In this way any conclusions that are drawn from one task can be confirmed by inspection of the other data sources. Subsequent analyses and interpretations are beyond the scope and rationale of this chapter.

A limitation of the postcard method (and to some extent participant-generated visual methods in general) is the need for some form of additional explanation after the creative process is complete to describe the thinking behind the work. This also helps to keep the data and its analysis independent of the researchers' subjective biases. However, when engaging in cross-cultural research the social context in which the images are produced and those who produce them have an impact upon them, which does benefit from critical reflection from both the producer and the researcher (Rose, 2002). Coming into this research both authors had very defined and established views of how a Tibetan community would see itself. The process of living with the community, establishing long-term friendships and engaging in these tasks ourselves allowed us to let the participants themselves re-define our own views and understanding.

Methods

Ethics

As the project was led by psychology staff, all ethical issues were duly considered and fully complied with the British Psychological Society (BPS) Code of Ethics.

As an international project, great care was taken to ensure that the research was sensitive to the needs and cultural expectations of the respective host communities. All participants gave informed consent for their words and artwork to be included in the research. Anonymity was ensured through the use of pseudonyms, participants were advised they could withdraw from the research at any time and all data were maintained confidentially through means of physical locked storage and password protection.

Participants

UK volunteers

Eight volunteer student teachers (six females) from Liverpool Hope University, UK were involved in the project over a 2-year period. Their ages ranged from 19 to 27 years and they studied a range of subjects. The student teachers represented all 3 years of undergraduate study and there were two postgraduates. None of the students had visited Asia before and they did not have any familiarity with the Tibetan community, either in the UK or in India. Two student teachers were placed in the Tibetan Hostel in Delhi in 2013 and three in 2014 (all females), one of whom had also been involved in the 2013 project; four student teachers (two females) were placed in the Tibetan Vocational Centre in Dehradun in 2014.

Tibetan volunteers

Seventy-two Tibetan students (thirty-six females) participated in the tasks. Thirty-four students (fourteen females) were studying a range of courses at the University of Delhi, India, and living at the Tibetan Hostel. They participated in Phases 1, 2 and 4 with representatives from this group participating in Phase 3. Twenty-eight students (eighteen females) were from the Tibetan Vocational Centre in Dehradun and they participated in Phases 1 and 2 of the tasks. Fifty-one students were born in India and twenty-one (nineteen exiled from Tibet) were born outside of the country. They ranged in age from 18 to 22 years. None of the students were trained in art. The backgrounds of the students varied. Some were brought up and educated in Tibetan Children's Homes, while others resided with their parents but received their elementary and secondary education in Tibetan schools in India. The group of students who were born outside of India received some of their very early education in those countries (Tibet, Nepal and Bhutan). All of the students reported that, prior to attending university, occasions were extremely rare for them to integrate socially and educationally with their Indian and Western counterparts.

Materials and procedure

As previously mentioned the tasks the students participated in were divided into four phases and are outlined next (see Figure 10.3):

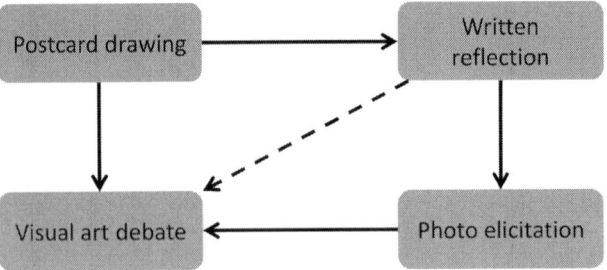

FIGURE 10.3 Schematic of phases in the use of visual representations.

Phase 1: Identity mapping as a means of developing a visual narrative of the relationship between the Tibetan students and their homeland

Within the refugee community it seemed that an important starting point for discourse about their beliefs would be to ask the Tibetan students to mirror the reality of what they believed a home like Tibet (Bhod) would look like. After initially checking that they were familiar with the concept of a postcard, the Tibetan students were asked to imagine they were going to send one to someone and wanted the illustration on the front of it to tell them something about how they saw Tibet. They were provided with a 10 cm x 15 cm white postcard and assorted coloured drawing materials and they were instructed to include as many social, ethnic and religious identities associated with Tibet as they could or they chose to. In addition, they could use drawings, colours, symbols, words or whatever other means they chose, to reflect how they saw Tibet (Katsiaficas *et al.*, 2011). They were also asked to record their personal details on the reverse of the postcard. The following page contains examples of the postcards (see Figure 10.4).

Phase 2: Speaking and writing about the imagery encapsulated on the postcards

The postcards not only served as a point of analysis for the student teachers from the UK to gain a greater understanding of the feelings and beliefs held by the Tibetan students about their exiled homeland but also as a prompt for the Tibetan students to write about what the postcards represented. This supplementary opportunity allowed the UK student teachers (see Figure 10.5) to gain an insight into the variation in skill level evident in the Tibetan students' writing and the confidence they seemed to have in communicating in English. The nature of the course demanded that the UK student teachers became familiar with the writing skills of the Tibetan students. It is common for people to feel more confident to write about what they know rather than impose something much more academically challenging in the early stages of an English language focused programme. The UK student teachers

FIGURE 10.4 Postcard examples completed in Delhi, 2013.

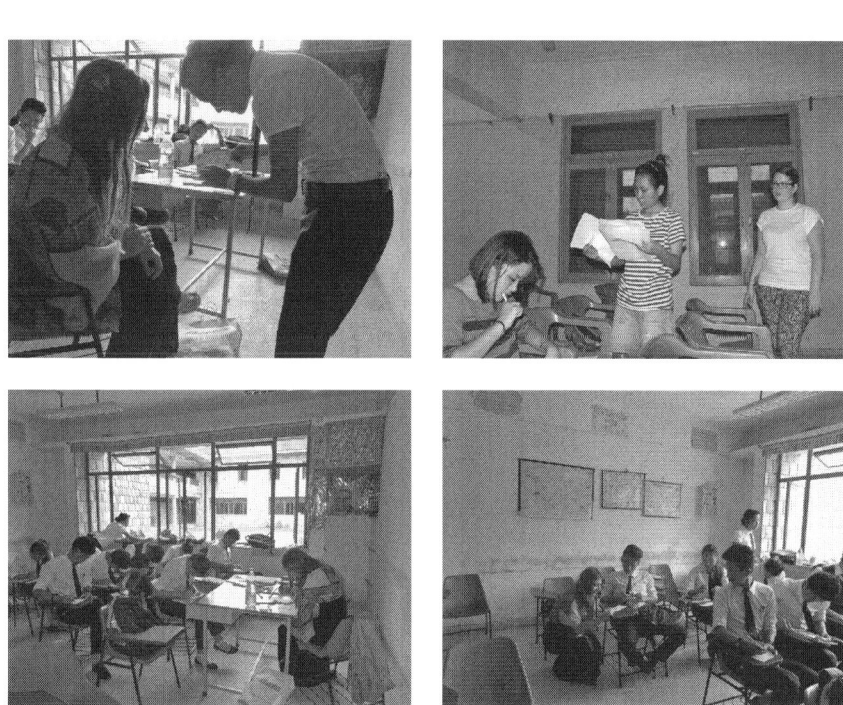

FIGURE 10.5 Two of the student teachers working on a postcard task in Dehradun, 2014, and Delhi, 2013.

provided feedback on this in the context of demonstrating an interest in the subject matter to the Tibetan students. The information gained provided them with a potential avenue to structure forthcoming sessions to support the development of those aspects of writing that required attention.

Phase 3: Photo-elicitation narratives on the relationship between Tibetan students and India

Six of the Tibetan university students (two females) reported earlier, volunteered to participate in this. This method was designed to encourage the students' expressive language skills. The UK student teachers provided the Tibetan students who had subsequently volunteered to participate in this phase with digital cameras permanently donated to the host country by the media services department of our home institution. The Tibetan students were asked to take photographs of modern Tibetan life as an extension to the postcard task which focused on the imagined (and in some cases real) experience of their homeland. They were encouraged to explore their relationships with others and the various social contexts they engaged in. Prior to the task, the students were instructed how to use the camera and provided with a practice opportunity. No formal training in photography skills was required. In addition, they were orientated to representing their views of 'Tibetanness' as part of a diasporic community within their images. It was left to the students to consider what they might conceptualise this to be. In contrast to previous outlines of this methodology, the individual students decided upon how many photographs they would need to accomplish this. Exemplar photographs are provided in Figure 10.6. Along with the other visual and verbal narratives obtained through the postcard task, they formed the basis of the open-ended interviews that were undertaken. The purpose of using multiple sources of information to inform the interviews was to encourage the development of ideas about the diversity and complexity of Tibetan diasporic identity so that new insights and understandings could be created (Moran-Ellis *et al.*, 2006; Smythe and McKenzie, 2010). The length of the interviews was directed by the Tibetan students and was largely dependent on the number of images they decided to present. On average, the interviews lasted approximately 1 hour.

The images were crucial to providing the Tibetan students with the confidence to find the language to describe their everyday lives and their feelings and emotions associated with them. For example, from some of the images Tenzin★ presented and the way he discussed them in the interview, it was clear music was a significant feature of his current lifestyle. It appeared to be a focal point for the group and other Tibetan exiles that he associates with and dominates their social activities. Our interpretation was that it provided a strong point of social cohesion between the Tibetan students and provided a means for self-expression. Even though he indicated an awareness of different styles of music, a photograph of a sign in his

★Names changed to protect identity

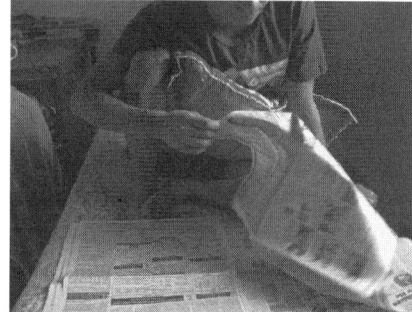

FIGURE 10.6 Examples of the photo-elicitation task.

accommodation stated 'Support Tibetan Music'. The interview allowed us to develop the symbolic importance of this further. It seems that Tenzin did not enjoy the sound of Tibetan music produced in India because of the influences within it from Indian music culture. Rather, he saw 'Tibetan music' from Tibet as a means of self-expression of negative viewpoints towards the Chinese Government of his homeland.

In contrast, Tsering★ tended to present a number of images of herself during different parts of a typical day, these included studying at university and visiting the Tibetan market. In all those images she either wore a T-shirt or carried a bag that proclaimed 'Free Tibet'. In class she would typically be dressed in a plain T-shirt and shorts. Consequently, the images provided open-ended prompts from which to create conversations about how the Tibetan students negotiate the multiplicity of their lives in India. It aroused descriptions of disparities that can lead to conflict and tensions between themselves and both their own community and those beyond it (Katsiaficas *et al.*, 2011). It also brought out the emotional highs and lows of their lives alongside the differences in their thinking about their situation, both within the Tibetan group and within themselves over time. For those who participated in this phase, it was clear that once they started talking, they wanted to tell us more. This evolved and formed the basis of the focus group debate in relation to identity and citizenship that occurred in Phase 4.

Phase 4: Focus group debate on the relationship between Contemporary Tibetan Art and the lived lives of the Tibetan community at the hostel

The focus group involved all the students and student teachers who were living at the Tibetan Hostel in Rohini, Delhi. The UK team's relationship with members of the Tibetan Art Collective in Delhi (e.g., Thupten, Tenzing, Tenzin, Gyurmey and Latika) provided a development opportunity to represent on film the discourse of the students when they were provided with direct visual imagery of Contemporary Tibetan Art from Tibetan artists and photographers. The activity within the focus group was developed in the style of a debate which the students would be familiar with. It was led by Thupten and Simon and recorded by Lorna. The Tibetan students asked questions, presented their views on art and the challenges they faced within their own lives. They also asked for clarification on, for example, 'What makes the art Tibetan?' Crucially, the students were provided with the opportunity to interact with other people in their community who they were unfamiliar with but who spoke English. This met a further aim by facilitating an understanding of the diversity of ways in which people can express themselves. In the second year of the project, this was followed-up with a visit from well-known Tibetan poet, Bhuchung D. Sonam, some of whose work focuses on feelings of isolation in exile.

Student reflections of the postcard task

We asked the UK student teachers and the Tibetan students about their experiences in participating in the task. They were given some pointers as a guide, for example:

- What were their initial thoughts about the task? What they were being asked to do?
- How did they find engaging with the task and with UK/Tibetan students?
- How useful was it in breaking down barriers in communication?
- What could be done to improve the learning experience?

The themes that emerged from the reflections (an overview is reported in Figure 10.7) suggest that prior knowledge and experience in using art in social or therapeutic situations will make the student more likely to engage with such methods in future projects. This included using images of self-identity to explore specific issues relating to confidence or suggesting ways in which the task could be extended within a research paradigm. For example, in examining:

> How religion affects perception: pretty much all the students drew empowering images of Tibet and I think this attitude is heavily influenced by their Buddhist beliefs. I think an orphan with no belief would draw something quite different.

> (UK student teacher)

One of the challenges is the similarity in narrative between the students when portraying images of Tibet, that is, many of the students produced work that was discursively culturally bound. From a researcher perspective this would not compromise the postcards as data because it would encourage an exploration into why the narratives were very similar. A student teacher questioned the imagery associated with a strong Tibetan cultural and community identity as

> to what extent are the [Tibetan] students giving what 'we' [Westerners] want to see/hear with regards to images and portrayals of Tibet as opposed to autonomous thought.
>
> (UK student teacher)

There are probably several points being made here. The idea of autonomous thought could be more related to the scripted ideas about what it is to be Tibetan; those ideas that are conveyed by the revered HH Dalai Lama and which are passed down through families. When conducting a thematic analysis of the postcards there were four main differences encapsulated in the following themes:

* paradise/beauty/nomad lifestyle
* before and after occupation by Chinese in 1959
* violence and aggression
* pollution.

Of note were the gender differences that emerged. For example, females did not depict any form of violence and aggression on their postcards. However, the majority of the postcards reflect the themes surrounding a sense of community, as a UK student teacher comments:

> Yaks, prayer flags etc. . . . This speaks volumes in that the group or community identity takes precedence over anything else.
>
> (UK student teacher)

In order to address the question regarding the degree of autonomy represented in the drawings, the student teachers suggest that

> perhaps if this was undertaken as a solo task, taken away overnight to complete, that could minimise 'peer pressure' to provide an image which fits with the group and allow more time for further introspection.
>
> (UK student teacher)

The theme of introspection was highlighted by the Tibetan students themselves, one of whom suggested that:

> My initial thoughts about postcard writing was of Bryan Lewis Saunder, where he drew 50 different portrait of himself after taking numerous drugs. I believe

postcard help us understand oneself . . . All expression of arts comes from knowing oneself, introspecting oneself. Never had in my life I had drawn a postcard or done any self-portrait. It was a little difficult at first to put everything about yourself at short notice.

(Tibetan student)

This suggests that the Tibetan students did find difficulty with the task. This was not so apparent to the UK student teachers who commented on how easily they adapted to it. It is also interesting that the Tibetan students viewed the task as synonymous with their own identity when, in actual fact, they were initially asked to draw what Tibet was like to them. The UK student teachers agreed that the Tibetan students 'didn't have much confidence in their English skills'. An advantage of the postcard task that the UK students identified was that

when asked to talk about something they [Tibetan students] were passionate about, their passion to express themselves seemed to override their fear of making mistakes while speaking.

Further, that the task also 'encourages a degree of openness between all participants and allows questions to be asked and answered' (UK student teacher).

However, as the quote below illustrates, conversely the Tibetan students struggled with the concept of openness:

It was at first difficult to breakdown certain stereotype and prejudice we had of people from west. Like, how should one make presentable in front of them, will they will be fine with our laid back attitude, or certain things during class. I had great session with them. We mostly stayed silent at first except for few nodding yes and no. Had they been silent like us, our class would have become meditation centre.

(Tibetan student)

In discussing the differences between themselves and the Tibetan students, the UK student teachers indicated that they became aware from the outset of the fundamental differences in thought processes.

The Tibetan students were far more ready . . . with an idea of who they were and what they could draw to represent this, for example, mountainous scenery or plains of Tibet.

(UK student teacher)

The student teachers also made comments about the practicalities of administering the task. For example, they queried, 'why the drawings needed to be done on postcards' with suggestions that if this was not 'necessary then it would be better to give them a bigger surface area to draw on'. Of interest, while Tibetan students questioned the research experience, they commended the opportunities for creative expression that the postcard task presented, particularly the opportunity for group discussion and subsequent activities,

> From my earliest memories of PhD student visiting our school, distributing questionnaire and conducting research on psychology of Tibetan student. Almost all their finding has same result: Low self-confidence, self-esteem. Not much is being done in school ... I think this program is small step towards breaking barrier in conversation between our students. Such program needs to reach schools.
>
> (Tibetan student)

> Programs like writing postcard, photography, movie screening and numerous group discussion are seldom done in schools. From what I had observed, such program are helping one in opening up to talk.
>
> (Tibetan student)

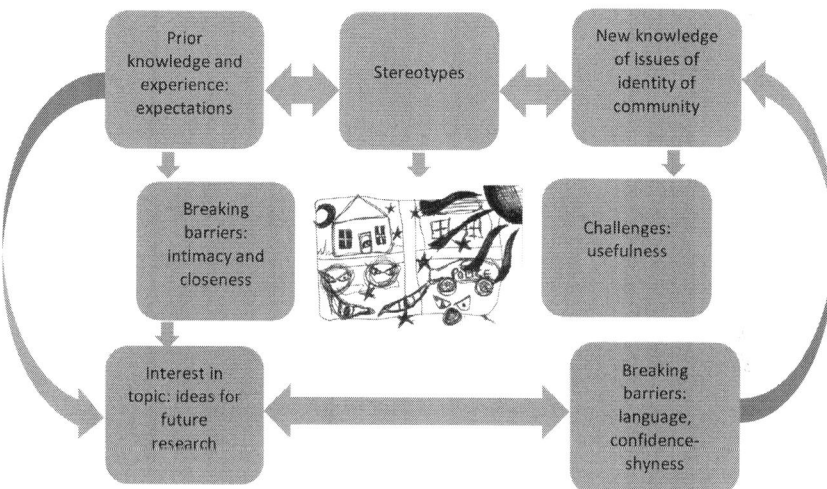

FIGURE 10.7 Overview of themes and reflective processes.

Our reflections

It has been important that our research design extrapolated meaningful data that moved away from Western pre-conceived stereotyping of Tibetan culture. In order to do this we had to be prepared to be open about our own thoughts, feelings and ideas to the students both before and during the experiences we were encountering. However, the dynamic of the relationship had to be balanced in order not to burden the students with any emotional fallout we might otherwise encounter. Although we both have different viewpoints at times, it is natural after working together on so many projects that there will be a synergy in outlook, for example, it never occurred to us that the group we were working with would not be part of the decision-making process in the materials we used. It was interesting when we read research relating to the use of photo-elicitation techniques (e.g., Harper, 2012) that typically the researchers take the photographs. It had not been a consideration that we would be the ones taking the photographs. Our focus was always on trying to find ways for the Tibetan students to decide on what they wanted to portray and talk about. This resulted in a collage of viewpoints and experiences.

Therefore, the use of visual methods led to changes in the way we approached and thought about interaction with our host communities. It became more focused on building up lasting friendships with individuals within the host community rather than past experience where commitment was largely with the host community to work with different individuals each year. In particular, this meant strengthening our resolve to encourage reciprocal arrangements in fostering cross-cultural learning. However, what we believe to be fair and equitable is not always possible due to current UK visa restrictions. This made us aware of potential setbacks which need to be considered when planning and designing projects of this nature.

More than anything this work has brought to the fore a conscious desire to see our partner communities as friends who are more than able to choose the direction that they want their voices to be heard. By being creative ourselves, and drawing on our experiences we have realised that we are in the privileged position to facilitate this process. The postcard task has provided us with an opportunity to engage more deeply with the individuals in the communities in Sri Lanka and India and gather rich meaningful data. Rather than perceiving these respective communities as a group we have a greater awareness and understanding of the individuals within, and the conflicts and tensions that consume their lives. This has encouraged us to take a more research-focused approach that subsequently has informed our teaching environment while overseas and at our home institution. We now have a far greater appreciation for the crossover of methods in teaching and research, which has impacted greatly on our practice as we gained confidence ourselves in trying new methods and pushing ourselves beyond our comfort zone.

Conclusion

This chapter focused on a number of international field trips and interventions which employed visual methods. The premise was that traditional research methods are dependent on cultural experience and outlook. However, cross-cultural environments are served particularly well by visual methods as differences in language are circumvented.

The tasks employed focused on participants' explanations of their feelings and experiences in a largely fluid and unstructured manner which gave them a freedom of expression. The postcard task had multiple uses because it allowed Tibetan students' views to be expressed about their homeland and also provided the UK student teachers with an opportunity to observe the English writing skill level among the Tibetan students. As an extension task, Tibetan students were asked to take photographs of the social context that they typically engaged in. Furthermore, interviews were conducted to elicit further information about Tibetan identity, with the photographs forming the basis from which to explore emotions regarding their everyday life. This revealed information about the multiplicity of their identities in India. Throughout the tasks, the importance of social context was considered and there was a further opportunity to be involved in a community-based focus group. Here, students presented their views on their life challenges, alongside identifying with and socialising with English speaking members of their community. Identities were closely aligned with a sense of community and traditional values.

With regard to the UK student reflections, the students saw the benefit in the tasks but concerns were raised regarding the individuality and autonomy of the thoughts and resultant drawings. However, while it was a seemingly collective identity, the Tibetan students had a clear idea of themselves and how to draw a representation of this. Further reflections from the UK students highlighted the perceived benefits of visual tasks in breaking down stereotypes and prejudices, particularly as language barriers were removed. Our reflections were that our interaction in this environment formed a patchwork of viewpoints and perspectives which subsequently changed our interaction with the Tibetans with whom we worked. The visual methods used allowed us a starting point to engage more deeply

REFLECTIVE ACTIVITIES

Below are four suggestions for reflective activities that can be based around the use of some of the visual methods reported in this chapter:

1   Postcard reflections
To help provide an insight into interpreting the identities drawn on the postcards, begin by drawing images of your own home and life. How do you feel about drawing rather than talking or writing about this?

2   Mind-mapping
Using a mind-map as an organisational device, document the process of using photo-production techniques in comparison to asking people to create a drawing. Do you expect the responses to differ between the two visual methods? What are the links between them? What overall conclusion can you draw?

3   Small group discussions
Using the images in this chapter, in small groups compare and contrast them in relation to your current understanding of ideas about culture and identity.

4   A dilemma
Picture this. You have given a camera to a fellow student. You think that this will provide a real insight into their lives. Discuss in pairs what the possible difficulties might be with this?

with the individuals and, their stories and more widely understand community life. Our experience of using visual methods has been an emergent journey that has appended our research toolbox but beyond that has informed our pedagogy and enriched our classroom practice.

Suggested reading

Bourke, L., Bamber., P. and Lyons, M. (2012). Global citizens: who are they? *Education, citizenship and social justice*, 7(2), 161–74.

Harper, D. (2002). Talking about pictures: A case for photo elicitation. *Visual Studies*, 17(1), 13–26.

Leitch, R. (2006). Limitations of language: developing arts-based creative narrative in stories of teachers' identities. *Teachers and Training: Theory and Practice*, 12(5), 549–69.

Reavey, P. (2011). *Visual methods in psychology: Using and interpreting images in qualitative research.* Hove, UK: Psychology Press.

References

Arnett, J. (2008). The neglected 95%: why American psychology needs to become less American. *American Psychologist*, 63, 602–14.

Biggs, J. and Tang, C. (2011). *Teaching for quality learning at university.* Berkshire, UK: McGraw-Hill.

Bourke, L., Bamber., P. and Lyons, M. (2012). Global citizens: Who are they? *Education, Citizenship and Social Justice*, 7(2), 161–74.

Brown S. and Knight, P. (1994). *Assessing learners in higher education*, London: Kogan Page.

Buckingham, D. (2009). 'Creative' visual methods in media research: possibilities, problems and proposals. *Media Culture Society*, 31(4), 633–52.

Entwistle, N. (2009). *Teaching for understanding at university: deep approaches and distinctive ways of thinking.* Basingstoke, UK: Macmillan Palgrave.

Frost, N. (2009). Do you know what I mean? The use of a pluralistic narrative analysis approach in the interpretation of an interview. *Qualitative Research*, 9(1), 9–29.

Graham, A. and Kilpatrick, R. (2010). Understanding children's educational experiences through image-based research. In J. Scott Jones and S. Watt (eds), *Ethnography in social science practice* (pp. 89–106). London: Routledge.

Harper, D. (2002). Talking about pictures: a case for photo elicitation. *Visual Studies*, 17(1), 13–26.

Harper, D. (2012). *Visual sociology.* Abingdon, UK: Routledge.

Heisley, D.D. and Levy, S.J. (1991). Autodriving: a photoelicitation technique. *Journal of Consumer Research*, 18, 257–72.

Henrich, J., Heine, S.J. and Norenzayan, A. (2010). The weirdest people in the world? *Behavioral and Brain Sciences*, 33, 61–135.

Hills, L.A. (2006). Playing the field(s): an exploration of change, conformity and conflict in girls' understandings of gendered physicality in physical education. *Gender and Education*, 189(5), 539–56.

Johnson, R.B., Onwuegbuzie, A.J. and Turner, L.A. (2008). Towards a definition of mixed methods research. *Journal of Mixed Methods Research*, 1, 112–33.

Katsiaficas, D., Futch, V.A., Fine, M. and Sirin, S.R. (2011). Everyday hyphens: exploring youth identities with methodological and analytic pluralism. *Qualitative Research in Psychology*, 8, 120–39.

Leitch, R. (2006). Limitations of language: developing arts-based creative narrative in stories of teachers' identities. *Teachers and Training: Theory and Practice*, *12*(5), 549–69.

Long, J. and Carless, D. (2010). Hearing, listening and acting. In M. O'Sullivan and A. MacPhail (eds), *Young people's voices in physical education and youth sport* (pp. 213–15). London: Routledge.

Morais, D.B. and Ogden, A.C. (2011). Initial development and validation of the global citizenship scale. *Journal of Studies in International Education*, *15*(5), 445–66.

Moran-Ellis, J., Alexander, V.D., Cronin, A., Dickinson, M., Fielding, J., Sleney, J. and Thomas, H. (2006). Triangulation and integration: processes, claims and implications. *Qualitative Research*, *6*(1), 45–59.

Phoenix, C. (2010). Seeing the world of physical culture: the potential of visual methods for qualitative research in sport and exercise. *Qualitative Research in Sport and Exercise*, *2*(2), 93–108.

Pink, S. (2012). *Advances in visual methodology*. London: Sage Publications.

Reavey, P. (2011). *Visual methods in psychology: using and interpreting images in qualitative research*. Hove, UK: Psychology Press.

Rose, G. (2002). *Visual methodologies: an introduction to the interpretation of visual materials*. London: Sage Publications.

Smythe, W.E. and McKenzie, S.A. (2010). A vision of dialogical pluralism in psychology. *New Ideas in Psychology*, *28*(2), 227–34.

Watt, S. and Wakefield, C. (2014). Picture it! The use of visual methods in psychology teaching. *Psychology Teaching Review*, *20*(1), 68–77.

PART III
Reflections

11

PRACTICAL APPLICATIONS OF TEACHING VISUAL METHODS

Sal Watt and Caroline Wakefield

Qualitative research continues to gain ground across the social sciences but while research has adopted creative methods of data collection, such creativity has often not translated significantly onto higher education curricula, where in the main qualitative techniques tend to focus on interviews, focus groups and observation. This chapter will consider the overarching benefits and challenges of using and teaching visual methods in higher education. We will focus on the preceding case studies, giving examples of good practice and offering practical advice and potential solutions for commonly arising issues. In addition to the many examples of good practice throughout the chapters that can be drawn upon, the following chapter refers to the bank of practitioner resources that can be found in Chapter 12, which we hope will be useful.

Learning and teaching

In teaching, like most other professions, time is always in short supply and whatever changes we consider usually necessitate an audit trail of form filling before we can instigate curricular change. However, in our experience and that of the other contributors in this text, introducing a visual method to the curriculum can be well worth the effort and time taken, particularly when we witness the creative work our students produce. Designing curricula is often a bit of a 'chicken and egg' situation; what comes first, the visual method to be taught, the learning objectives, mode of teaching, the assessment and so it goes on. At the outset, we would recommend investing considerable time in thinking through the many factors involved when changing or embedding new material into a curriculum.

In determining the type of visual methods to be taught, there is a range of questions that need to be considered. For example, is there a visual method that might lead on from, or complement, another method of data collection that students have already experienced? In our case, students had already gained experience of conducting a simple observational study and, in doing so, had already some experience of devising a basic floor plan. Through an exemplar, we had illustrated to students the usefulness of a visual floor plan that detailed the contents of an observational setting, for example, the seating or furniture in the setting, the use of male and female symbols to denote gender alongside a five-bar gate strategy that quantified the number of each within the setting. As the students had already completed a drawing of a simple floor plan that would visually complement observational field notes, the progression seemed to make sense to our students. For example, one student reflected,

> the more I find out and think about visual methods and visual ethnography the more I value it as a research method. Images have an instant impact and breach age, class, language and cultural divides (music and dance similarly have this characteristic), whereas writing is not so universal this subsequently provides a methodological equality.

As the student quote above illustrates, a natural trajectory existed with one visual method flowing into another that our students had previously experienced. When embedding visual methods into the curriculum, we would recommend such a trajectory as advantageous conceptually because it provides theoretical continuity for students, which then aids both confidence and practical application.

Once it is established how a visual method could lead on from other methods taught, then the focus shifts to establishing associated learning objectives and assessment criteria, but in doing so it becomes necessary to think about the kind of projects and topic areas students could undertake. In our experience not all students immediately embrace the creative nature of using a visual method and we have found it beneficial to invest time in talking through possible options with students. Resource One in Chapter 12 provides a number of ideas and scenarios we have built up over time when working with students. The breadth of topic areas is wide, and assessing what is ethically viable takes time. A further advantage of investing time in working through topic options with the students, is that it adds a collaborative dimension to the student work which importantly seems to give students confidence, particularly those who might shy away from the creativity of the chosen method. While most students engage with the new technique and its creative nature, some do not. In Edd Pitt's chapter, he talks about those students who ask the question, 'what do I draw?', while we have experience of students asking 'what shall I photograph?' We share Edd's experience that if, as teachers, we invest time in developing a working relationship with our students, this facilitates discussion and is particularly important in establishing topic areas and associated procedural and creative practicalities. In short, ongoing working relationships and discussion break down the unfamiliar and enable the students to widen their imagination about what is possible.

New to teaching visual methods, we learned a hard lesson very quickly when we realised that our students needed much clearer dissemination of the aims of the visual project and how these linked in with the module's wider learning outcomes and assessment. Therefore, investing time at the planning stage is essential for both the students and the practitioners and we would suggest posing the following questions might be helpful.

- What do I want my students to learn from such a method?
- How feasible is the task being set?
- What is the practical application of the chosen visual method beyond university study?
- Will the chosen visual method upskill and prepare the student for the workplace?
- How will I evaluate the student experience?

These are just a few of the questions that must be firmly addressed in order to ensure the learning outcomes set are meaningful and doable. Designing curricula is necessarily cyclic in nature and therefore it is not possible to set learning outcomes without mapping these onto assessment (and vice versa). In determining these respective parameters, as the earlier chapters have illustrated, it is crucial to engage students in a method that has relevance or incorporates real life through 'everyday real life examples'. Our chosen method capitalised on the practice of taking photographs as a method that would reflectively speak to students in respect of their everyday lives. In Chapter 7, Julie Taylor's experience working with students was predicated on bricolage as a means of drawing together diverse methods (some but not all visual) whereby students set about devising an intervention that responded to a social issue. Similarly in Chapter 5, Moira Lafferty's work with students in incorporating film in the curricula provided opportunity for students to reflect on psychological sporting scenarios where fieldwork would not be possible.

Resource Two in Chapter 12 provides a list of possible learning outcomes. The list is not exhaustive but a starting point from which to consider discipline-specific outcomes. One approach illustrated in Chapter 7 through Julie Taylor's teaching is to include students in the design of a project assessment, which necessarily then impacts through to learning outcomes and ensures student knowledge of, and therefore engagement with, the associated criteria. Good research often evolves to meet the project's aims and the same can be said of teaching when responding to the needs of students or, as in the case of the students in Julie's classes, when responding to a social issue or problem. Therefore, while overarching learning outcomes can be established, how these can be achieved can open up exciting and creative avenues for collaborative discussion with students. Joel Rookwood in Chapter 8 also makes the point that collaborative working both in research design and through the methods employed in sessions makes a valid contribution in developing student understanding and as such enhances student experience. The point made earlier was that aspects of curriculum design cannot be neatly compartmentalised but, instead, the process is a cyclic conundrum that oscillates between aims and objectives, learning outcomes, assessment, evaluation, student experience and so on. In addition to the questions posed above, Resource Three lists further key questions that need careful consideration and which feed forward into the other aspects of curriculum design. Once it has been established which visual method, or combination of methods is viable and draft learning outcomes have been determined, our attention must turn to ethics.

Ethical considerations

Despite the prevalence of imagery through social media and everyday practices of taking photographs we must, of course, ensure that when teaching visual methods we instil good practice into our students around consent, inclusion and, in particular with visual methods, participant rights of privacy. As Julie Scott Jones has illustrated throughout Chapter 3, ethical issues are wide, far-reaching and present particular problems in respect of visual methods of data collection. Too often ethics is thought of as a tick-box exercise but teaching visual methods offers an opportunity to bring alive and explore, often through personal experience of social media, how taking photographs or filming can lead to deception and/or the infringement of human/participant rights if we do not put adequate measures in place. Therefore, some of the unique ethical issues that can emerge when using visual methods provide us with ideal opportunity to unpack ethical concerns and teach students that ethics is a necessary and relevant process; that it is not simply about adhering to ethical codes of practice but a practice that must be integrated into every stage of the research process and embodied by researchers and student researchers alike.

As outlined in Chapter 4, the projects we have set our students have found them taking on the dual role of being both the researcher and the researched, which has necessitated the students negotiating ethics from both perspectives. In the first instance, once the topic area is established, issues of consent must be addressed as a matter of course. For example, if students are taking photographs of human participants or using existing photographs, then informed consent must be obtained (see Resource Four for an exemplar). If taking photographs or filming in a public space then, as determined by disciplinary bodies such as the British Sociological Association (BSA) or the British Psychological Society (BPS), this should only take place in public spaces where individuals might ordinarily expect to be photographed or filmed. In complying with our home institution and the BPS Code of Research Practice, our students completed an ethics checklist and ethics application form, (see Resource Four), prepared an information sheet and an informed consent form (see Resources Five and Six for example guidance). In the case of a member of the public querying with the students what they were doing, students also prepared a public information sheet (see Resource Seven).

The assessment we determined for our students was a group assessment whereby the students shared their photographs with each other. In terms of ethics, this added another dimension that needed careful consideration in respect of issues of trust and responsibility. We encouraged the students to spend time thinking through these issues and requested that an ethical agreement must be collaboratively constructed to ensure each group member was clear about the handling of each other's photographs and in agreement with any other related ethical issues the group identified. This element of the assessment took on a life of its own. The dual role of both researcher and researched found students engaging from a personal perspective as they debated the appropriate usage of their respective photographs. The embodiment of ethics was best illustrated through the ethical agreements that the students drew up. One such agreement, which we identified as an example of good practice, can be found in Resource Eight.

Throughout the chapters in this text, a number of distinct ethical issues and points have been raised. In Chapter 8, Joel Rookwood makes the point that in order to fully consider ethical issues and relay these to students, tutors are required to have sufficient training and/or practice of incorporating visual methods into the curriculum to ensure that the level of familiarity with the process impacts through to ethical considerations. For Julie Taylor's students (Chapter 7) who engaged in the various methods via a bricolage approach, this raised the potential of particular ethical dilemmas involved in creating specific and participant-orientated interventions.

Ethical considerations associated with fieldwork can be particularly problematic. For example, Janet Speake in Chapter 9 identifies the problems of taking photographs of others covertly/overtly. While our practice of using visual methods may be determined by a disciplinary code of practice when in the UK, once we take students on field trips abroad then further and wider ethical considerations must be given serious thought. Ethical practices considered acceptable in the UK should not be automatically generalised to other countries where ethical and cultural practices may be quite different. In Chapter 10, Simon Davies and Lorna Bourke, highlight the need to be sensitive to the expectations and needs of specific communities. In particular, their work in Sri Lanka and more recently with Tibetan communities makes us acutely aware of the ethical considerations necessary when working with an international population. The diversity of ethical considerations noted across the chapters highlights that ethics cannot be approached as a 'one size fits all' exercise but rather that a carefully considered specific thought process is needed from one project to the next. With ethical considerations met, we must now turn our attention to the methods that we utilise.

Methods

Earlier in this chapter, we suggested that it was advantageous to teach a visual method that naturally followed on from a method that students had already experienced. In our case, the natural progression from visual floor plans was to photographs.

However, a natural trajectory might not always be possible and the method could also be determined by the remit of the project or by the group being studied. Across this text, we have seen various visual methods deployed in the classroom to good effect. In Chapter 5, Moira's students presented 3-minute film clips and associated academic research that exemplified one of the core topics discussed in the module, by way of a summary or revision session. These were then drawn together by the tutor to ensure that the students could fully appreciate the relevance of the work to their studies. Acutely aware that novel approaches such as film could evoke anxiety, Moira also produced worksheets that scaffolded student learning and helped in staving off undue anxiety. In Chapter 6, Edd Pitt's pedagogic research required students to draw their experiences of assessment and feedback in higher education. These were then used as a basis for subsequent student interviews, which provoked valuable discussion between the researcher and student participant. Drawing in itself can be considered a novel approach, particularly to those students who find the prospect of drawing intimidating or inhibiting. However, here again, we can see good practice at work with students engaging in warm-up activities and receiving constant reassurance that it was the students' expression of feedback based on the drawings that was under scrutiny and not the students' drawing ability.

Julie Taylor's work with students provided a fascinating insight in unleashing student creativity through the development of a social intervention (Chapter 7). The diversity of a bricolage approach and a collaborative set-up which saw students working with stakeholders and service users is both highly creative and proactive in utilising those methods that are best fit for purpose. Using visual methods to design an intervention that met the needs of service users to tackle a societal problem or concern further highlights the creativity that the methods offer.

The case studies examined so far illustrate some of the different visual methods that can be employed, but we also need to think about the most appropriate methods to use when undertaking fieldwork in countries beyond the UK. Joel Rookwood in Chapter 8 explains how he has undertaken research across the world making films about several sporting experiences including mega-events and global projects. These have then been shown as part of lecture sessions to promote discussion about sporting engagement and participation across various population groups at both national and international level. Similarly, Janet Speake (Chapter 9) has worked nationally and internationally using visual methods with under-graduate students. Here students have undertaken a number of tasks including taking and reflecting upon a series of photographic images on topics such as regeneration, writing reflexive accounts about a landscape and their engagement with it, through to using a thematic approach of photographs in projects and dissertations. Possibly one of the most challenging and creative approaches is that taken by Simon Davies and Lorna Bourke (Chapter 10) who have worked internationally with Sri Lankan students, encouraging them to produce postcard pieces of art that visually represent love/happiness in their respective cultures, supplemented by short essays. While working with Tibetan students, a similar postcard task was completed and alongside photo-elicitation the student participants were asked to take photographs of modern Tibetan life, write a short essay and take part in an interview-based task. Each of the methods used informed the subsequent interviews and helped to develop an appreciation of the complexity and intricacies of Tibetan identity and culture.

Assessment

The methods used in the chapters outlined are varied, with Edd Pitt's informing pedagogic research, and Simon Davies and Lorna Bourke's international research and teaching informing summative feedback. Closer to home and in most cases, the methods taught have fed forward to formative assessment. With our own students, assessment has been made up of a group presentation (worth 50 per cent of the module) and an individual written report (making up the other 50 per cent). Students either took or identified existing photographs that they then shared with their group members. Each group member wrote a short reflective piece on both their own and others' photographs. As a group, they then came together to share their reflective interpretation of each other's photographs and a group thematic analysis pulled their respective themes together. The group presented their work orally and produced an A3 poster of the group's collaborative themes. For more details of the project we set for our own students see Resource Nine. In Chapter 12, other related resources are available; for example Resource Ten provides a bank of ideas for student projects. As reflexivity is crucially important at each stage of visual methods work, throughout the process we encouraged students to be self-reflective and reflexive, and Resource Eleven provides a template for a reflexive diary. At the outset, we also provided students with an outline for the required assessment project (Resource Nine) and the presentation feedback sheet (Resource Twelve) to encourage early engagement with the criteria and develop an understanding of expectations.

Similarly, the assessment set by Moira Lafferty (Chapter 5) was made up of 50 per cent group presentation and 50 per cent practical report. Moira discusses the ethical issues of group working and students' generalised perception that weaker students can score well if placed in a strong group. Therefore, a group processes rubric sheet can be introduced in order that group members' contributions can be evaluated. In Moira's assessment this rubric did not attract or deduct any marks (unlike the example found in Resource Thirteen), but more generally such rubrics can have a positive self-policing or monitoring effect, which goes some way to assuaging concern. Moira raises the interesting point that students often do not engage in continued learning, but rather think of assessment as tied discretely to a module's learning outcomes, only to be forgotten when it is completed. It raises questions such as, how do we encourage our students to think of the skills that they are learning as lifelong tools that can be referred to or used whenever the opportunity arises? The film clips that Moira's students identified carried no marks for identifying and sourcing the clips per se, but marks were awarded for the associated analysis. Students had to be reminded of this, which emphasises that however clear module handbooks, learning outcomes and so on are, there is a need to continually remind students of the aims and objectives of the assessment along with clear, transparent marking criteria. Edd Pitt (Chapter 6) advocates the need to be clear on how a visual method impacts beyond the assessment through to clearly mapped learning outcomes; essentially focusing on the learning rather than the assessment. However, students can pay scant regard to learning outcomes without fully understanding the synergy between learning outcomes and assessment. We would suggest that a student task that actively deconstructs the outcomes and illustrates how they map on to the assessment is the way forward here. Julie Taylor in Chapter 7 suggests that true student engagement is needed with the marking criteria in order to facilitate students attaining the highest grade bands, and the criteria, again, will differ from project to project. In Julie's case, students focused on intervention development and as such the marking criteria needed to be highly specific in respect of issues of access, inclusivity, range of methods used and consideration of related issues relevant to the intended target population, with marks being awarded for the process, the evaluation behind the intervention and the associated evidence. The work undertaken by Julie's students highlights the need for assessment marking criteria to be highly specific in order that the true worth of using a visual method is fully and appropriately rewarded.

As the previous sections have illustrated, designing curricula that use visual methods needs careful thought in respect of which visual method can be deployed, the potential ethical issues to be addressed and the assessment to be set. Introducing visual methods to curricula, like any curricular change, inevitably brings with it challenges. The following section will outline such challenges, using the case studies as examples.

Challenges

Throughout this text we have laboured the point that sufficient time and consideration are needed when changing the curriculum to include a visual method. The same of course is true of all curricular change but introducing visual methods brings with it unique challenges around, for example, ethics, student familiarity and confidence with the task set, and student ability to engage with its creativeness. First we will consider the issue of ethics. In our first year of teaching photo-elicitation as a visual method, either by using existing photographs or taking new photographs, our instruction to our students was that each student had to produce five photographs that fell into the topic area chosen by the group. The instruction from us was that topic area had to be driven by a psychological concept and had to approved by us as tutors. The topics largely revolved around the construction of identity with students taking photographs of their student life or reverting back to old school or family photographs. However, at the presentations the extent to which a few students had delved into their identity was a cause for concern (see Watt and Wakefield, 2014) and it was this experience that drove home to us the need to slow things down and give greater consideration to some aspects of the work. Our concern around ethics and duty of care to the students found us the following year taking a very cautious approach that determined the topic area of 'Place and Space' as a safer area where perhaps students could photograph how individuals interacted in a particular place or space. However, the pendulum swung the other way and the creativity of the work the students produced was too constrained (see Wakefield and Watt, 2015). We fell into the trap that Becker (2004) identified of being overly anxious about the ethical implications to the extent that we then stifled the work of our students. However, this does illustrate that time and care thinking through what you really want to achieve is time well spent. Therefore in our case we have pondered whether we needed to be more realistic regarding our expectations and even questioned the veracity of getting things right first time, given that we always need to be flexible to the needs of different student groups. Therefore, decisions around topic can be a challenge to practitioners but also to students. Despite our imposition, we also found that some students can feel very overwhelmed by having to think through a topic area. We had experience of one group in our first year who debated for hours what topic to choose and despite all our suggestions found it difficult to settle and agree a topic area. Eventually the group came up with the topic of representation of emotion. Initially we pondered how this might pan out as a photo-elicitation project but the time and care that particular student group took culminated in one of the best projects we have experienced (see Watt and Wakefield, 2014).

It is not just topic area that can be challenging with regard to student response, the actual methods themselves can equally stifle creativity or induce anxiety in respect of ability. In Edd Pitt's research (Chapter 6), he found that students asked the question, 'What should I draw?' in the same way as some of our students asked 'What should I photograph?' Edd makes the point that drawing is not a typical activity for individuals and is one that may be considered daunting with students trying to get it 'right' or more generally feeling intimidated or inhibited because they could not draw. Therefore while some basic level of ability is required to draw per se, a level of maturity is also required to recognise and be assured that the task is not about ability but one of expression, however abstract that might be. In Edd's research he makes the point that such abstraction is not a problem when it can usefully be explored by means of an interview. However, the difficulty that drawing does pose when used as an assessment is in respect of marking. Complemented by another method such as an interview that explores the expression, drawing is a useful research tool. In isolation drawing as a means of comparison between groups or students becomes less useful and difficult to mark because of its subjective nature. However, the same can be said to be true of any visual method and, therefore, issues of marking and subjective preference need to be carefully considered ahead of any planned assessment.

The issue of subjectivity is yet another challenge that needs to be considered is practitioner use of visual stimuli. Joel Rookwood (Chapter 8), responding to student criticism, took to making films for teaching in order to ensure that topic relevance was clear to the students and to eliminate the former damaging practice they had experienced of tutors randomly inserting clips, resulting in students' negative prior experience skewing their perceptions. Such selectivity (which is often unavoidable) as previously experienced by the students prevents the whole picture from being available, which can skew the subsequent reflections. While this might at times be unavoidable, it must at the very least be acknowledged by both the tutor and the student group, and measures considered to avoid this, such as those developed by Joel in Chapter 8.

A further challenge to teaching visual methods is the need to scaffold student learning and to build confidence. Janet Speake (Chapter 9) suggests that in order to ensure that the students have the necessary grounding to excel and fully appreciate the tasks set, a longitudinal approach to learning which scaffolds and supports students should be adopted with careful consideration being given to achievement at all levels. The question of student understanding and interpretation of the task being set is a challenge again in terms of subjective and cultural understanding. Instruction to one population may require additional explanation to another. Simon Davies and Lorna Bourke's (Chapter 10) work with international populations illustrates how cultural differences may require further clarification or explanation for the participants, for example the meanings that underpinned their postcard task. This additional consideration ensures that there is less subjective bias in interpretation and avoids the potential for students to produce socially desirable responses to, for example, drawing requests and interview tasks. Further, in some international populations, freedom of expression may not always be possible. For example, the images produced by the Tibetan students were culturally bound and are therefore similar between participants. While there are clear and unique benefits to working with an international population, so too are the cultural challenges that the practitioners experience. The challenges of teaching visual methods as this text has illustrated are many but so too are the benefits.

Benefits

Despite the many challenges there may be in using visual methods, these are far outweighed by the extensive range of benefits. In terms of learning and teaching, embedding visual methods into the curriculum increases interaction and debate between students and tutors. We see evidence of this throughout the chapters, whether in the films and film clips introduced by Moira (Chapter 5) and Joel (Chapter 8), drawing introduced by Edd (Chapter 6) and Simon and Lorna (Chapter 10) or through our own work with photographs. Our experience of talking through topic areas with students, in particular issues of ethics when our students have taken on the dual role of researcher and researched, have been gratifying experiences where we have seen our students embrace the embodiment of research and ethics. Without doubt the close working relationships we have built up have facilitated this. The wealth of visual techniques illustrated across the case studies of this text have illustrated how students' contextual understanding of topics through the use of visual methods has been enhanced, and furthering their engagement has led to developed student understanding in relation to assessment.

For example we can see through the work undertaken by Joel (Chapter 8) that the novel and creative approach of making films can be used to the tutor's advantage. Not only is it new and exciting for students compared to some more well-established methods, but it illustrates a broader acknowledgement of the lived experiences of others, one that is often not sensitive to language differences but which can facilitate students exploring differences in culture and identity, as we have further seen through Simon and Lorna's work in Chapter 10.

The methods in the case studies not only offer new opportunities to experience visual methods but also can expose students to distinct and sometimes marginalised groups, which broadens their wider understanding. We can see this through the work of Julie Taylor's students (Chapter 7) who from a bricolage approach used a range of techniques to reach specific and sometimes vulnerable groups in such a way that traditional methods may not. This is also true of Simon and Lorna's work (Chapter 10) with international populations where cross-cultural experience and appreciation of other ways of being have been gained and preconceived ideas about different cultures have been challenged. Further, both their work and that of Janet (Chapter 9) provides opportunity for students to engage in research and use methods that span language barriers. In Moira's work (Chapter 5) we can see how the use of film clips can replace practical training or working with clients to give a sense of 'doing' some practical application or creating a real-world experience. Direct experience of such factors is often limited for professional or ethical reasons, and therefore would not otherwise be possible. The film clips provide opportunity for students to see how theory can be applied to real life.

As teaching practitioners, for us the most rewarding benefit was witnessing our students' development. There is no question that using visual methods is empowering, drawing on student creativity, inducing reflection and engaging students in the reflexive process both in terms of their learning and personal development. All of the case studies identified that students were reflective of their learning experience and, in the main, enjoyed the creative process. Julie's students (Chapter 7) reported they felt empowered by their experience of developing a social intervention and working with their respective groups resulting in feelings of confidence that they now knew how to put theory into practice. The reflexive practice is perhaps best highlighted through Janet's experience (Chapter 9) of working with students on fieldtrips and developing their understanding of how the same image can be viewed and interpreted by different people in different ways. This, in demonstrating the role of positionality and the potential for varying interpretations, enhances student knowledge and understanding of the potential modes that can be used for collecting visual data but, importantly, also develops their skills of reflexivity about their own engagement and that of other people. Student development across the case studies is enhanced beyond traditional research methods to ones that promote creativity through the means of photography, film and bricolage. Further, in the case of Edd's (Chapter 6) and Simon and Lorna's (Chapter 10) research and teaching, drawing and art are used as a structure that can help both participants and student researchers in organising their own thoughts and ideas. In particular visual methods can provide a starting point from which students engage with deeper meaning and empathy both as individuals and when working with others.

Drawing it all together

Our experience of using visual methods occurred through chance. By working collaboratively with our Ironman our interest in visual methods was captured (see Resource Fourteen), but less by chance, it found its way into our teaching and the classroom. In teaching research methods our aim has always been to equip our students with the research tool box they will need as they leave us as graduates in preparation for the workplace. However, we are also staunch advocates that in equipping our students with these tools they must be encouraged to employ the most appropriate research method that is fit for purpose in meeting a project's aims. The advantage of visual methods is that they hold the potential to sit alongside more traditional research methods and hold out the option to triangulate the research approach taken. There are many things we wish we had known before we started teaching visual methods and we thought it might be useful to include these for those practitioners who are inspired to teach visual methods in some form.

The reflections from the case studies in this text highlight the necessity of the inclusion of a range of visual methods across both undergraduate and postgraduate curricula. While it is important for such work to be strongly grounded in the pedagogical literature base, we believe that it is crucial with regard to developing students with balanced and well-rounded research methods training and the necessary skills to utilise visual methods as a meaningful qualitative technique in collecting data. We encourage practitioners to be enthused, brave and reflective in implementing these techniques and we wish you the very best of luck for what will surely be a fulfilling and fruitful journey.

References

Becker, H.S. (2004) Afterword: photography as evidence, photographs as exposition. In C. Knowles and P. Sweetman (eds), *Picturing the social landscape: visual methods and the sociological imagination* (pp. 193–7). London: Routledge.

Wakefield, C. and Watts, S. (2015). A double take: the practical and ethical dilemmas of teaching the visual method of photo elicitation. *Psychology Teaching Review*, 20(2), 143-55.

Watt, S. and Wakefield, C. (2014). Picture it! The use of visual methods in psychology teaching. *Psychology Teaching Review*, 20(1) 28–35.

12

PRACTITIONER RESOURCES

This chapter aims to provide readers and practitioners with a bank of resources that may be useful when embarking upon teaching visual methods in a higher education setting.

The contents for this chapter are below:

- Resource 1: Bank of ideas
- Resource 2: Bank of learning outcomes
- Resource 3: Key questions for consideration
- Resource 4: Ethics checklist
- Resource 5: Guidance notes for participant information sheets
- Resource 6: Example participant consent forms
- Resource 7: Example information sheet for the public
- Resource 8: Example group agreement form
- Resource 9: Example student project outline
- Resource 10: Example student projects
- Resource 11: Template for reflexive diary
- Resource 12: Example student feedback sheets
- Resource 13: Peer and self-assessment form
- Resource 14: Ironman poster
- Resource 15: Useful reading

Resource 1: Bank of ideas

The following page consists of a bank of ideas and scenarios for practical implementation. These are, in part, based on the reflective activities of each chapter. You will see from the diagram that many of the ideas are closely intertwined with each other. Initially, we suggest that you choose one of the ideas and then experiment with broadening this with different cohorts. Clearly, each of these ideas comes with a distinct set of ethical considerations and these should be explored prior to embarking upon projects. The diagram is by no means exhaustive, nor are the links made between the areas, therefore several other ideas may stem from this or occur independently.

BANK OF IDEAS

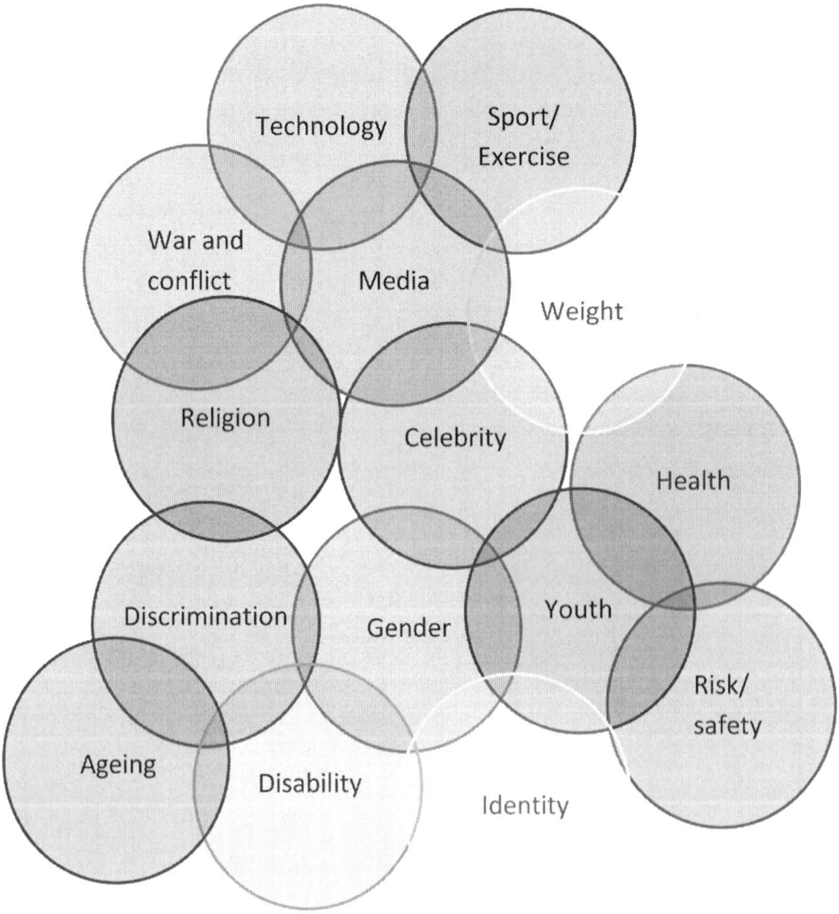

Technology

Sport/ Exercise

War and conflict

Media

Weight

Religion

Celebrity

Health

Discrimination

Gender

Youth

Risk/ safety

Ageing

Disability

Identity

Resource 2: Bank of learning outcomes

The following page contains suggested learning outcomes regarding the use of visual methods in higher education curricula. These can be adapted for levelness depending on the stage at which visual methods are introduced and the requirement for autonomy and reflexivity within the projects completed. Obviously it will be necessary to ensure that these are in line with the marking criteria of the associated assessment.

BANK OF LEARNING OUTCOMES

- Demonstrate skill in choosing and employing one of the visual methods

- Critically analyse the use of a visual methods technique as a research tool

- Demonstrate knowledge of a range of visual methods techniques and have the ability to evaluate their effectiveness

- Effectively conduct a reflexive piece highlighting your involvement in group-based assessment activities

- Exhibit understanding of the dual role of participant and researcher and the implications that this has for the research process

---

Resource 3: Key questions for consideration

The following page explores some of the key issues that are pertinent when considering the use of visual methods as a teaching and assessment tool. We recommend that the teaching team carefully considers each of these questions prior to introducing the assessment to students. However, some of the questions offer the opportunity for trial and error, and should therefore be reconsidered at regular intervals. You will probably find that several other questions arise from discussions with the teaching team, particularly if your team is varied in terms of background and visual methods experience.

KEY QUESTIONS FOR CONSIDERATION

- How do we ensure that assessment remains central to learning?

- How do we force students to engage with the marking criteria? Indeed, do we involve students in the production of these criteria?

- How do we ensure a sufficient power balance between participants and researchers?

- To what extent should we involve the students in the design of the assessment?

- Should a graded approach to the introduction of visual methods be undertaken, from undergraduate to postgraduate level?

- What role, if any, should self- and peer assessment be a contributing factor to the assessment? How should this be managed/calculated?

- To what degree should the students be given free rein over their chosen assessment or choice within specified boundaries? Should this be consistent or fluid between student groups? How could this be managed in relation to equity of experience and learning outcomes?

- What do we need to put in place to ensure that ethical considerations are fully thought through?

Resource 4: Ethics checklist

An example of a checklist that can be offered to students prior to completion of a visual methods project is shown below. This will allow them to consider the range of associated ethical issues and promote discussion about ethics as something which should be embodied, rather than just a process to be completed. We also recommend that students are encouraged to read Chapter 3 of this book to develop a broader understanding of ethics.

ETHICS CHECKLIST

Tick when considered

Governing Ethics

Is it worthwhile? How have you assessed this? ☐

Will it be useful? ☐

Does it make a useful contribution to the field? ☐

Does it make a positive difference? ☐

Who will it benefit? ☐

Procedural Ethics

Are all participants able to provide informed consent? ☐

Have the participants been given an information sheet? ☐

Have the participants provided informed consent? ☐

How will you ensure anonymity? ☐

How will you ensure confidentiality of participant data? ☐

What are your procedures for data storage and use? ☐

How are you going to ensure the avoidance of harm? ☐

Have you completed a risk assessment? ☐

Have you considered relevant child protection issues? ☐

Have you gained approval from the relevant bodies? ☐

If necessary, has an information sheet been provided to members of the public who may have questions about the research? ☐

Resource 5: Guidance notes for participant information sheets

When completing a participant information sheet, there are a number of key areas to be considered and information that must be included to ensure that the participants have enough information to make an informed decision about participation. A set of guidance notes that may be useful to students when producing such an information sheet is shown below.

PARTICIPANT INFORMATION SHEET – GUIDANCE NOTES

When undertaking any research project, it is important to write a Participant Information Sheet. This is given to potential participants (in any type of research project) so that they are fully informed about what they would be expected to do, should they agree to take part in your study. The form should be given to participants when they are invited to participate and it should be retained by them.

N.B. The information sheet should be attached when the ethics form is submitted.

Potential recruits to your research study must be given sufficient information to allow them to decide whether or not they want to take part. An Information Sheet should contain information under the headings given below where appropriate, and in the order specified. It should be written in simple, non-technical terms and be easily understood by a lay person. Use short words, sentences and paragraphs. [You might want to ask a friend who is not studying psychology to read over your sheet to make sure that it reads clearly.]

1.   **Study title**
Is the title self-explanatory to a lay person? If not, a simplified title should be included.

2. **Invitation paragraph**
This should explain that the participant is being asked to take part in a research study. The following is a suitable example:

> 'You are being invited to take part in a research study. Before you decide, it is important for you to understand why the research is being done and what it will involve. Please take time to read the following information carefully. Ask us if there is anything that is not clear or if you would like more information. Take time to decide whether or not you wish to take part.'

3.   **What is the purpose of the study?**
The background and general aims of the study should be given here. You should also mention the duration of the study – participants should be fully informed of how long it will take, as they are often busy and need to know if they can spare the time (you should do the study yourself or practice on a friend to measure how long it will take).

You do not need to reveal all the details and expectations regarding your study. Sometimes you may need to keep some aspects hidden, as participants may alter their behaviour if they know exactly what you expect. This is an ethical consideration – weighing up the balance between keeping participants fully informed and not biasing their responses.

4.   Why have I been chosen?
You should explain how the participant was chosen and how many other people will be studied.

> e.g., if your study is looking at belief in paranormal phenomena among women, you will be looking to recruit women only;

>> 'We are seeking to recruit 160 women, as we are interested in women's beliefs in paranormal phenomena.'

5.   Do I have to take part?
You should explain that taking part in the research is entirely voluntary. You could use the following paragraph:-

> 'It is up to you to decide whether or not to take part. If you do decide to take part you will be given this information sheet to keep and may be asked to sign a consent form. If you decide to take part you are still free to withdraw at any time and without giving a reason.'

6.   What will happen to me if I take part?
You should say how long the participant will be involved in the research, how long the research will last (if this is different), what exactly will happen e.g., tests, interviews, etc., what the participant's responsibilities are. Set down clearly what you expect of them.

7.   Will my taking part in this study be kept confidential?
You will need to obtain the participant's permission to allow restricted access to the information collected about them in the course of the study. You should explain that all information collected about them will be kept strictly confidential. A suggested form of words may be used:

> 'All information which is collected about you during the course of the research will be kept strictly confidential and may not be accessed by other individual outside this project.'

8.   Contact for further information.
You should give the participant a contact point for further information. This can be your name or that of a supervisor involved in the study. You should also be able to provide a general information sheet for the general public in case this is requested.

<u>**Remember to thank your participant for taking part in this study!**</u>

Resource 6: Example participant consent forms

Following the production and distribution of a comprehensive participant information sheet, it is important to complete (and have participants complete) an accompanying consent form. The following pages demonstrate two different example consent forms. Clearly these will need to be adapted to reiterate the key points from the information sheet and for the specifics of the study, but should act as a guide regarding level of details required.

'STUDY TITLE'
CONSENT FORM

The purpose of this study has been explained to me and I understand that my rights as a volunteer participant are as follows:

- That I have been invited to take part in an interview but that it is purely voluntary and I am under no obligation to do so

- That my identity will remain anonymous and that my name will be anonymised through the use of a pseudonym (false name)

- That my data will be kept securely and confidentially in a locked cabinet/password protected

- That I have the right to decline any questions or line of questioning that I do not wish to answer

- That I have the right to withdraw from this study at any time up to the date specified and that my data would then be excluded

- That should I chose to withdraw I understand that I need to contact the researcher via his/her contact details as specified

- That I have the right to request a copy of the typed transcript of my interview

- That I have the right to a summarised copy of the findings of this study

- That the data from this study may be used for publication purposes

Signature:..

Date: ....

INVESTIGATION INTO 'INSERT TITLE'
CONSENT FORM

I have read the Participant Information Sheet and have had the opportunity to ask any questions about this study. I give my informed consent to participating in this investigation.

Name (print):   _____

Signature: _____

Date: _____

I would like to receive a copy of my transcript   YES/NO

I would like to receive a summarised report of the overall
findings of this study   YES/NO

My email address is   _____

My address is   _____

       _____

       _____

If you have any questions at any time, please contact:

[Student name and contact] as below

       _____

OR [Supervisor name and contact] as below

       _____

Resource 7: Example information sheet for the public

As reported by Rose (2014) official guidance is somewhat limited regarding the public involvement in projects such as these. In line with the recommendations offered in Chapter 3, it is sensible to follow some basic standards when videoing or taking photographs in public places. Wherever possible, the images should not portray members of the public in a way such that they could be identified (for example, in the foreground). However, if this is not possible to avoid, pixilation can be used in the final images. Clearly the public retain the right to ask questions about the project and request not to be photographed or that their image be removed from the data. It is always useful to devise an information sheet for members of the public and an example is shown below.

PUBLIC INFORMATION SHEET

As part of a university project, I am collecting visual data regarding...
[OUTLINE OF THE PROJECT]

_____

_____

_____

_____

_____

_____

You will not be able to be identified from images in the final project (through pixilation or distance from the camera). However, if you would like all images of yourself to be removed from the project, please just ask the researcher.

If you have any further questions about the nature of the project or the data therein, contact:

STUDENT NAME AND CONTACT DETAILS

_____

or TUTOR NAME AND CONTACT DETAILS

_____

Resource 8: Example group agreement form

When conducting group work, particularly that of a sensitive and personal nature, it is crucial for the members of the group to form an agreement about the use of the data. While the requirements of this will alter depending on the nature of the project and the degree of personal investment in the data, the example below can act as a guide for groups. In our experience, completion of such an agreement allows the students to think about ethics in terms of personal involvement rather than as a process, and the security provided by this agreement contributes to the production of deeper and more meaningful personal reflections in the project work.

GROUP AGREEMENT FORM

- While taking photographs I will endeavour to respect all individuals and their property. I will not take photographs from which individuals can be identified.
- The photographs taken by each group member and their associative narrative are both personal and special. I endeavour to respect this and treat this data in an appropriately sensitive manner. I consent for my data to be used without being anonymised.
- I will only use the photographs and associated narratives for the purpose of this academic project, including the presentation and written report. I will not publish or use this data for any other purposes. I will store all data related to this study in accordance with the Data Protection Act (see below).

Data Protection Act

I understand that my own data will be stored by other team members and I will store some of their data relating to the participation in this study; this will be stored on a computer. I will anonymise files relating to other team members, and files containing information about me will be made anonymous by others. I agree to the other team members recording and processing this information about me. I understand that this information will be used only for the purpose of this study.

By signing this form, I agree to voluntarily participate in this study. I have read and understood the above information. I have had the opportunity to discuss any ethical concerns with the group.

Group member name: _____

Signed: _____ Date: _____

Group member name: _____

Signed: _____ Date: _____

Group member name: _____

Signed: _____ Date: _____

Group member name: _____

Signed: _____ Date: _____

Resource 9: Example student project outline

When beginning our journey in visual methods and considering how these could be incorporated into a meaningful teaching and assessment tool, we put a great deal of thought into how the assessment would be devised and presented to the students. Given the relatively abstract and creative nature of the assessment, we found that the students benefited from a comprehensive outline of the expected output. Clearly, levelness should be considered when devising and outlining student projects to ensure that they are appropriate for the experience of the student group. The following page contains the guidelines that were provided to the students for one of the projects that we employed.

VISUAL METHODS ASSESSMENT

STUDENT GUIDANCE

Assessment remit
- Group presentation of 6 to 8 minutes: Allowing 2 minutes per person in groups of three to four people.
- 1,500 word *individual* write up: Thematic and reflexive analysis of self-selected photographic images together with a critical and reflexive discussion of the process used.

Guidance

Presentation guidance
PowerPoint must be used for all presentation. You must email your presentations including the images the Friday prior to your presentation.
Your presentations must be to a professional standard and must be rehearsed beforehand. **It is important that your presentation does not exceed the allotted time.**

This assessment point provides you with an opportunity to be creative and to build on and demonstrate your presentational skills. You should consider your presentation from an audience perspective thus ensuring it is unambiguous and timely.

Your presentation mark will be a group mark and you will be marked in the following areas:

- Preparation and research
- Engagement and presentation
- Communication – clarity
- Organisation of materials
- Timing of presentation

Report guidance

Your report **must be** double or 1.5 line spaced using size 12 font Times New Roman.

It must be professionally presented with a title, contents and reference pages. You **must** state clearly the word count at the end of the report. On this occasion please submit both a paper copy of your report to the administrator and an e-copy to TUTOR EMAIL.

The structure of the report should be as follows:

Title page – For example, this should inform the reader clearly of what your project topic is about. Please ensure your name is clearly indicated and the course code.

Introduction – Ordinarily this would be a full literature review of a chosen research topic, however, in this instance the introduction should just be a very short paragraph that briefly explains the purpose and importantly the aims of your visual study. In qualitative research you **must always** have a research question and you must clearly state this (Third person and **approx. 50–100 words.**)

Methodology, method and data analysis (approx. 700 words) – As a research methods course, nearly half of your report should be outlining your methodology, the method applied and the analysis technique you have chosen to adopt. Remember you always need to ground your work theoretically through academic theories and references.

- **Methodology** – For example, in this section you need to write about and justify the background of your study and the approach you have taken. Any visual method will still fall under the umbrella term of interpretivism but in the main this is where you might write about CAP and certainly, photo-elicitation. Again you can write in first person when justifying your group's chosen philosophical approach.
- **Method** – In the main your method of data collection is the taking of photographs; however, some of you may incorporate other creative data collection techniques that fall under the criteria of CAP. You must clearly state all the methods of data collection you have employed, theoretically and reflexively outlining and justifying these. But do be careful if employing methods beyond the taking of photographs because you still need to remain within the word count.
- **Ethics** – While the tutors will have agreed the ethics of your project topic areas, you must write about any ethical issues and the practical measures that may impact or affect the handling of your collective data. You should **collaboratively** agree how the data will be handled. For example, if you are sharing photographs, you should agree that practically those

© 2017, *Teaching Visual Methods in the Social Sciences*, Sal Watt, Caroline Wakefield, Routledge

photographs are not for public consumption beyond your group or beyond the purpose of the class assessment, that is, photographs should be respected and should not, for example, be put on the web.

As a group you should collaboratively construct a group informed consent form that you each individually sign and which **must** be included in the appendices.

- **Data analysis** – You will need to tell the reader the exact step-by-step process you undertook in analysing your data. The process and the order you undertook should be clearly illustrated and labelled in your appendices.

NB: You must include the entire analysis process in your appendices, that is, all your rough workings etc. and the process whereby you 'collapsed down' or determined your themes – we cannot give you credit for your hard work if we have no evidence of the process you took.

Findings (600 words)

- You should introduce the themes and reflexive thoughts and feelings that emerged from your data analysis here. Once you have stated what these are you should write about them in the same order. Each theme should have a theme title (make it interesting).
- When you present themes I would suggest you follow the order suggested below by Chenail (1995):
  - Present the theme – state what emerged.
  - Give examples, that is, direct quotes from the reflexive accounts to highlight and support what you have just presented (quotes should be indented and identified through quote marks, for example, ' . . . ' and *italicised*. Insertion of the relevant photographs to illustrate your point/theme would also be beneficial. **Remember:** Direct quotes do not count towards the word count for the assessment.
  - You should go on to interpret the theme that you have highlighted, exemplified through the quote/s you've chosen.
- As you will see from the above, following this sequence helps the reader to follow your train of thought, and when you have exhausted one theme then move on to the next. Following this pattern makes writing about your data more manageable and more user friendly for the reader – qualitative writing is about guiding the reader through a logical chain of events/reflection/thoughts and building your argument/rationale.
- When all your themes have been exhausted, then you need to think about a solid conclusion that brings your themes together and illustrates what they say about how you own or your group's experiences (again you can supplement by the use of photographs). Remember the double hermeneutic is about the researcher trying to step into another's world

view and trying to understand how the participant makes sense of his/her world. In this instance, some of you may be trying to step into the world views of your group members and these may be very different to your own understanding and experiences; therefore, please be respectful; this project must be inclusionary and every group member's voice must be heard and respected.

Reflexive account (approx. 200–300 words)
- This is an exploration and discussion of your thoughts and feelings about the research process. Some questions that might be helpful in thinking about what to write here might include (but don't just focus on these, do think about your own experience!):
  - How did you feel about undertaking a visual method?
  - How did you feel about sharing your photographs and your thoughts and/or feelings with your group members?
  - Did you identify with your participants' worldview? Did that cloud your interpretation when you analysed your data?
  - How did you (and indeed, did you?) overcome your biases towards the method or your peers' interpretation? (We all have biases . . . and we **must** write about them.)
  - Did it feel judgemental interpreting your group members' reflective or reflexive comments? Did it feel intrusive?
  - Are you happy with how you conducted the process? Or analysed your data? Or how this report has turned out?
  - Were your thoughts and feelings about the process taken into account by your group members? If not, what was your part in this?

  Be reflexive!

- Do not think that writing negatively about the process, or your experience of it, will mean that we use your critique to bring your mark down. Your mark is far more likely to be affected if you DO NOT write reflexively. You cannot leave out this section. It is really important that you are open and honest about YOUR thoughts and feelings. (If by this point you are seriously running over the word count, then you can summarise the key aspects you are being reflexive about and write a fuller account which you can then refer to and include in your appendices.)

Reference list (NB: This list, along with the appendices content list and the appendices is not included in the word count.)
- You should follow the accepted referencing style for your discipline, that is, Harvard or if you are a psychology Master's student, APA. Please state clearly which reference system you are using after the title 'Reference List'.
- At this level of study we expect work to be appropriately referenced and subsequently listed to a high standard.

Appendices

You should have an appendices list that indicates the order of the appendices and their respective number. You must also clearly label each of your appendices. Below is a quick example of what your Appendices List must include.

Appendix 1   Tutor-signed ethics form
Appendix 2   Group ethics/consent form
Appendix 3   Copy of presentation slides
Appendix 4   Copy of A3 photographic presentation sheet
Appendix 5   All evidence of data analysis (you **must** include all your rough workings of your analysis)
Appendix 6   Reflective comments and/or focus group transcriptions

Resource 10: Example student projects

This page contains a list of ideas that could be used within student projects. If there are a small number of students, a greater degree of free rein can be offered and closely monitored. However, when at the initial stages of incorporating visual methods, or if you are conducting projects with first- or second-year undergraduates, it is worth considering being quite prescriptive with the boundaries of the projects.

EXAMPLE STUDENT PROJECTS

- Group members could identify a local tourist location and capture photographs which best represent a city

- Group members could devise the script to a short play which is based on the lived experiences of a specific population group

- Group members could identify a local 'grot-spot' and consider what constitutes or identifies an area in this way

- Group members could take five photographs that represent meaningful places in their lives, which can then be shared with the rest of the group

- Group members could draw pictures of how they represent different emotions, and complete subsequent elicitations

- One group member could give permission for their peer group to shadow them while undertaking an activity (such as visiting the zoo), then five photographs can be selected from those captured as being significant or important

- Group members could make and share videos that they believe represent their life in a meaningful way

- Group members could produce a resource to assist children in developing understanding of a particular life issue (e.g., bullying, bereavement)

- Group members could be asked to draw a timeline of their significant life events

---

Resource 11: Template for reflexive diary

Reflexivity forms an important part of engaging in any research project (either quantitative or qualitative in nature). However, it is crucial in the production of good visual methods research and teaching. The following page provides a template which may be provided to the students to frame the reflexivity and promote a deep engagement with the process. However, it is also worth noting the highly subjective and personal nature of reflexivity. Therefore, while the following template may act as a guide, it is not a definite list of considerations and should not in any way limit the depth of the reflexivity conducted.

TEMPLATE FOR REFLEXIVE DIARY

Consider the events/experiences you have encountered.

- What are your thoughts and feelings relating to these?

- Are there any potential biases? How did you overcome or allow for these? How might you have influenced the research?

- Did you represent your participants ethically and appropriately?

- How did you engage with the method?

Consider the methodological and epistemological choices you made/ continue to make.

- What were the limitations of the technology you used?

- What was your motivation for photographing/videoing/drawing what you did?

- How did you work together as a group?

- What is your part in the interpretation?

Resource 12: Example student feedback sheets

The following pages provide example feedback sheets that can be used for both written work and presentations of visual methods projects. These should be adapted to ensure that they are closely tied in with the learning outcomes and marking criteria provided to the students. Owing to the creative nature of many of the projects, it is also crucial that an effective second-marking and moderation procedure is in place.

VISUAL PHOTO ELICITATION REPORT

Student name: _____

Report sections	Excellent	Very good	Good	Fair	Poor	Fail
Introduction						
Methodology						
Methods						
Ethics						
Data analysis						
Findings						
Conclusion						
Reflection/reflexivity						
REPORT STYLE						
Writing style						
References						
Presentation						

Tutor comments:

Grade: _____ %

Resource 12 – continued

VISUAL PROJECT – PRESENTATION ASSESSMENT SHEET

Student name: _____

Marking Criteria	Excellent	Very good	Good	Below average	Weak	Fail
Methodology						
Engagement and presentation						
Communication – clarity						
Organisation of materials						
Timing of presentation						

Feedback:

Mark Awarded: _____

Signed: _____

Resource 13: Self- and peer assessment form

In our experience, group work can be problematic, particularly on occasions where students are awarded a group mark. However, group work is an essential life skill and is at the heart of many visual methods projects. Therefore, we devised a system to guard against unfair allocation of work among the student group. Following the completion of group work, students can be asked to confidentially and individually complete the form below regarding their own and their group members' contribution to the work completed. Marks can then be awarded proportionately. We have typically followed a system whereby groups are awarded a mark for their work and the individual mark is then calculated as the group mark, minus ten, plus the average mark awarded on the contribution sheets. While this can only make a difference of a few marks, in our experience this is enough to satisfy disgruntled group members who feel that they have taken on a large proportion of the work. However, it also seems to have the added bonus of encouraging individuals to reflect honestly on their own contributions and to work more cohesively with the rest of the group from the outset. This could also be achieved by awarding individual marks to the group members, but this is often problematic when the project itself is so integrated.

PRESENTATION SELF- AND PEER ASSESSMENT FORM

Please complete the form below, giving each group member a score (out of 10) for each component of the presentation process. This will remain confidential, so please be as honest as possible.

Component / Group member name	Preparation: background reading	Preparation: compiling the presentation	Presentation delivery
1.			
2.			
3.			
4.			

Resource 14: Ironman poster

The following page is an example of a conference poster presentation that we conducted on research that employed a visual method (see Chapter 4). We used this research project as a vehicle to explain the premise of visual methods and act as a real-world example of how they could be used in research. We found that the students engaged with the process themselves more readily following this as they were able to ask questions about ethics and the decisions made throughout the research process. We would encourage anyone considering incorporating visual methods in their curriculum to conduct a piece of research using visual methods to gain first-hand experience and allow them to be positioned well to answer questions about the process.

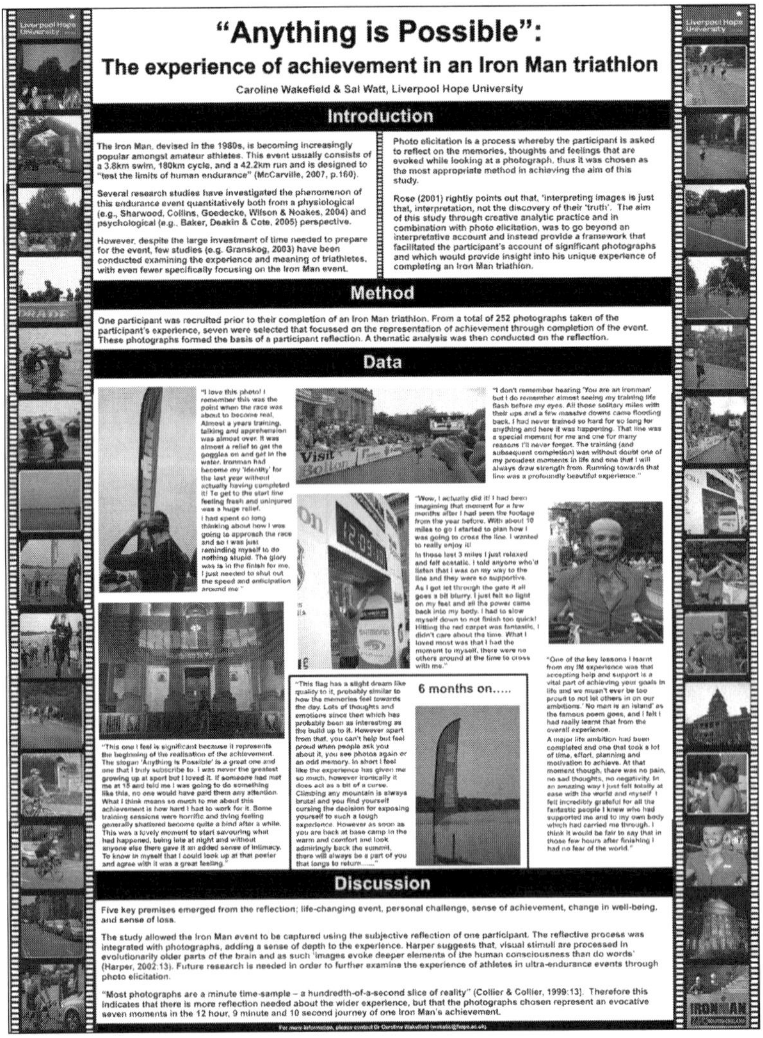

Resource 15: Useful reading

Below is a reference list of useful reading across the spectrum of visual methods. These are taken from the suggested readings in each chapter and form a comprehensive guide of research on this topic.

USEFUL READING

Berk, R.A. (2009). Multimedia teaching with video clips: TV, movies, YouTube, and mtvU in the college classroom. *International Journal of Technology in Teaching and Learning*, *5*, 1–21.

Bourke, L., Bamber., P. and Lyons, M. (2012). Global citizens: who are they? *Education, Citizenship and Social Justice*, *7*(2), 161–74.

Bryans, P. and Mavin, S. (2006). Visual images: a technique for surfacing conceptions of research and researchers. *Qualitative Research in Organizations and Management: An International Journal*, *1*(2), 113–28.

Bulmer, M. (1980). Comment on 'the ethics of covert methods'. *The British Journal of Sociology*, *31*(1), 59–65.

Burgess, J. and Green, J. (2009). *YouTube: online video and participatory culture*. Cambridge: Polity Press.

Calvey, D. (2008). The art and politics of covert research: doing 'situated ethics' in the field. *Sociology*, *42*(5), 905–18.

Carrabine, E. (2012). Just images: aesthetics, ethics and visual criminology. *The British Journal of Criminology*, *52*(3), 463–89.

Clark, A., Prosser, J. and Wiles, R. (2010). Ethical issues in image-based research. *Arts & Health: An International Journal for Research, Policy and Practice*, *2*(1), 81–93.

Denzin, N.K. and Lincoln, Y.S. (eds) (2011). *The SAGE handbook of qualitative research*. London: Sage.

Doyle, J. (2007). The neutral lens: Constructing a visual critique of football for peace. In J. Sugden and J. Wallis (eds), *Football for peace? the challenges of using sport for co-existence in Israel* (pp. 155–71). Oxford: Meyer and Meyer.

Edwards, J. (2010). Teaching and learning about psychoanalysis: film as a teaching tool, with reference to a particular film, *Morvern Caller. British Journal of Psychotherapy*, *26*, 80–99.

Enyon, R., Fry, J. and Schroeder, R. (2008). The ethics of internet research. In N.G. Fielding, R.M. Lee and G. Blank (eds), *The SAGE handbook of online research methods* (pp. 23–41). London: Sage.

Gardner, R. and Davidson, R. (2010). Hypothesis testing using the films of the three stooges. *Teaching Statistics*, *32*, 49–53.

Hall, T. (2009). The camera never lies? Photographic research methods in human geography. *Journal of Geography in Higher Education*, *33*(3), 453–62.

Harper, D. (2002). Talking about pictures: a case for photo elicitation. *Visual Studies*, *17*(1), 13–26.

Hodge, S. (2005). Participation, discourse and power: a case study in service user involvement. *Critical Social Policy*, *25*(2), 164–79.

Homan, R. (1992). The ethics of open methods. *The British Journal of Sociology*, *43*(3), 321–32.

Resource 15 – continued

Kearney, K.S. and Hyle, A.E. (2004). Drawing out emotions: the use of participant-produced drawings in qualitative inquiry. *Qualitative Research, 4*, 361–82.

Leitch, R. (2006). Limitations of language: developing arts-based creative narrative in stories of teachers' identities. *Teachers and Training: Theory and Practice, 12*(5), 549–69.

Literat, I. (2013). A pencil for your thoughts: participatory drawing as a visual research method with children and youth. *International Journal of Qualitative Methods, 12*, 84–98.

Pauwels, L. (2008). Taking and using: ethical issues of photographs for research purposes. *Visual Communication Quarterly, 15*(4), 243–57.

Reavey, P. (2011). *Visual methods in psychology: using and interpreting images in qualitative research*. Hove, UK: Psychology Press.

Ritchie, J., Lewis, J., Nicholls, C.M. and Ormston, R. (eds). (2013). *Qualitative research practice: a guide for social science students and researchers*. London: Sage.

Rookwood, J. and Palmer, C. (2009). A photo-ethnography: a picture-story-board of experiences at an NGO football project in Liberia. *Journal of Qualitative Research in Sports Studies, 3*(1), 161–210.

Rose, G. (2008). Using photographs as illustrations in human geography. *Journal of Geography in Higher Education, 32*(1), 151–60.

Rose, G. (2012). *Visual Methodologies: an introduction to researching with visual materials*. London: Sage.

Rose, G. (2014). On the relation between 'visual research methods' and contemporary visual culture. *The Sociological Review, 62*(1), 24–46.

Shell, L. (2014). Photo-elicitation with autodriving in research with individuals with mild to moderate Alzheimer's disease: advantages and challenges. *International Journal of Qualitative Methods, 13*, 170–84.

Spencer, S. (2011). *Visual research methods in the social sciences: awakening visions*. London: Routledge.

Stiles, D.R. (2004). Pictorial representation. In C. Cassell and G. Symon (eds), *Essential guide to qualitative methods in organizational research* (pp. 123–39). London: Sage.

Ventura, S. and Onsman, A. (2009). The use of popular movies during lectures to aid the teaching and learning of undergraduate pharmacology. *Medical Teacher, 31*, 662–4.

Wakefield, C. and Watt, S. (2012). 'There will always be a part of you that wants to return': A reflective photo elicitation of an Ironman triathlon. *Qualitative Methods in Psychology, Special Issue: Focus on Sport and Performance, 2*(14), 40–52.

Wakefield, C. and Watt, S. (2014). A double take: the practical and ethical dilemmas of teaching the visual method of photo elicitation. *Psychology Teaching Review, 20*(2), 145–57.

Watt, S. and Wakefield, C. (2014). Picture It! The use of visual methods in psychology teaching. *Psychology Teaching Review, 20*(1), 68–77.

Wiles, R., Coffey, A., Robinson, J. and Heath, S. (2012). Anonymisation and visual images: issues of respect, 'voice' and protection. *International Journal of Social Research Methodology, 15*(1), 41–53.

INDEX

Locators in *italics* refer to figures and those in **bold** to tables.

 Taylor & Francis eBooks

Helping you to choose the right eBooks for your Library

Add Routledge titles to your library's digital collection today. Taylor and Francis ebooks contains over 50,000 titles in the Humanities, Social Sciences, Behavioural Sciences, Built Environment and Law.

Choose from a range of subject packages or create your own!

Benefits for you

- » Free MARC records
- » COUNTER-compliant usage statistics
- » Flexible purchase and pricing options
- » All titles DRM-free.

 REQUEST YOUR **FREE** INSTITUTIONAL TRIAL TODAY

Free Trials Available
We offer free trials to qualifying academic, corporate and government customers.

Benefits for your user

- » Off-site, anytime access via Athens or referring URL
- » Print or copy pages or chapters
- » Full content search
- » Bookmark, highlight and annotate text
- » Access to thousands of pages of quality research at the click of a button.

eCollections – Choose from over 30 subject eCollections, including:

Archaeology	Language Learning
Architecture	Law
Asian Studies	Literature
Business & Management	Media & Communication
Classical Studies	Middle East Studies
Construction	Music
Creative & Media Arts	Philosophy
Criminology & Criminal Justice	Planning
Economics	Politics
Education	Psychology & Mental Health
Energy	Religion
Engineering	Security
English Language & Linguistics	Social Work
Environment & Sustainability	Sociology
Geography	Sport
Health Studies	Theatre & Performance
History	Tourism, Hospitality & Events

For more information, pricing enquiries or to order a free trial, please contact your local sales team: www.tandfebooks.com/page/sales